International Perspectives on Disability Exceptions in Copyright Law and the Visual Arts

This book provides an overview of disability exceptions to copyright infringement and the international and human rights legal framework for disability rights and exceptions. The focus is on those exceptions as they apply to visual art, while the book presents a comprehensive study of copyright's disability exceptions and the international and human rights law framework in which they are situated.

3D printing now allows people with a visual impairment to experience 3D reproductions of paintings, drawings and photographs through touch. At the same time, the uncertain application of existing disability exceptions to these reproductions may generate concerns about legal risk, hampering sensory art projects and reducing inclusivity and equity in cultural engagement by people with a visual impairment. The work adopts an interdisciplinary approach, with contributions from diverse stakeholders, including persons with disabilities, cultural institutions and the 3D printing industry. The book sketches the scene relating to sensory art projects. Experts in intellectual property, human rights, disability and art law then critically analyse the current legal landscape relating to disability access to works of visual art at both international and regional levels, as well as across a broad representative sample of national jurisdictions, and identify where legal reform is required.

This comparative analysis of the laws aims to better inform stakeholders of the applicable legal landscape, the legal risks and opportunities associated with sensory art and the opportunities for reform and best practice guidelines, with the overarching goal of facilitating international harmonisation of the law and enhanced inclusivity.

Jani McCutcheon is Associate Professor in the Law School, University of Western Australia.

Ana Ramalho is Copyright Counsel at Google, and Guest Assistant Professor at Leiden University.

International Perspectives on Disability Exceptions in Copyright Law and the Visual Arts

Feeling Art

Edited by
Jani McCutcheon and
Ana Ramalho

Routledge
Taylor & Francis Group
LONDON AND NEW YORK

First published 2021
by Routledge
2 Park Square, Milton Park, Abingdon, Oxon OX14 4RN

and by Routledge
605 Third Avenue, New York, NY 10017

First issued in paperback 2022

Routledge is an imprint of the Taylor & Francis Group, an informa business

Publisher's Note
The publisher has gone to great lengths to ensure the quality of this reprint but points out that some imperfections in the original copies may be apparent.

British Library Cataloguing-in-Publication Data
A catalogue record for this book is available from the British Library

Library of Congress Cataloging-in-Publication Data
Names: McCutcheon, Jani, editor. | Ramalho, Ana, 1976– editor.
Title: International perspectives on disability exceptions in copyright law and the visual arts : feeling art / edited by Jani McCutcheon and Ana Ramalho.
Description: Abingdon, Oxon ; New York, NY : Routledge, [2020] | Includes bibliographical references and index.
Identifiers: LCCN 2020017531 (print) | LCCN 2020017532 (ebook) | ISBN 9780367359300 (hardback) | ISBN 9780429342677 (ebook)
Subjects: LCSH: Copyright—Art. | Museums—Law and legislation. | People with visual disabilities—Legal status, laws, etc. | Museums and people with visual disabilities. | People with visual disabilities and the arts.
Classification: LCC K1460 .I58 2020 (print) | LCC K1460 (ebook) | DDC 346.04/82--dc23
LC record available at https://lccn.loc.gov/2020017531
LC ebook record available at https://lccn.loc.gov/2020017532

ISBN: 978-0-367-55346-3 (pbk)
ISBN: 978-0-367-35930-0 (hbk)
ISBN: 978-0-429-34267-7 (ebk)

DOI: 10.4324/9780429342677

Typeset in Galliard
by codeMantra

Contents

Contributors

Lida Ayoubi is a senior lecturer at Auckland University of Technology (AUT) Law School where she teaches intellectual property (IP) and human rights law. In 2016, she received her PhD degree from Victoria University of Wellington (New Zealand). Her doctorate investigated access to copyright works for the blind and visually impaired persons as an example of the interface of human rights and IP law. For this, she received the John Miller Award in Social Justice & Community Development. She also holds an LLB degree from University of Tehran (Iran) and an LLM in International Human Rights and Intellectual Property Law from Lund University (Sweden). During her LLM studies, she conducted research at the Raoul Wallenberg Institute of Human Rights and the World Intellectual Property Organization. She has presented and published her research (for which she received funding) on various aspects of the interface of human rights and IP. She is also an executive member of the Asian-Pacific Copyright Association (APCA).

Ann Blokland has been a Curator of Education at the Van Gogh Museum since 2006. In this capacity, she is responsible for museum interpretation and education for adult visitors. Serving an international audience of millions, she is always looking for the best methods and media to tell Van Gogh's story. More recently, she has focused on inclusive interpretation for blind and partially sighted visitors, resulting in the Feeling Van Gogh programme. Ann studied art history at the University of Amsterdam (MA) and has also worked as a curator and exhibition maker. She has written various articles and art catalogues.

Sérgio Branco has a PhD and a master's degree in civil law from the Rio de Janeiro State University (UERJ), and an undergraduate law degree from UERJ. He is a guest researcher and professor at the University of Montréal. He has undergone an extension course in intellectual property at the Pontifical Catholic University (PUC-Rio) and also in film documentary (FGV). He is one of the co-founders and director of the Institute for Technology & Society of Rio de Janeiro (ITS Rio).

Caine Chennatt is an arts administrator and facilitator fostering inclusive and future-focused communities through arts and cultural engagement. He recently commenced in the role of associate director for cultural collections at the University of Tasmania, where he nurtures an approach of cultural humility to bridge fine art and science collections with diverse audiences.

A Churchill Fellow researching inclusive galleries and arts accessibility, he has presented at conferences and workshops, within Australia and internationally, on areas of audience engagement, digital access, inclusion and access programmes for visitors with varying abilities. Formerly as audience engagement manager at the Lawrence Wilson Art Gallery, he has curated numerous inclusive programmes, events and access exhibitions in partnership with various organisations in Western Australia. He is currently developing the Arts and Cultural Access Consortium, an informal network of individuals and arts organisations that work towards becoming more accessible.

Outside the arts sector, Caine is an accredited mediator and conflict-resolutionist. He applies this facilitative outlook to projects bringing communities together in exploring contemporary issues in society and the self.

Noël Daemen works as an independent end-to-end 3D printing consultant, supporting companies and institutions with implementing of 3D printing with an integrated approach on technical, economic and social aspects. He regularly speaks at events and moderates workshops for SME/startups as well as academic students. Noël holds a master's degree in economics /international management (Maastricht University, 1995) and a master's degree in international law (Maastricht University, 1995). From the Massachusetts Institute of Technology (MIT), he holds a grade in Additive Manufacturing for Innovative Design and Production (2019), and he was certified as an Ultimaker expert in 2016.

Andres Guadamuz is a senior lecturer in intellectual property law at the University of Sussex and the editor-in-chief of the *Journal of World Intellectual Property.* His main research areas are on artificial intelligence as well as on copyright, open licensing, cryptocurrencies and smart contracts. Andres has published two books, the most recent one of which is *Networks, Complexity and Internet Regulation*, and he regularly blogs at Technollama.co.uk. He has acted as an international consultant for the World Intellectual Property Organization and has done activist work with Creative Commons.

Lucie Guibault is associate professor of intellectual property law and associate director of the Law and Technology Institute at the Schulich School of Law of Dalhousie University in Canada. She was formerly affiliated with the Institute for Information Law at the University of Amsterdam. She holds a PhD from the University of Amsterdam. She has specialised in international and comparative copyright and intellectual property law. Her general research interests revolve around the critical and normative analysis of the copyright system, primarily looking at the impact of technological change on the balance of interests between rights owners and users. She has countless publications on topics relating to copyright and related rights in the information society, exceptions and limitations. She was co-author with J.-P. Canat of the WIPO Study on museum exceptions (2015).

Paul Harpur is an associate professor at the University of Queensland Law School, an Academic Fellow with the Harvard Law School on Disability, an International Distinguished Fellow with the Burton Blatt Institute, Syracuse University, a Fulbright Future Scholar and a former Paralympian. He is an acclaimed international and comparative law scholar, board director and has been admitted to practice law.

Tianxiang He (China P. R. 1984) is assistant professor at the School of Law, City University of Hong Kong. He holds an LLB degree (Huaqiao University, China, 2007) and a master's degree in international law (Jinan University, China, 2009). He holds a PhD degree in IP law from Maastricht University (the Netherlands, 2016). He received an honorable mention in the Ius Commune Prize 2014, and is the author of the book *Copyright and Fan Productivity in China: A Cross-jurisdictional Perspective* (Springer, 2017).

Sabine Jacques is an associate professor in IP/IT/media law at the University of East Anglia. Her monograph, *The Parody Exception in Copyright Law*, published with Oxford University Press, focuses on the parody exception in copyright law using a comparative methodology.

Her research in the area of copyright exceptions has given rise to publications in the field-leading journals, like the *EIPR* and the *JIPLP*. Additionally, she was awarded the Dean Moore Prize as recognition of her qualities as a researcher and was granted the Golding Essay Prize 2015 by the Competition Law Association. Recently, she received the Routledge Prize for best presentation at the EIPTN in 2017. She was also an associate researcher at CREATe where she led a project investigating the impact of automated anti-piracy systems on cultural diversity.

Peter J. Karol is Professor of Law and director of the Intellectual Property Law Certificate Program at New England Law | Boston. Peter teaches a wide range of intellectual property courses, including law and the visual a, intellectual property and human rights, and copyright law. His recent scholarship focuses on the relationship between copyright, contract and trademark law and conceptual, post-representational and reproducible art practices. His latest scholarly law review article, Permissive Certificates: Collectors of Art as Collectors of Permissions, appeared in the Washington Law Review in fall 2019. Prior to joining the New England Law faculty, Peter was a partner in the Intellectual Property Litigation, Trademark and Copyright practices groups at Sunstein, Kann, Murphy & Timbers in Boston, where he remains of counsel. He received his Juris Doctorate, cum laude, from Harvard Law School in 2004.

Joseph Lelliott is a lecturer in the School of Law at the University of Queensland, where he teaches courses in the field of international human rights law (with a focus on the rights of the child) and criminal law. He has bachelor degrees in law and arts and a PhD from the same university. He has published various articles on issues intersecting with rights and has presented papers in Australia and internationally. Joseph has also served as an expert consultant to the United Nations Office on Drugs and Crime.

Jani McCutcheon is an associate professor at the University of Western Australia Law School, where she teaches intellectual property law, creative expression and the law and business law in practice, and is the deputy head of school (Learning and Teaching). Jani has also practised as an intellectual property law solicitor and worked as a legal research officer for a Member of Parliament. Jani has a Master of Laws by research, writing her major thesis on the 'new signs' under the Australian Trade Marks Act. She has published numerous articles in reputed Australian and international journals and has presented at Australian and international conferences and seminars on intellectual property law issues. She has been a visiting scholar at Berkeley Law School (2016). Jani has co-edited and co-authored *The Research Handbook on Art and Law* (Edward Elgar, 2020), and is currently writing a monograph *Literary Characters in Intellectual Property Law* (Edward Elgar 2021). Her research traverses a number of issues concerning the interface between copyright, moral rights and literature, the nature of the work in copyright law, the copyright doctrines of originality, authorship and fixation, the interface between law and art and disability exceptions in copyright and moral rights law for artistic works. Jani co-convened the International Experts Feeling Art Workshop in June 2018 at Maastricht University, convened the Art in Law in Art conference hosted by the University of Western Australia Law School at the Art Gallery of Western Australia in July 2017, and the Art After Death Symposium at the Lawrence Wilson Art Gallery in 2013.

Beatriz Nunes is a Specialist in Intellectual Property (PUC-Rio), and has an Undergraduate Law Degree from Fundação Getulio Vargas (FGV-Rio), having dedicated her thesis to 3D Printing and its implications on Consumer and IP Law. She currently works as Freelance Translator for articles and other documents both related and non-related to Intellectual Property and Law.

Ana Ramalho is Copyright Counsel at Google and Guest Assistant Professor of Intellectual Property Law at Leiden University. Previously, she was an assistant professor at Maastricht University, where she was also the Director of the Indie Art Legal Clinic, a pro bono legal advice service for artists and cultural entrepreneurs based in the Faculty of Law of Maastricht University. Ana holds a PhD in copyright and European law from the University of Amsterdam (2014), a Research Master in intellectual property law from the University of Lisbon (2008), an LLM in intellectual property and competition law from the Munich Intellectual Property Law Center (2007) and a 5-year advanced

LLB from the University of Lisbon (1999). Throughout her career, she has taken on commissioned research and consultancy on a range of international and European IP topics for several private and public institutions, including the World Intellectual Property Organization, the European Patent Office and several EU institutions. She is the recipient of numerous competitive grants and fellowships, such as the Erasmus+ Jean Monnet activity, the Fellowship Researcher Invitation Programme from the Institute of Intellectual Property of Japan or World Universities Network Research Mobility Award. Ana is a member of the Editorial Board of the *Journal of World Intellectual Property*. Ana has been a guest lecturer and/or speaker at several foreign Universities, and she has convened and co-convened international conferences and workshops, notably the Innov-AI-tion Law for Technology 4 Conference (April 2018), the Feeling Art Workshop (June 2018) and the Value-less Data Symposium (December 2018)

Anthony Rosborough is a research associate and lecturer at the Schulich School of Law at Dalhousie University in Canada. Anthony works primarily within Schulich's Law & Technology Institute, teaching and researching in the intellectual property area. He holds an LLM from the University of Glasgow (Intellectual Property) as well as a Juris Doctor from the Schulich School of Law and a Bachelor of Arts (Political Science) from the University of King's College. Anthony's research interests focus on the shifting concept of ownership in an increasingly automated and service-oriented digital environment. Anthony is particularly interested in the effects of this new technological paradigm on the functioning of the copyright system.

Simone Schroff is a lecturer in Law at the University of Plymouth. She specialises in the inter-disciplinary qualitative, quantitative and comparative analysis of copyright law and policy. Her main areas of interest are copyright and related rights in the digital context. She researched Japanese copyright law as a Visiting Scholar at Waseda University, Tokyo.

Fernando Torrente's main professional activity is as a psychotherapist. He also works as an advisor on school inclusion and education and technological aids for blind and partially sighted children from 6 to 18 years of age. He deals with art accessibility issues from the perspective of visually impaired people. Over several decades, he has coordinated workshops, conducted research and provided expert consultation on art accessibility, in addition to speaking at conferences and organising museum events. Since 2018, he has coordinated the National Commission on Cultural Heritage and Art Works of the Italian Union of the Blind and Partially Sighted.

Vivian van Saaze is an associate professor at the Department of Literature and Art at the Faculty of Arts and Social Sciences of Maastricht University. She specialises in the study of museum practices, focusing on institutional challenges and opportunities arising from digitalisation and the acquisition and display of contemporary art (focusing on installation art, technology-based art and performance art). Her interdisciplinary approach builds on museum studies, ethnographic methods and science and technology studies. Van Saaze is co-founder and director of the Maastricht Centre for Arts and Culture, Conservation and Heritage (MACCH) and Director of Studies of the master's programme Arts and Heritage: Policy, Management, and Education.

Lisa Waddington holds the European Disability Forum Chair in European Disability Law at Maastricht University in the Netherlands. The Chair was established by Maastricht University in collaboration with the leading organisation of disabled people in Europe. She works in the field of European, international and comparative disability law, with a focus on non-discrimination and human rights. Professor Waddington is the disability coordinator of the European Network of Experts on Gender Equality and Non-Discrimination and was a member of the Scientific Board of ANED (Academic Network of European Disability experts).

In addition to working with the European Commission, Professor Waddington has collaborated on reports for the European Parliament and the Fundamental Rights Agency of the European Union, as well as written reports for the Council of Europe and spoken at the UN Committee on the Rights of Persons with Disabilities, and worked with numerous Disabled Peoples' Organisations across Europe.

Andrea Wallace is a lecturer in law at the University of Exeter. She has a PhD in cultural heritage law from the University of Glasgow and previously received an LLM from Radboud University in the Netherlands, a JD from DePaul University College of Law in Chicago and a BFA from the Art Institute of Chicago. Andrea explores legal issues surrounding copyright, heritage institutions and the public domain. Her research considers the impact of digital technologies on the preservation, interpretation and dissemination of cultural heritage and the obstacles and opportunities presented by the digital realm. She frequently writes and presents on open culture and meaningful access to our common cultural heritage in the public domain.

1 Introduction

Jani McCutcheon and Ana Ramalho

This book critically reviews disability exceptions to copyright infringement in key jurisdictions and the international legal framework for disability rights and exceptions, with a focus on how they apply to visual art. Disability access to copyright works is a universal issue. The book therefore undertakes a comparative analysis of the laws in select yet diverse jurisdictions, with a view to better inform stakeholders of the applicable legal landscape, the legal risks and opportunities associated with disability access and the opportunities for reform and best practice guidelines. It has an overarching goal of facilitating international harmonisation of the law.

The new terrain of disability access to visual art

The book's attention to visual art seeks to complement and correct the concentrated scholarship and reform relating to disability access to literary works in accessible format copies, which led to the Marrakesh Treaty. This treaty, in turn, prompted a number of states to modify or introduce exceptions insulating infringements made to facilitate disability access to copyright works (mostly literary works). Because accessible format copies almost invariably involve making reproductions of copyright works, they may infringe copyright and moral rights unless exempted. In the context of visual art, three-dimensional (3D) printing technology now permits paintings, drawings and photographs to be rendered in 3D form so that persons with a visual impairment (PVI) can haptically perceive the art. This book was prompted in part by a curiosity to know whether new and existing disability exceptions to infringement apply to these sensory art translations and reproductions. Consistent with the tenor of the Marrakesh Treaty, we hypothesised that the exceptions would focus on, or assume a limitation to, access to literary works, and expected their application to visual art to be uncertain or even non-existent, particularly due to the novelty of 3D art reproduction and the multiplicity of actors involved in it. We knew that disability exceptions had received scant scholarly examination and differed across jurisdictions. We wondered how technology-neutral they were, and whether they were able to encompass contemporary digital practices. From an inclusivity perspective, we were concerned that the lack, inadequacy or uncertainty of exceptions to infringement of copyright may hamper sensory art projects for PVI beneficiaries and reduce inclusivity and equity in cultural engagement by PVI. We realised that a comprehensive overview of disability exceptions was necessary, overdue and timely, particularly as those exceptions apply to visual art and 3D printing technology.

An interdisciplinary approach

In order to capture a holistic picture of the legal and policy landscape surrounding disability access, particularly to art, this book adopts an interdisciplinary approach, with contributions from industry stakeholders, social scientists and experts in intellectual property law, human rights law, disability law and art law. Part 1 considers the social, cultural and technical challenges of 3D printing 2D art works. It explores sensory art projects in cultural institutions; issues of open access to art and the practices and policies of galleries, libraries and archives and museums; 3D printing in arts and heritage; and the issues from the perspective of PVI and a 3D printing service. Part 2 canvasses the disability exceptions under international law and the international human rights framework. Part 3 gives an overview of the EU framework for disability rights and exceptions. Part 4 then maps and critiques the copyright and moral right exceptions framework in the individual representative jurisdictions of Australia, the United States, Canada, Brazil, the UK, China, Costa Rica, Japan and New Zealand, exploring whether and how they apply to visual art, and identifies major issues and strengths and weaknesses in the system.

The sensory art landscape

Historically, questions and concerns surrounding disability exceptions and visual art may have been largely theoretical, because the technology facilitating the manipulation of art into 3D form was relatively immature. However, the existence and growing sophistication of 3D printing, particularly its embryonic but potentially capacious use by cultural institutions to foster access to artworks by PVI, now compels the consideration of these issues. For some time, cultural institutions have engaged in programmes facilitating access to art through tools such as audio tours and Braille descriptions, and touch tours of replicas of existing 3D artworks. However, it is only with the advent of 3D printing that PVI have been empowered to 'see' *two-dimensional* art through touch for the first time. Recent projects include those undertaken by the Lawrence Wilson Art Gallery at the University of Western Australia,[1] Madrid's Museo del Prado,[2]

1 See 'For Visitors with Visual Impairment: Audio Description and Tactile Tour', at http://www.lwgallery.uwa.edu.au/events (accessed 23 March 2020).

2 https://www.museodelprado.es/en/whats-on/exhibition/touching-the-prado/29c8c453-ac66-4102-88bd-e6e1d5036ffa (accessed 23 March 2020).

the Canadian Museum for Human Rights,[3] the Oxford University Museums,[4] The Van Gogh Museum,[5] the Belvedere Museum in Vienna,[6] the Smithsonian American Art Museum,[7] The Virginia Historical Society,[8] The Panhandle-Plains Historical Museum[9] and the Art Institute of Chicago.[10] Increasingly, PVI can also organise their own 3D versions of paintings, drawings and photographs through platforms such as the Thingiverse website.[11] Characters from the French book *Le Petit Prince* (1943)[12] and Dr. Seuss' classic *The Cat in the Hat*[13] have been transformed into 3D printable models for children with visual impairment. PVI can now also capture photographic moments in 3D form, as revealed in the short documentary 'Touchable Memories', in which one of the film's subjects says, 'If I could touch the picture, I could make the memory tangible again'.[14] Organisations like 3DPhotoWorks,[15] Versus Art,[16] The Unseen Art Project,[17] artecontacto[18] and The VRVis Center for Virtual Reality and Visualization's Tactile Paintings research project[19] are all committed to enhancing access to the cultural heritage of two-dimensional art by PVI.[20] This technology allows these works to be haptically 'seen' for the first time, or experienced in more effective ways. Anecdotal evidence suggests that these sensory art projects are beneficial to PVI.[21]

3 https://humanrights.ca/explore/exhibitions/sight-unseen/3d-images-and-tech (accessed 23 March 2020).
4 http://globalaccessibilitynews.com/2016/10/30/new-project-to-improve-museum-experience-for-people-with-vision-disabilities/ (accessed 23 March 2020).
5 https://www.vangoghmuseum.nl/en/whats-on/feeling-van-gogh (accessed 23 March 2020).
6 https://www.belvedere.at/bel_en/exhibition/gustav_klimts_kiss_at_your_fingertips_ (accessed 23 March 2020).
7 http://americanart.si.edu/education/verbal/ (accessed 23 March 2020).
8 https://www.3ders.org/articles/20171023-virginia-museum-uses-3d-printed-tactile-artefacts-in-touch-tours-for-visually-impaired.html (accessed 23 March 2020).
9 https://www.youtube.com/watch?v=6ySUoGXJOaQ and see http://www.newschannel10.com/story/38090144/going-beyond-the-visuals-new-exhibit-at-panhandle-plains-museum-provides-art-to-the-visually-impaired (both accessed 23 March 2020).
10 http://www.nytimes.com/2013/10/27/arts/artsspecial/welcoming-art-lovers-with-disabilities.html
11 http://www.artic.edu/aic/resources/resource-tag/11071 (accessed 23 March 2020).
12 https://3dprintingindustry.com/news/3d-printing-is-helping-blind-people-see-the-world-around-them-66480/ (accessed 23 March 2020).
13 https://all3dp.com/3d-printing-supporting-blind-people/ (accessed 23 March 2020).
14 http://blog.drupa.com/3dprinting-blind/ (accessed 23 March 2020).
15 http://www.3dphotoworks.com/ (accessed 23 March 2020).
16 http://verusart.com/ (accessed 23 March 2020).
17 http://www.unseenart.org/ (accessed 23 March 2020).
18 http://www.artecontacto.org/ (accessed 23 March 2020).
19 http://www.vrvis.at/research/projects/tactile-paintings/ (accessed 23 March 2020).
20 Those with other disabilities may also benefit from tactile interaction with art, such as those with Alzheimer's disease or who are on the autism spectrum.
21 One beneficiary of a sensory art project describes his frustration with visual art programmes that rely on the sighted to describe the work, giving a 'Reader's Digest version of a painting'. The beneficiary spoke of the interpretive autonomy facilitated by 3D printing:

Human rights justifications

All of this combines to enhance the human rights of PVI and persons with a cognitive impairment. These rights are contained in Article 27 of the Universal Declaration of Human Rights (1948), confirming the 'right freely to participate in the cultural life of the community, to enjoy the arts and to share in scientific advancement and its benefits',[22] and in the United Nations Convention On the Rights of Persons with Disabilities (CRPD),[23] Article 30.1 of which recognises 'the right of persons with disabilities to take part on an equal basis with others in cultural life', and requires state parties to 'take all appropriate measures to ensure that persons with disabilities... enjoy access to cultural materials in accessible formats'. Article 30.3 of the CRPD also requires State Parties to 'take all appropriate steps, in accordance with international law, to ensure that laws protecting intellectual property rights do not constitute an unreasonable or discriminatory barrier to access by persons with disabilities to cultural materials'. Article 30 is consonant with Article 15 of the International Covenant on Economic, Social and Cultural Rights (ICESCR), which provides that State Parties recognise the right of '*everyone* ... to take part in cultural life'.[24]

Perceptions and implications of legal risk

Our early investigations indicated that, worldwide, only a handful of sensory art projects have been undertaken. The potential reasons for this may be manifold. Of particular interest to this book, however, is whether and to what extent perceptions of legal risk, real or imagined, may contribute to this relative paucity of sensory art translation. Concerns about legal risk may explain why existing sensory art projects have targeted public domain works in which copyright has expired. However, that excludes millions of contemporary art works from the scope of accessible works.[25] This is art which PVI may have a deep interest in

> when you have the chance to put your hands on an actual painting and you can feel the faces and the crevices on their faces, I can get my own interpretation of what it's like without it being censored by someone else. I'm free to figure out what I think is important in the picture.

Quoted in Melissa Locker, '3-D Technologies Help the Blind Experience Art More Fully' *Fast Company*, 3 November 2016, at https://www.fastcompany.com/3057520/3-d-technologies-help-the-blind-experience-art-more-fully (accessed 22 March 2020).

22 *Universal Declaration of Human Rights*, GA Res 217A (II), UN GAOR, UN Doc A/810 (10 December 1948).

23 *Convention of the Rights of Persons with Disabilities*, opened for signature 13 December 2006, 2515 UNTS 3 (entered into force 3 May 2008).

24 *International Covenant on Economic, Social and Cultural Rights*, opened for signature 16 December 1966, 993 UNTS 3 (entered into force 3 January 1976) art 5. Emphasis added.

25 'Many of the museum's modern and contemporary holdings are still not in the Creative Commons, however, due to copyright restrictions held by artist's estates, foundations, galleries, and various artists-rights organizations'. http://www.artnews.com/2017/02/07/

experiencing,[26] as suggested by one beneficiary of a sensory art project run by 3D Photoworks at the Canadian Museum of Human Rights, who urged innovators to give her access to Jackson Pollock:

> You would get a sense of the shapes and feel and movement of it … If I could feel that, I would get a sense of the movement of that painting, even though there's no specific picture or shape. Feeling it would give me a sense of what you're seeing. You know it's splashed all the way across the canvas, but unless I can feel it, I don't know that.[27]

The risk of infringing intellectual property rights may also be diminished by obtaining relevant licenses and consents through contract. However, negotiating with the complex mix of potential stakeholders along the 3D art translation continuum is likely to be cumbersome, if not impossible. This is at least partly due to the separation of ownership of the art chattel from the ownership of the copyright and moral rights, potentially splitting between three or more people. Numerous entities deal with the physical chattel, and this may mandate dealings with the owner of the chattel, the entity in possession of the chattel (the gallery, museum or archive, and third parties engaged in the 3-D printing process), the owner of the copyright and the 'owner' of the moral rights. Additional property rights and claims may follow as third parties enter the matrix and provide services, generating intermediary modifications of the artwork, including photographic surrogates of the art object, digital files and the 3D printed objects themselves. Further, it may be impossible to identify or locate rights holders with respect to many artworks which are 'orphaned' and have no known or contactable author. This may lead to a tendency to treat orphan works as copyright works, giving them the benefit of the doubt, another example of risk aversion. In addition to being unwieldy, a system based on individually negotiated consents also excludes works which have not been the subject of such negotiations, excluding access to the majority of works. This practical quagmire likely contributes to the mix of factors which may deter sensory art projects, correspondingly reducing access to artworks by PVI. This complex mesh of legal, property and other interests reinforces the need to ensure the existence of a globally robust disability exception framework, which would accommodate the accessibility of

---

metropolitan-museum-of-art-puts-375000-public-domain-images-in-creative-commons/ (accessed 22 March 2020).

26 *The Art Newspaper*'s annual surveys demonstrate that 'Leading US museums, many with collections that span centuries if not millennia, now devote nearly half of their temporary exhibitions to shows of contemporary art'. Julia Halperin, 'Contemporary Art Dominates US Museums, Our Visitor Surveys Confirm' *The Art Newspaper*, 30 March 2017.

27 Melissa Locker, '3-D Technologies Help the Blind Experience Art More Fully' *Fast Company*, 3 November 2016, at https://www.fastcompany.com/3057520/3-d-technologies-help-the-blind-experience-art-more-fully (accessed 22 March 2020).

copyright extant works like Pollock and avoid the legal and practical quagmire of negotiating individual contractual solutions to disability access.

Obstacles to disability access

Disability exceptions are only one small part of a constellation of factors affecting inclusive access to cultural material. The chief difficulty is that the disability exceptions presuppose access to the copyright material in order to make the exempted reproduction. The exceptions forgive otherwise infringing reproductions, but they do not confer a positive right *to* access. Essentially, the PVI is reliant on the whims of the copyright owner in permitting access to the reproduced material. A media organisation, for example, might arrange for a famous soccer player to share his winning goal with his blind daughter through a 3D print of their match footage.[28]

The peculiar nature of artistic works raises unique issues for disability access. While some rare editions of books may not be generally available, virtually uncountable copies of books exist in digital and analogue form in myriad repositories. Therefore, it is usually the case that one of potentially millions of copies of a book can be easily transformed into a braille, audio or large text format. Further, these days, the copy from which the alternative format is generated is usually in digital form, and thus the quality of the copy is excellent. Art objects, on the other hand, particularly paintings and sculptures, tend to exist in rarefied, individual, material instantiations.

Generating a quality 3D print depends on scanning the original object or a high-resolution photograph of it. The vast majority of cultural objects housed in galleries, libraries, archives and museums are not digitally accessible. Access to the physical object for the purposes of taking a high-resolution photograph depends on the discretion of its custodian, and contractual terms often prohibit the taking of photographs in museums and galleries, or regulate how digital surrogates can be used. The person who has custody of that article will therefore determine the usefulness of the disability exception. Special concessions would need to be demanded based on the disability exception.

Online access to high-resolution photographs of the original objects may solve the physical access problem, and the PVI can theoretically arrange the 3D printing themselves if they have the wherewithal and requisite knowledge.[29] However, as already mentioned, online access to copyright material is rare, and, in any event, most digital surrogates lack the requisite high-resolution quality for 3D printing. A technological method of constraining viral, market harming reproductions of photographs has been to limit access to low-resolution, thumbnail versions while withholding high-resolution images. This is likely due to concerns

28 Anon, 'Roger Dreams Big for Blind Daughter' *World Para Swimming*, 29 June 2017, at https://www.paralympic.org/news/roger-dreams-big-blind-daughter (accessed 22 March 2020).

29 Perhaps aided by the ubiquitous YouTube DIY video, such as https://blog.prusaprinters.org/from-2d-to-3d-how-to-turn-a-picture-or-a-photo-into-a-3d-model (accessed 22 March 2020).

that the provision of high-resolution imagery to facilitate disability access might virally release the image beyond the limited permissible disability purpose.

Resolving this access conundrum is not easy. It may seem tempting to impose a positive obligation on relevant stakeholders to take reasonable steps to facilitate access for the limited disability purpose;[30] however, who should bear the cost of this? Many well-intentioned cultural institutions are already too financially impoverished to fund sensory art projects. The problem is captured well in a recent white paper:

> Overstretched small disability agencies and small cultural organizations cannot fill such yawning gaps on their own. It takes government commitment to create a national perspective, vision and strategy for change. Committed practitioners are all too aware of how much cultural accessibility projects still rely on personal initiative and short-term funding. This leads almost invariably to faltering project legacies. Knowledge gained is not being passed on.[31]

An additional practical constraint on the efficacy of the disability exceptions is due to the reality that, if high-resolution digital surrogates of artistic works are available, they tend to be of public domain works. Many institutions are reluctant to provide open access to digital surrogates of *copyright* art works.[32] Again, it is reasonable to assume that this reluctance is at least partly due to the practical impossibility of limiting user reproductions to those with a permissible exempted purpose, including the disability purpose.

A number of authors in this book have also observed how technological protection measures and legal constraints on circumvention devices and services may pose an obstacle to gaining access to copyright material in a suitable format.[33] Similarly, several authors also observe how contractual provisions may

30 Analogous to the duty, in Australia, to make 'reasonable adjustments' in s 5(2) of the *Disability Discrimination Act 1992* (Cth), if default in the duty means that persons with a disability are treated less favourably than a person without the disability would be treated in circumstances that are not materially different.

31 Marcus Weisen, *International Perspectives on the Cultural Accessibility of People with Disabilities* Project Access White Paper, at http://www.artbeyondsight.org/mei/wp-content/uploads/WP_International_Perspectives-REV.pdf (accessed 22 March 2020).

32 Some cultural institutions controversially claim copyright in the photographs of *public domain* works in their collection, which, if correct, would render virtually all digital surrogates copyright material. See, for example, Andrea Wallace's chapter in this book; Jani McCutcheon, 'Copyrighting Culture: Photography and the Public Domain' (2018) 11 *Photography and Culture* 261, and Jani McCutcheon, 'Digital Access to Culture: Copyright in Photographs of Two Dimensional Art under Australian Copyright Law' (2017) 7:4 *Queen Mary Journal of Intellectual Property* 416.

33 For example, the Australian Law Reform Commission has observed that '[t]he widespread use of technological protection measures (TPMs) is creating significant barriers to access for people with disability'. Australian Law Reform Commission, *Copyright and the Digital Economy* Report No. 122 (2014), para 16.1.

conflict with, and thereby undermine, exceptions. While some exceptions tackle this potential problem directly, for example, by declaring any such provision void, most exceptions are silent on the issue.

Other issues complicate the practical efficacy of disability exceptions. For example, it is conceivable that the PVI may be less interested in art housed in cultural institutions and more interested in having the same access to more everyday images circulating on social media as the sighted. Countless technical infringements occur by the minute as endless users circulate, share, download and otherwise reproduce images posted on the Internet. The vast majority of these infringements are tolerated by either indifferent or ignorant copyright owners, at least until their economic or privacy interests are affected. The same is likely to apply if PVIs wish to generate 3D reproductions of 2D art so that they, too, can experience shape and form. It is likely to antagonise copyright owners only where they perceive a missed licensing opportunity. However, it would be impractical, for example, to provide 3D versions of the uncountable images washing through the Internet on an hourly basis. And yet, for the PVI to truly enjoy a level playing field with their sighted peers in experiencing this ocean of images, it should be permissible for them to convert the image into a tactile form. Having said this, the process of 3D printing is currently still relatively laborious and expensive, and somewhat inaccessible, and for those reasons it is anticipated that the disability exceptions would rarely be utilised to facilitate this level of access. This may change as technology develops to enable quick and cheap conversion of images in-house and in real time, such as the recent camera design allowing the image to be felt on a touch screen.[34] In the meantime, the PVI would doubtless continue to avail themselves of existing and affordable technology which permits them to 'read' images, like Microsoft's Seeing AI app, the iPhone's VoiceOver Image Recognition[35] and Twitter's Compose Image Descriptions setting (where it is utilised).[36] These tools, however, diminish the PVI's interpretive autonomy

34 See the example at https://www.yankodesign.com/2018/02/22/a-camera-and-touch-screen-for-the-blind/ (accessed 22 March 2020). Note, however, that this technology may not crystallise copyright infringement issues. For one thing, it seems primarily directed at converting targeted 3D form into 3D form on the camera. There is also a question about whether there is a sufficiently permanent reproduction of the captured form to constitute an infringing reproduction.

35 See also the technology mentioned in Matt Burgess, 'Tech Is Helping the Blind to See' *Wired*, 28 September 2017, at http://www.wired.co.uk/article/blind-technology-accessibility-ar-voice-aria (accessed 22 March 2020). The question of whether this image to text transformation is a reproduction or adaptation within the exclusive rights of the copyright owner is interesting, but beyond the scope of this particular chapter which focuses on 3D manifestations. However, it is noted that, for example, the definition of adaptation in the Act extends only to the reverse, namely, text to image transformations. See the definition of 'adaptation' in s10(1), which includes 'a version of the work in which a story or action is conveyed solely or principally by means of pictures'.

36 Aatif Sulleyman, 'Little-Known Twitter Feature Can Help Blind and Visually Impaired People Use the Site' *Independent*, 5 January 2018, at https://www.independent.co.uk/life-style/gadgets-and-tech/news/twitter-blind-users-alt-text-accessibility-features-ios-android-app-website-compose-image-a8143391.html (accessed 22 March 2020).

which seems very important, with one PVI explaining how '[t]he feeling of being able to see it and form my opinion is like breaking down another wall as a blind person'.[37]

The law's role in disability access

The discussion here suggests that the efficacy of disability access exceptions ultimately depends on a number of factors beyond the form and content of the exception. It is impacted by the access policies of stakeholders and individual institutions, which are not always clear or easy to find; lawfully circumventing any technological protection measures; and avoiding contractual overrides of exceptions.

This book demonstrates the complexity of the interfacing factors supporting and constraining disability access to visual art. There are a number of problems chilling disability access to culture. This book does not profess to claim that clarification of the law will cure all problems hampering disability access to culture. However, it does suggest that the law plays a part, potentially a significant part, in the matrix of complex issues that contribute to enhanced disability access. We hope the book plays an important role in explaining and unravelling the legal and human rights matrix regulating PVI access to art across a number of jurisdictions, and thereby enhancing increased inclusivity access to art.

37 Natasha Daly, 'The Blind Can Now 'See' Priceless Paintings by Touch' *National Geographic*, June 2017, at https://www.nationalgeographic.com/magazine/2017/06/explore-3D-painting/ (accessed 22 March 2020).

Part 1

Social, cultural and technical challenges of 3D printing 2D art works

2 Reality through interaction

Ann Blokland and Caine Chennatt

Introduction

Often, when conversing with colleagues and collaborators about the possibilities and the importance for art galleries and museums to create meaningful engagement opportunities for visitors with blindness or vision impairment (PVI), this can prompt puzzled expressions and well-intentioned questions such as 'how would that work?', 'if they can't *see* the art, what's the point' or 'won't they be bored?'

These are understandable questions considering how much of the art sector relies on sight – from creating art, transportation, display (managing sightlines), discussion ('so tell me, what do you see?'), to the market (acquisitions of that which is tangible and viewable). This position also makes sense because few exchanges take place between people with disabilities, beyond their immediate circle of care, and those without.

Furthermore, the art world is not renowned for inclusivity. A simple database search reveals a number of commentators arguing that a certain elitism exists within art institutions.[1] This can create a gulf between the art and its audiences through such things as superfluous statements, long-term storage of art, and exhibition displays that often feel incomplete without jargon-laden parallel texts.[2]

This gap is amplified for certain visitors. We already know that for PVI, museums and art galleries can be uninteresting or inaccessible altogether.[3] Persons with disability can be adept at finding alternative ways to access what they seek. However, galleries and museums are increasingly subscribing to the social model of disability (which locates the disability within the designed and attitudinal aspects of society rather than the person with the disability)[4] and offering different ways to foster participation in the arts. For PVI visitors, these include basic

1 Justin Paton, *How to Look at a Painting* (Awa Press, 2012).

2 Gilda Williams, *How to Write about Contemporary Art* (Thames & Hudson, 2015).

3 ABC News SA (ABC1 Adelaide); Time: 19:00; Broadcast Date: Saturday, 7th April 2018.

4 Matthew Molineux, 'Social Model of Disability', in *A Dictionary of Occupational Science and Occupational Therapy* (Oxford University Press, 2017). Available at: https://www.oxfordreference.com/view/10.1093/acref/9780191773624.001.0001/acref-9780191773624-e-0565 (last accessed 5 March 2020).

options such as producing 'Large Print' or Braille copies of the exhibition catalogues, as well as highly technical proprietary methods of 3D printing artwork replicas that are faithful to the original aesthetically, yet robust enough to be touched. This chapter outlines a number of examples of galleries and museums engaging in sensory art inclusivity for PVI, and later in the chapter, we look at a case study from the Van Gogh Museum's *Feeling Van Gogh* project, widely accepted as an exemplar of multi-sensory art experiences designed for PVI across a number of criteria – from community consultation, curation, technical approaches to alternatives, all the way to design and testing.

Given these precedents, one might be forgiven for wondering why all galleries and museums have not adopted such an inclusive stance in their exhibitions, displays and programming. In interviews with the second author during his Churchill Fellowship to investigate inclusive practices within arts organisations, many galleries have cited resourcing deficits – lacking dedicated staff, in-house budgets, capacity and skills. At the heart of this is that inclusion is not part of the museum's governance. In what follows, we seek to highlight several themes that emerged in the first author's analysis of successful inclusive programming, specifically as it relates to sensory art projects. This is by no means exhaustive, but it should help to both describe the nascent sensory art cultural landscape and aid galleries and museums in developing such projects.

Collective impact and collaboration

As already mentioned, an important practical factor for museums and galleries concerns the investment into staffing for accessibility initiatives. This can vary widely across a number of alternatives:

1 No dedicated accessibility staff.
2 No dedicated accessibility staff, but an inclusion 'champion' is present, usually employed through another capacity (e.g. audience engagement, education, visitor services).
3 No dedicated access staff, but access initiatives are distributed within a network of select committed individuals employed in other capacities.
4 One access / inclusion staff employed (often curator of access programmes, or special projects).

While significant work can be achieved through the work of one individual, organisations that rely on one individual to instigate accessibility actions face the risk of staff movement and burn-out. The organisations with most long-term potential for positive impact with sensory art projects were those with access programmes / initiatives that have the additional benefit of shifting the overall organisation to becoming more inclusive. How is this encouraged? One approach is through the *collective impact model* – a framework that requires broad cross-sector collaboration performing an isolated intervention derived from a common agenda, with mutually reinforcing activities and continuous communication, and the availability of backbone support.[5]

The Mori Art Museum (MAM) in Tokyo is perhaps a good indicative microcosm of this framework in practice. With no dedicated access staff (at the time of interviews), but strong curatorial and education teams in place, MAM embraces their organisation's 'open mind open life' motto by offering their gallery as a platform for collaborating with non-profit organisations that provide services for visitors with blindness. At the time of writing, each of their fortnightly verbal description tours had been fully booked.[6] In the United States, LightHouse for the Blind has been making 3D printed tactile maps and images for PVI, aiding in their independence.[7] These 3D printed maps and images have been utilised by councils as well as museums. VocalEyes in London offers a similar service to galleries and museums all across the UK. A registered charity, focused on offering verbal descriptions for performances and tours, recently supported the Museum of Liverpool to develop multi-sensory experiences in the exhibition environment.[8] In addition to tactile images (produced in collaboration with the design firm Tactile Studios), they offered three different smell stations available for visitors to support their visit.[9]

Nothing about us, without us

One of the key criticisms of the collective impact model is its failure to require that meaningful engagement to take place with the community they are supporting. *Nothing about us, without us,* the slogan adopted circa 1993 for the disability rights movement,[10] is an important guiding principle for all sensory art projects. The San Francisco Museum of Modern Art (SFMOMA) collaborated with accessibility consultant and entrepreneur Sina Bahram in developing a digital interactive with universal design principles, enabling a blind visitor to navigate the screen in an 'eyes-free mode' through touch gestures,[11] with the option

5 John Kania and Mark Kramer, 'Collective Impact' (2011) 9:1 *Stanford Social Innovation Review* 36.

6 Mori Art Museum. (2019). *Access Programs | Learning | Mori Art Museum.* [online] Available at: https://www.mori.art.museum/en/learning/category/cat5/ (last accessed 5 March 2020).

7 Caine Chennatt. (2017). *3D Tactile Map Work in Progress at Lighthouse San Francisco.* [image] Available at: https://photos.app.goo.gl/JjkaBgFSEBDcblw29 (last accessed 5 March 2020).

8 VocalEyes UK. (2019). *Blitzed: Liverpool Lives, Photographs Made Accessible.* [online] Available at: https://vocaleyes.co.uk/blitzed-liverpool-lives-accessible-exhibition/ (last accessed 5 March 2020).

9 VocalEyes UK. (2019). *Small Stations.* [image] Available at: https://vocaleyes.co.uk/wp-content/uploads/2019/07/Smell.jpg (last accessed 5 March 2020).

10 James Charlton, *Nothing About Us Without Us* (University of California Press, 2000).

11 Henrik Kam. (2018). *Touch-Wall Showing Three Adjacent User-Stations Each Two Screens Wide. From Left to Right: Theme Story 'The Eyes Have It;' Theme Story 'Found Objects;' and Artworks Up Close; 'Frieda and Diego Rivera'.* [image] Available at: https://mw17.mwconf.org/wp-content/uploads/2017/01/Bahram_Fig1_SFMOMA_People_at_wall_in_218_Henrik_Kam_2016.jpg.

of listening to hundreds of audio descriptions of the artworks in the collection.[12] Bahram also collaborated with the Andy Warhol Museum in developing a mobile app that delivers guided tours paired with tactile reproductions of Warhol paintings *Self-portrait*, 1986, and *Camouflage*, 1986. The tours included verbal descriptions as well as tactile descriptions to guide the visitor in touching each reproduction to get an understanding of the textures, elevations and outlines present and compare how they relate to the original artwork.[13]

Dedicated collection and commissions

While most sensory art projects exist in the form of developing a reproduction (albeit, often highly sophisticated), an original work, if robust enough to be touched, could be the preferred experience for the PVI visitor. It is for this reason The Metropolitan Museum of New York identified and dedicated a small subset of their collection, *the Touch Collection,* to be used for tactile tours. These include a first-century Roman marble foot and a twentieth-century Eskimo sculpture of a mother and child.[14] Taking this one step further, the Museum of Contemporary Art Australia in Sydney opened the Bella Room, a dedicated sensory space where students with disabilities (sensory or intellectual) can explore art in an interactive approach guided by artist educators.[15] Each year, an artist is commissioned to develop a sensory art project, which, through mediation by an educator, is tailored to meet the needs of any access requirement.

Bridging communities

The Prado Museum (officially known as Museo Nacional del Prado) in Madrid also exists as an exemplar of inclusive museum practices. Pioneering in research regarding rapid prototyping (with additive manufacturing / 3D printing in particular), the Prado developed proprietary 3D printed 'reliefs' of paintings – each relief was also coloured, responding to the fact that many PVI visitors can still perceive colour. The technical process called 'didu' used a chemical ink which, through ultraviolet exposure, created volume in the paint, providing texture and

12 Sina Bahram, Peter Samis, Thomas Ryun, and Scott Thiessen, 'Completing the Picture: How A Graphical Interface for Understanding Modern Art Is Meeting the Touch of Non-Sighted Visitors', *Museums and the Web Conference* 2017. Available at: https://mw17.mwconf.org/paper/whats-right-with-this-picture-how-a-graphical-interface-for-modern-art-is-meeting-the-touch-of-non-sighted-visitors/ (last accessed 5 March 2020).

13 Andy Warhol Tactile Reproductions and Mobile Application. (2018). [Blog] *Prime Access Consulting*. Available at: https://pac.bz/projects/andy-warhol-tactile-reproductions-and-mobile-application (last accessed 5 March 2020).

14 Met Museum. (2019). *For Visitors Who Are Blind or Partially Sighted.* [online] Available at: https://www.metmuseum.org/events/programs/access/visitors-who-are-blind-or-partially-sighted (last accessed 5 March 2020).

15 Richard Cann, 'MCA Brings Art Education into the Digital Age' (2012) 93:5 *Education* 17. Available at: http://search.proquest.com/docview/1022642120/ (last accessed 5 March 2020).

outlines. Importantly, the social process included working with a member of the PVI community to determine what might be 'readable' by touch, and working with a curator to determine which artwork would be suited to this process.[16] While the exhibits were primarily intended for PVI visitors, the Prado Museum also offered visitors with sight opaque glasses to block their vision, in order to recreate the experience from the perspective of PVI, bringing together PVI with sighted visitors in a shared experience.

At the Van Gogh Museum case study we visit later, this was precisely the case. The project leaders were surprised that an outcome beyond inclusion was an awareness among the sighted of the experience for PVI. Within the museum staff, there were initial questions about why PVI might be interested in visiting a museum that is largely visual-based. Sensory art projects resulted in a wider recognition of the importance and usefulness of such programmes for those visitors with disabilities. This, in turn, results in the inclusion of similar programmes within the strategic plans of cultural organisations.

Representation and expression

Author Orhan Pamuk remarked that the success of a museum should be in its capacity to reveal the humanity of individuals.[17] This suggestion of a shift from national identities to individual narratives and from histories to personal stories, including the stories of PVI, can be best highlighted in the Wellcome Collection's permanent exhibition *Being Human* (2019), which explores, through 50 artworks and objects, what it means to be human in the twenty-first century.[18] Consulting widely and including contributions from key disability advocates, the exhibit design made space for visitors with disabilities to see themselves represented in the exhibition.

The Lawrence Wilson Art Gallery in Perth, Western Australia, commissioned a disability advocate, consultant and performer Grace King and artist Elizabeth Bills to develop an exhibit for an inclusive arts campaign exhibition. The collaboration resulted in a participatory art and sculpture titled *Tactile Art*. Over two sessions, visitors were invited to interact with the installation which consisted of four opaque hooded plinths with a narrow opening which led to a plush sculpture inside, unlit and hidden from sight. Visitors would need to place their hand through the opening and feel their way through the sculpture to 'view' the

16 Adrian Murphy, 'Touching the Prado: A Hands on Approach to Accessibility' (2015) ***Museums + Heritage Advisor***. Available at: https://advisor.museumsandheritage.com/features/touching-the-prado-a-hands-on-approach-to-accessibility (last accessed 5 March 2020).

17 Orhan Pamuk, 'This Is the Museum of the Future: Nobel Laureate Orhan Pamuk Explains Why He Built a Museum Dedicated to the Glory and Tragedy of One Fictional Couple's Love' ***Newsweek***, 3 September 2012. Available at: https://search-proquest-com.ezproxy.library.uwa.edu.au/docview/1035124819?accountid=14681 (last accessed 5 March 2020).

18 Wellcome Collection. (2019). ***Being Human***. Available at: https://wellcomecollection.org/exhibitions/XNFfsxAAANwqbNWD (last accessed 5 March 2020).

works. In addition, the room guide was printed entirely in Braille, offering no alternative, creating a designed dependency of the visitor on King, who read the Braille interpretative text aloud.[19]

Feeling Van Gogh

The mission statement of the Van Gogh Museum is to 'make the life and work of Vincent van Gogh and the art of his time accessible and reaches as many people as possible in order to enrich and inspire them'.[20] Accessibility of the art collection and corresponding information has always been an important aspect of the Van Gogh Museum's work, as is stated earlier in the mission statement. More recently, inclusion has become part of the Van Gogh Museum's strategic plan for 2018–2020.[21] The Van Gogh Museum has stated more strongly that it:

> believes that it is important to be an inclusive organisation in the broadest sense of the word. [...] society is changing; new audiences are emerging who are less likely to visit the museum as a matter of course and who are yet to become properly acquainted with the museum. Inclusivity therefore needs to be a driving policy principle in the years ahead. In order to remain relevant to a wide audience, the museum's inclusivity policy focuses on young people, young residents of Amsterdam, people with a physical disability and vulnerable elderly people.[22]

With the launch in 2015 of *Feeling Van Gogh*, a content-driven programme for PVI, the Van Gogh Museum took a first step in the direction of becoming a more inclusive museum.

Reaching your audience

Programmes for PVI offered in Dutch museums were few some five years ago. One example of good practice is the Museum Beelden aan Zee with a large sculpture collection, which has been organising touch tours for PVI for many years. The Van Abbe Museum launched a programme in 2014 called *Special*

19 Lawrence Wilson Art Gallery. (2017). *Image of a Gallery Visitor with Her Hand Placed in Elizabeth Bills Artist Work Tactile Tour. Collaborator Grace King.* [image] Available at: https://photos.app.goo.gl/s5MZbtucutqEomCv9 (last accessed 5 March 2020).

20 https://www.vangoghmuseum.nl/en/organisation/mission-and-strategy (last accessed 5 March 2020).

21 Van Gogh Museum. (2018). *Van Gogh Aspires. Strategic Plan 2018–2020.* Available at: https://www.vangoghmuseum.nl/en/organisation/mission-and-strategy (last accessed 5 March 2020).

22 Van Gogh Museum. (2018). *Van Gogh Aspires. Strategic Plan 2018–2020*, 38. Available at: https://www.vangoghmuseum.nl/en/organisation/mission-and-strategy (last accessed 5 March 2020).

Guests, making the museum 'accessible to anyone who is curious, whether they are blind or visually impaired, deaf or hard of hearing'.[23]

Feeling Van Gogh primarily aims to cater to PVI visitors, but most of them need a guide and often are looking for an experience they can share together with someone. After all, a museum visit is a social outing for most of us. The Museum wanted to develop a programme for PVI and their sighted friends, family or companions, and make it enjoyable for both. This way the Museum not only makes Vincent van Gogh's work accessible to a new audience but engenders a positive effect on their participation in culture and society.

Special need programmes are often developed without sufficient dialogue with their intended beneficiaries. *Feeling Van Gogh* was set up from the start with close coordination with PVI representatives of Dutch organisations in the field of visual impairment: Kubes (Art for the blind and partially sighted), Oogvereniging (Association of the blind and partially sighted) and the European Blind Union (Access to Culture project).[24] They were involved from concept phase until launch – testing materials, advising on services, training of staff and marketing. The programme was co-funded with a substantial financial contribution from the Oogfonds (The Dutch Eye Fund). Prior to the launch, the Museum organised two test sessions via blind organisations to see if it is set up and objects, smells and sounds would meet their needs. Teaming up the Museum's expertise on art interpretation with the expertise of the target group proved very efficient and was the key to the success of the programme.

Star material: 3D paintings

The Van Gogh Museum Collection – premium quality relief reproductions of Van Gogh's paintings – was the starting point of *Feeling Van Gogh*. The special 'Reliefography' technique combines a 3D scan with a high-resolution print to resemble the original as accurately and faithfully as possible, not only the front but also the back of the painting. The 3D reproductions were developed by the Museum and Fujifilm at an earlier stage for commercial and educational purposes but proved to be star material for a programme for PVI.

Van Gogh often used expressive brushwork in his paintings and a technique with which he applied various layers of thick oil paint on the canvas. This painting technique is very suitable for 3D reproduction. Now Van Gogh's characteristic style, with vibrant brush strokes, became accessible through touch for the first time. As one visitor commented:

> I've never been able to see more than the difference between light and darkness. Because of that I've never been able to experience what's depicted on

23 https://vanabbemuseum.nl/en/research/highlighted-projects/special-guests (last accessed 5 March 2020).

24 http://www.euroblind.org/working-areas/access-to-culture (last accessed 5 March 2020).

> a painting. The Van Gogh Museum Relievos are a great solution: I was able to touch the 3D printed paintings.[25]

The tactile quality of the 3D paintings opens a new possibility for PVI to discover Van Gogh's art. However, feeling only the brushwork will not give them a clear image of the work. Explanation, description and other learning methods, focusing on the other senses, are necessary to experience what is represented and what the ideas and aims of the artist were. It is very important to stress that offering only a tactile painting or other tactile art objects will never be sufficient to experience the art fully; other actions of interpretation are needed as well.

Interactive and multi-sensory

The Van Gogh Museum's Department of Education and Interpretation seeks to meet audience expectations of a social and accessible museum with an interpretative mix of various media. It looks for an 'educational mix' that dovetails with diverse learning styles, diverse senses and diverse target groups. In this case, the diversity of eye conditions of participants corresponds with Museum policy to offer more than one tool or medium. It is not providing either this *or* that, but rather a rich variety. Using multi-sensory activity, where PVI can touch, hear or smell, the participants make the paintings their own at their own pace, no matter what their impairment is. There is also a lot of room for interactivity between the educator and the participant, and among the participants themselves. Interactive guided tours are the Van Gogh Museum's specialty, using, amongst others, visual thinking techniques.

Feeling Van Gogh is a two-hour programme and consists of two parts: (1) a guided tour through the museum galleries followed by (2) a multi-sensory session in the Museum's studio.

Guided tour

First a group of 10–12 persons is taken by a trained museum educator through the galleries. They will stop at the paintings that will be part of the multi-sensory session later on.

Combining object description with interactive techniques, for example, asking questions to spark a dialogue, makes it interesting to both the PVI visitors and their sighted companions. They can enjoy a museum visit together, and share the experience of the hustle and bustle of the galleries and standing in front of (real) icons, like Van Gogh's *Sunflowers*.

25 Quote from interviews with participants of Feeling Van Gogh, 26 February 2015.

Multi-sensory session

The noise and crowded galleries can be challenging for this particular group, therefore the multi-sensory session takes place in the quiet studio. Participants are seated in two separate groups around tables. Besides the 3D paintings, the museum educator starts to introduce other materials related to two paintings for each group. The Museum chose Van Gogh's paintings *Sunflowers, The Bedroom, Wheatfield under Thunderclouds* and *Landscape at Twilight* because of their thick, tactile brushwork. They are also key works in Van Gogh's story as an artist. The Museum additionally offers the following:

- Artist materials like the type of linen Van Gogh used for his canvases and a reproduction of his palette.
- Simplified tactile images to clarify the composition of the painting without the criss-cross brush strokes. These raised images are successful material for educating PVI.
- Objects like a characteristic nineteenth-century vase, used in the Provence to preserve duck's fat, similar to the one depicted in the *Sunflowers.* These pots can still be found in antique shops, and it makes the painting come alive. Also the texture of smooth glazing versus the rough pottery works very well.
- A scale model of *The Bedroom* painting is the museum's showstopper. It was made by someone who creates dollhouses, and everything is there in detail: the bed, the little side table with the towel next to it, the paintings on the wall and so forth.

The museum also provides other materials that tickle the senses:

- The overwhelming landscape of the *Wheatfield*, with its fresh green colours and hint of summer rain (Van Gogh painted it a couple of weeks before his death in July 1890) is translated in the scent of wet grass. The smell of clean, fresh sheets from the bed –mentioning jokingly that maybe Van Gogh's beddings were not that clean– is called up with a simple bar of Marseille soap. Through smelling, the places where Van Gogh stayed can be brought back to life.
- Reading out Van Gogh's letters to his brother Theo brings the artist himself back to life. He describes what he is working on, what colours he uses or what he wants to express with his work. Getting close to Van Gogh's most private thoughts is an impressive experience.

Moving forward

In March 2015, the Museum launched *Feeling Van Gogh* based on four sessions a year; following overwhelming interest, it was increased to eight sessions a year. Since 2017, the Museum has a permanent area for an independent, multi-sensory experience. Furthermore, in 2018, the Museum extended the programme with in-gallery tours for temporary exhibitions, without a separate touch session. This allows the educators to work with smaller-size materials that are easy to bring in a docent's bag and can be passed around amongst the participants while standing in front of the original artwork.

A brand new addition to the programme is a 3D printed bust of Van Gogh that can be touched. Participants had suggested earlier that they would be interested in learning what Van Gogh looked like. There is only one photograph known of Van Gogh as an adult; therefore, his many self-portraits have always served as the most reliable images of the artist: red beard, green eyes, square face, strong brow. Having only paintings for reference of Van Gogh's face, a 3D model was needed to create a touchable face.

The Vincent van Gogh House in Zundert, Van Gogh's birthplace, recently received a beautifully sculpted head of Van Gogh in bronze on loan. It was a model made by André Schallens, a sculptor who was commissioned in the 1950s to make a monument for the artist on the Museumplein in Amsterdam – the very same square where the Van Gogh Museum would arise in 1973. The monument gives a striking image of an impassioned painter with his brush up in the air surrounded by rays of sun and birds, figures of a peasant woman and a miner, important sources of inspiration, at his feet. This expressive image fits the popular image of the artist as passionate and suffering, but it also comes very close to Van Gogh's self-portraits – the main source of reference for Schallens.

Hane3D by Casper Hanegraaf made a 3D model of the original study head by Schallens by taking photos from every angle and applying software to recreate it in3D. This free model was then used to 3D print the bust we have now. Again, as with the 3D paintings by Van Gogh, this head was not designed especially for PVI; it is a work of art by itself, coarsely sculpted, not smooth with all the details easily recognisable. Nevertheless, the expressive face with the protruding cheekbones, deeply sunk eyes and coarse beard will communicate the physical characteristics of Vincent and will hopefully spark a discussion of the mythical image we have created of him.

Concluding comments

Despite various museums and galleries showing us what is possible, a number of lingering questions remain. One is whether a mediated experience using reproductions is going 'to be the same'. Did the visitors to the *Tactile art* installation 'miss out' on seeing the original sculpture hidden within the plinths? Could we argue that also for the person with sight, our memory creates a representation and transforms this object every time it is recalled, (re)making sense of this in relation to our immediate everyday experiences? This issue of the richness, purpose and efficacy of the mediated experience, and the diversity of models and methods for providing it, also raise the question of how we best achieve the optimal experience for PVI. It was never the intention to definitively resolve these questions in this chapter, nor in this book. However, it seems clear that merely offering a tactile object as a proxy is insufficient to experience the art fully; other actions of interpretation and interaction are needed – verbal descriptions and conversation exchanges of ideas between visitors contribute to the overall experience for both PVI and sighted. And, of course, the perennial questions of how to proliferate inclusivity programmes in galleries and museums, and who should design and fund them, remain.

The physicist Carlo Rovelli poetically declared that 'all reality is interaction'.[26] Indeed, each of the sensory art projects described had multiple layers of interactions, bringing various groups of people together under a mutual interest and commitment through constant communication. Each sensory art project has overcome normative, technical and practical challenges, even navigating, or supported by, the legislative and international instruments discussed in this book. However, we must not forget the key goal that makes the programme worthwhile: social inclusion. As one of the participants of *Feeling van Gogh* expressed it:

> I had visited the Van Gogh Museum before, but it was mainly something that the other members of my family enjoyed and I was simply dragging my feet. This time I felt I was also participating.[27]

This chapter's overview of the contemporary sensory art cultural landscape demonstrates that we do not have to give up engaging with art and the stimulation and joy it provides, even when our sensory and intellectual capacities change and the details escape us. We conclude with the words of one access programme participant: 'I won't remember what you said, but I'll remember how you made me feel'.[28]

26 Krista Tippett, 'Carlo Rovelli – All Reality Is Interaction' 2017 podcast. Available at: https://onbeing.org/programs/carlo-rovelli-all-reality-is-interaction-apr2018/#transcript (last accessed 5 March 2020).

27 Quote from interviews with participants of Feeling Van Gogh, 26 February 2015.

28 Quote from conversation between the second-named author and an arts patron living with Alzheimer's, on 7 August 2017.

3 Accessibility and Open GLAM

Andrea Wallace

Introduction

The quest to make artworks accessible using new technologies is neither new nor has it only been led by heritage institutions.[1] Disability activism, anti-discrimination legislation and human rights treaties, technological innovation, and increased awareness of disabled audiences and their legal rights to participate in culture have accelerated institutions' efforts to translate visual works to tactile, haptic, aural, or other sensory experiences.

While this book examines how copyright can impede these acts, heritage institutions are not without recourse. Reproductions might be so transformative that questions of infringement can be set aside.[2] In addition, institutions can avoid copyright entirely by translating public domain works. Yet access to those translations is not always guaranteed. First, people with visual impairments (PVI) must physically visit an institution to participate in most accessibility programs.[3] This practical limitation excludes less-mobile and non-local PVI audiences. Second, although technologies enable the rapid transfer (and printing) of digital data worldwide, another barrier arises when a *new* copyright is claimed in the newly accessible work, which impedes access and reuse by digital PVI communities.[4] Finally, despite the growing number of institutions joining the Open

1 See Yvonne Ericksson, 'What Is the History of Tactile Pictures?' in Elisabeth Salzhauer Axel and Nina Sobol Levent (eds), *Art Beyond Sight: A Resource Guide to Art, Creativity, and Visual Impairment* (Art Education for the Blind, Inc and AFB Press of the American Foundation for the Blind 2003).

2 Moral rights concerns might be settled by, for example, using historic practices signaling the new work's connection to its source: "After [artist's name]".

3 Exceptions include deaf and hearing-impaired tours made accessible to non-local audiences through Facebook Live. See Elena Goukassian, 'Metropolitan Museum Aims for Accessibility with Sign Language Tours on Facebook Live' *Hyperallergic* (18 April 2018) <https://hyperallergic.com/436294/metropolitan-museum-accessibility-asl-facebook-live/> accessed 2 April 2020.

4 Whether that copyright claim is valid is a legal question, the outcome to which might depend on variations between the source and final format, decisions made before, during, or after the work's capture, or even the technology used.

GLAM (Galleries, Libraries, Archives, and Museums) Movement[5] to release data for public reuse, few acknowledge disabled audiences within the scope of their policies. In general, website terms categorically exclude any acknowledgement of online PVI audiences, let alone how they should legally access and reuse digital content (in standard formats) according to disability exceptions. Even fewer meet the W3C Web Accessibility Guidelines.[6] Thus, the need to reconsider and more holistically integrate disability access in museums onsite *and* online is both apparent and long overdue.

This chapter explores accessibility's potential against copyright's barriers and incentives to analyze the impact on access for PVI communities. It argues that while legal measures currently set *minimum* compliance standards and provide copyright exceptions for in-copyright works and accessibility, they fail to adequately consider institutional obligations around out-of-copyright works and accessibility. In doing so, the chapter analyzes accessibility initiatives and sensory art projects in order to critique IP and access policies in practice. The analysis reveals a risk that accessibility programs and legal measures could perpetuate a climate of *in*accessibility via the new IP arising, which positions accessibility as an "opt in" rather than default approach. To counter this risk, the following sections are framed by questions that scholars, lawmakers, the GLAM sector, and their plural audiences should be – or already are – asking about sensory art projects, IP, and open access. These include the following:

- What is access (which implies exclusion is default) in an age of greater inclusivity? How might this question be answered differently by the law than by the GLAM sector, or even a digital audience, depending on the audience? And how might "open" in combination with open access therefore become problematic depending on those context(s)?
- As applied to visual art, what is an accessible format copy in an age of rapidly developing technologies? And how do we ensure that equity, and not just equality, is extended through different iterations of an artwork according to need?
- Finally, how might legal exceptions or recommendations put forward by this book apply to the *new* works generated by GLAMs, especially with regards to translations of public domain works?

Within this inquiry, themes emerge around the ableist nature of visual culture, communication, copyright, and access. These questions and themes guide the discussion and expose how visabled assumptions are deeply embedded in IP management and access to heritage. The chapter concludes with workable

5 Douglas McCarthy and Andrea Wallace, 'Survey of GLAM Open Access Policy and Practice' (*Google Docs*, 2018) <https://docs.google.com/spreadsheets/u/1/d/1WPS-KJptUJ-o8SXtg00llcxq0IKJu8eO6Ege_GrLaNc/edit?usp=embed_facebook> accessed 2 April 2020.

6 'Accessibility - W3C' (*Web Accessibility Initiative*) <https://www.w3.org/standards/web design/accessibility#wai> accessed 2 April 2020.

suggestions for institutions, lawmakers, and the plural public and recommends gradated access policies more aligned with social inclusion goals.

Aiming for accessibility

Access in an age of greater inclusivity

Before proceeding, we must discuss terminology. This chapter uses the term visabled to describe ableist conditions resulting in the exclusion of PVI (and other disabled) audiences, both onsite and online. To be clear, this is no attempt to introduce a new word into the discourse of disability. Rather, "visabled" serves a narrow purpose for the argument, which seeks to capture and confront the specific kind of ableism impeding access to visual culture embedded in accessibility initiatives *and* copyright due to historical misunderstandings of blindness.[7] It is also because more neutral phrases like "non-disabled", "sighted", or "non-PVI" are generally imperfect and overbroad: imperfect, because people can assume PVIs to be non-PVIs when the disability is not (visually) apparent,[8] and overbroad, because non-PVIs are not always non-disabled. Indeed, non-PVIs could have a cognitive or learning disability affecting their perception of visual information.[9]

As always, there is a danger in reducing a rich spectrum of individuals to binary categories. David Bolt argues such a reduction fortifies a homogeneity inconsistent with a breadth of people from varied demographics, potentially with more than one disability.[10] This chapter's use of "PVI" and "visabled" thus confronts and reminds us of the binaries perpetuating the designs of many cultural and legislative initiatives, and it captures the specific visual ableism reflected in mainstream societal conditions. This ableism, for example, assumes that an apparently- or partially-sighted person might sufficiently perceive a visual work; visual perception is the only or best method for meaningful consumption of visual art; or non-visually impaired persons are best placed or equipped to lead PVI accessibility projects.[11] In reality, research shows accessibility initiatives are of value to PVI audiences, as well as to wider disabled and non-disabled

7 See 'The Tenacious Life of the Hypothetical Blind Man,' in Georgina Kleege (ed), *More Than Meets the Eye: What Blindness Brings to Art* (Oxford University Press 2018) 14–28.

8 See Georgina Kleege, *Sight Unseen* (Yale University Press 1999).

9 For a discussion of psychosocial disabilities and accessibility, see Paul Harpur, *Ableism at Work: Disablement and Hierarchies of Impairments* (Cambridge University Press 2019); Paul Harpur, Ursula Connolly and Peter Blanck, 'Socially Constructed Hierarchies of Impariments at Work: Example of the Austrian and Irish Workers' Access to Compensation for Injuries' (2017) 27 *Journal of Occupational Rehabilitation* 507.

10 David Bolt, 'Terminological Typology and the Social Model of Disability' (2005) 20 *Disability and Society* 539, 539.

11 Many examples can be found in Kleege (n 7); Amanda Cachia, 'Talking Blind: Disability, Access, and the Discursive Turn' (2013) 33 *Disability Studies Quarterly* 35.

audiences, through more enriched learning experiences[12] and for increased awareness of disabled communities.[13] If access is the goal, intersectional and inclusive principles must drive that process.

As we shall see, visabled regimes prevent our society from realizing the potential of enabling environments, which now encompass the digital realm. But despite the technologies available, accessibility has yet to embrace its digital potential and move past temporary exhibitions or periodic programs designed for PVI audiences who are local, more mobile, or have support.[14] Online, building accessibility information remains separate from general visitor information, and tour information for disabled visitors remains separate from general tour information. Such web pages may exist separately for functional efficiency: screen readers are better able to locate relevant information than if displayed among block text. However, few institutions' websites are web-accessible.[15] Moreover, overbroad terms prohibiting any use of text, data, and images fail to account for user rights and general copyright exceptions, let alone exceptions for disabilities. These visabled systems carry the segregated approaches of early exhibitions over to contemporary digital spaces, thereby sustaining the creation of separate spaces and experiences for PVI and visabled audiences.[16]

Let us consider this in context with the Tate and British Museum.[17] The Tate Gallery hosted the first major touch exhibition in the UK in 1976, but did not allow PVI visitors to bring sighted friends.[18] At the time, visitors noted difficulties, from navigating the exhibition to finding objects they were meant to touch.[19] Today, the Tate's onsite program considers visitors who are blind and visually impaired, deaf and hearing impaired, have learning disabilities, dyslexia,

12 Fiona Candlin, 'The Dubious Inheritance of Touch: Art History and Museum Access' (2006) 5 *Journal of Visual Culture* 137, 138; Catherine Kudlick and Susan Schwiek, 'Collision and Collusion: Artists, Academics, and Activists in Diaglogue with the University of California and Critical Disability Studies' (2014) 34 *Disability Studies Quarterly*; Georgina Kleege and Scott Wallin, 'Audio Description as Pedagogical Tool' (2015) 35 *Disability Studies Quarterly*.

13 Kleege (n 8); Cachia (n 11).

14 Exceptions are discussed *infra* in Making Art Accessible. For a review in the law's responsibility here, see Paul Harpur, 'From Universal Exclusion to Universal Equality: Regulating Ableism in a Digital Age' 40 *Northern Kentucky Law Review* 529.

15 Lawsuits are increasing against US galleries with non-accessible websites in violation of the Americans with Disabilities Act. See Eileen Kinsella, 'More Than 75 New York Galleries Are Slammed with Lawsuits for Allegedly Violating the Americans with Disabilities Act' (*artnet News*, 29 January 2019) <https://news.artnet.com/art-world/dozens-of-new-york-galleries-slammed-with-lawsuits-for-ada-compliance-on-websites-1450276> accessed 2 April 2020.

16 See Kevin Hetherington, 'Accountability and Disposal: Visual Impairment and the Museum' (2003) 1 *Museum and Society* 104.

17 Programs began prior to the Disability Discrimination Act 1995. See also Anne Pearson, 'Please Touch: An Exhibition of Animal Sculptures at the British Museum' (1984) 3 *Museum Management and Curatorship* 376.

18 Hetherington (n 16) 104–105.

19 Ibid.

autism, or require mobility provisions.[20] This information is online, but Tate's digital space is used to advertise onsite initiatives rather than reach digital disabled audiences.

Parameters around digital access are further compounded by IP: copyright is claimed in all content, and digital surrogates of public domain works are released © Tate, CC BY-NC-ND (3.0 Unported).[21] While the terms permit reproduction "for the non-commercial purposes of research, private study, criticism and review, or for limited circulation within an educational establishment", they prohibit "inaccurate or distorted reproduction, colour treatments, alterations or adaptations of website content" and "unauthorized text/data mining of website content and metadata".[22] Tate's terms incorporate fair dealing and select UK copyright exceptions, but disability access either is not one or, at the least, conflicts with many reuse restrictions designed around visabled engagement.

In 1990, the British Museum installed the first UK *permanent* touch tour using objects in the Egyptian and Graeco-Roman sculpture galleries[23] and added the touch gallery outside the Parthenon Galleries in 1998.[24] PVI communities and their families planning visits will find only basic information and no photos of either tour online.[25] The Egyptian tour is more accessible: users can download a large-print guide, a Braille book with raised drawings, and the tour's audio files.[26] But while the Museum's *Sketchfab* hosts 254 3D models for download CC BY-NC-SA,[27] no mention is made on the Egyptian Touch Tour web page that four of the nine sculptures[28] – or any other models for that matter – are available for download on *Sketchfab*.[29] The CC license reserves commercial rights in 3D scans, which makes downloading and ordering a 3D print from a commercial printer difficult. Few 3D-printed replicas are available on *The British*

20 Tate Modern, 'Accessibility' (*Tate*) <https://www.tate.org.uk/visit/tate-modern> accessed 2 April 2020.

21 Tate, 'Website Terms of Use' (*Tate*) <http://www.tate.org.uk/about-us/policies-and-procedures/website-terms-use> accessed 2 April 2020.

22 Ibid.

23 Hetherington (n 16) 104–105.

24 Ibid. 111.

25 'Egyptian Touch Tour' (*British Museum*) <https://www.britishmuseum.org/learning/access2/egyptian_touch_tour.aspx> accessed 28 June 2019; 'Room 18: Greece: Parthenon' (*British Museum*) 18 <https://www.britishmuseum.org/visiting/galleries/ancient_greece_and_rome/room_18_greece_parthenon.aspx> accessed 28 June 2019. Google Arts & Culture Street View provides views of the Egyptian touch tour, but ends outside the Parthenon Galleries. Street View: British Museum' (*Google Arts & Culture*) <https://artsandculture.google.com/project/street-view> accessed 2 April 2020.

26 No online equivalent exists for the Parthenon installation.

27 Models are released under a CC BY-NC-SA license. '3D Models by the British Museum (@britishmuseum)' (*Sketchfab*) <https://sketchfab.com/britishmuseum/models> accessed 2 April 2020.

28 This includes: (1) seated statue of Amenhotep III (about 1390-1352 BC, granodiorite); (2) lion statue of Amenhotep III (about 1390–1352 BC, red granite); (2) Sarcophagus (about 2400 BC, red granite); and (9) colossal scarab beetle (about 200-100 BC, quartz diorite). See ibid.

29 'Egyptian Touch Tour' (n 25).

Museum Shop Online.[30] This approach reinforces material assumptions about accessibility and physical sites of inclusion, and misses an opportunity to enable offsite engagement through use of the Braille and audio guides with 3D-printed models. That said, translating onsite initiatives to online audiences will not always be practical. With the Egyptian Touch Tour, the pieces are mostly there, but the Museum's execution fails to comprehensively consider and connect the dots for digital PVI communities.

In addition to their operational responsibilities, institutions must adapt polices to legal and cultural developments as necessary. Consequently, institutions operate within complicated set of legal norms, interpretations, and customs that can vary from one institution to the next.[31] However, some legal measures, like human rights and international law, bind only state parties. For example, states party to the 2006 UN Convention on the Rights of Persons with Disabilities[32] must ensure disabled persons can enjoy access to cultural materials in accessible formats and participate in creative, artistic, and intellectual production for individual and societal enrichment.[33] Notably, Article 30 obligates states to "take all steps, in accordance with international law, to ensure that laws protecting intellectual property rights do not constitute an unreasonable or discriminatory barrier to access by persons with disabilities to cultural materials".[34] Although signatories number 161, comprehensive reform to satisfy Article 30 has been slow to materialize.[35] Nor has the convention infiltrated institutional operations similar to other conventions, like the 1970 UNESCO Convention on the Means of Prohibiting and Preventing the Illicit Import, Export and Transport of Ownership of Cultural Property.[36]

As the introduction describes, competing interests in favor of IP protection can frustrate access-driven goals. The Marrakesh Treaty also aims to improve access to in-copyright (textual) works.[37] States party to the Treaty must implement copyright exceptions for making accessible format copies and allowing their transfer across borders,[38] but a 2017 WIPO scoping study on disability

30 3D printed replicas are priced around £200. 'Sculpture - Replicas' (*British Museum Shop Online*) <https://www.britishmuseumshoponline.org/sculpture-replicas/sculpture.html?p=1> accessed 2 April 2020.

31 See Andrea Wallace and Ronan Deazley, 'Display at Your Own Risk' <http://displayatyourownrisk.org/> accessed 2 April 2020.

32 UN Convention on the Rights of Persons with Disabilities (2006).

33 Article 30(1)–(2).

34 Article 30(3).

35 Other chapters explore implementation gaps. See also Julia Hoffmann and Aliaa Dakroury, 'Disability Rights between Legal Discourses and Policy Narratives: An Analysis of the European and Canadian Frameworks' (2013) 33 *Disability Studies Quarterly* 6

36 See Patty Gerstenblith, 'The Meaning of 1970 for the Acquisition of Archaeological Objects' (2013) 38 *Journal of Field Archaeology* 364.

37 Marrakesh Treaty to Facilitate Access to Published Works for Persons Who Are Blind, Visually Impaired or Otherwise Print Disabled adopted (2013).

38 The Treaty was implemented and subsequently transposed across EU Member States via Directive 2017/1564 and Regulation 2017/1563.

access found states "varied significantly in their coverage" and "have taken a diverse set of approaches to accessibility and copyright".[39] Some seem designed to protect the rightsholder's market for commercialization in PVI markets rather than to ensure uninhibited inclusive access. For example, the UK excludes visual impairments that may be corrected by contacts or glasses, and only authorized entities are permitted to make accessible format copies and extend access for personal use.[40] The law therefore distinguishes between valid and invalid visual impairments and mandates reliance on physical public institutions for limited forms of copying, instead of empowering PVI communities to design solutions themselves. These distinctions are all the more disabling when applied to access around reproductions of public domain works.

Meanwhile, the need to find financial support for operations can entrench approaches that prioritize commercialization above open access goals. National disability rights legislation requires compliance, but such legal measures, if followed, set a floor for minimum conduct rather than a meaningful standard towards holistic inclusion. Rarely is such legislation accompanied by financial support.[41] Consequently, institutions can be hesitant to waive rights in material perceived to generate revenue, like copyright in digital surrogates of public domain works.[42] More complex projects may be realized through private funders, specific funding schemes, or third-party partnerships, with each setting its own access parameters. For example, funding may carry obligations to generate revenue through IP exploitation[43] or, conversely, to openly license data.[44] IP can attract partnerships, bringing the technology and know-how, but programs are at a risk of having access defined by third-party interests, as well as transplanting non-diverse and visabled assumptions into projects for PVI audiences.[45] Accessi-

39 Blake Reid and Caroline Ncube, 'Scoping Study on Access to Copyright Protected Works by Persons with Disabilities' (World Intellectual Property Organization 2017) 2.

40 Copyright Designs and Patents Act 1988.

41 In addition to austerity measures gutting cultural funding worldwide, WIPO reported "a general lack of government support for people with disabilities" Reid and Ncube (n 39) 4. The Parthenon touch gallery was funded through private American donors, Lawrence and Barbara Fleischman. Hetherington (n 16).

42 Simon Tanner, 'Reproduction Charging Models & Rights for Policy Digital Images in American Art Museums' (2004) <http://www.kdcs.kcl.ac.uk/fileadmin/documents/USMuseum_SimonTanner.pdf>.

43 See Adrian Harvey, 'Funding Arts and Culture in a Time of Austerity' (Arts Council England and New Local Government Network, 2016).

44 See Effie Kapsalis, 'The Impact of Open Access on Galleries, Libraries, Museums, & Archives' (Smithsonian Institutes 2016).

45 Kleege (n 7) discusses visabled audiences misappropriating Braille with examples of the Alabama state quarter and the FDR Memorial. Kleege notes the quarter's Braille was impossible to read at such a tiny size, and unnecessary, since coins are already recognizable by touch, weight, and size. For the FDR Memorial, artist Robert Graham used Braille on bronze bas relief plaques four- to five-times larger than standard Braille with uneven spacing, placing some plaques higher than seven feet. Graham's intent was to invite touch and communicate graphic qualities of layering using relief and Braille. Kleege asks: "invitation to whom?" Kleege (n 7) 46–49.

bility requires, but fails to receive, adequate and sustainable government investment to enable holistic integration for more inclusive missions.

As discussed earlier, institutions are not always at liberty to set broad open-access policies around their own IP. GLAMs are bound by national copyright and disability rights legislation when managing collections and extending access. But the core of this latter activity is rooted in contract law and institutional policy-making. More often than not, public domain collections are treated as sources of revenue generation rather than ripe for a reproduction agenda prioritizing access and inclusive design. While claiming copyright may seem antithetical to the purpose behind the work's translation, it is often supported by law,[46] especially with format shifts from 2D to 3D, or vice versa.[47] And without the economic benefits envisioned by copyright, many complex projects with third-party partners risk never being realized. In this way, IP incentives can pit greater inclusivity against the commercial market of potential PVI (and other) consumers, shaping how disabled audiences are able to participate in culture and creative industries.

Translations (and copyright) in an age of rapidly developing technologies

So far, we have considered broader operational and legal conditions producing a visabled system of accessibility, onsite and online. We will now highlight concrete aspects of copyright and disability exceptions that are incompatible with holistic access.

To begin with, our normative legal notions of what constitutes a reproduction, adaptation, translation, communication, and even what "value" is within an IP framework have been shaped by ableist assumptions about a functioning society. These notions have been historically defined and measured by systems founded upon sighted experience.

Copyright exceptions can be similarly underscored by ableist assumptions, especially when designed to accommodate a single type of disability, medium, use, or specific act. The end result protects the exclusionary right secured to the rightsholder for a small market at the expense of more inclusive access and cultural enrichment.[48]

A visabled copyright system is disabling to non-visual audiences, leads to further restricted access, and undermines the potential of our collective cultural attainment. Indeed, the nature of art and inclusive cultural growth resists rigid forms of exclusivity. Art celebrates multiple perspectives, and technology now enables low-cost reproduction in various digital formats. Yet the public remains

46 Thomas Margoni, 'The Digitisation of Cultural Heritage: Originality, Derivative Works and (Non) Original Photographs' (2014) Institute for Information Law (IViR) ID 2573104.

47 For example, this might include 2D paintings captured by 3D scanning, or 3D objects captured by 2D photography. Issues arise when the output fails to satisfy the legal threshold of creativity. See Wallace and Deazley (n 31).

48 Lionel Bently and others, *Intellectual Property Law* (5 edition, OUP Oxford 2018) 259.

largely dependent on heritage institutions to reproduce and disseminate works in their collections. The combination of ownership of the object with a copyright claim in the reproduction reduces the potential spectrum of new perspectives to one produced by the host institution. Nor is there much opportunity for independent public creation. As Georgia Kleege argues, the failure to embrace and value disability with its learning benefits for all reinforces a monolithic experience of pictorial representation.[49] This monolithic experience is further bolstered by the law.

This critique is especially relevant to the suitable accessible format copy.[50] First, what *is* suitable and to whom? The UK legal exceptions permit reproduction for personal and educational use and adaptation only to the extent necessary to enable the disabled person to enjoy a work to the same degree as someone without a disability.[51] With respect to moral rights, under the EU Directive, a copy must also respect "the integrity of the work or other subject matter".[52] These visabled framings are problematic. Not only do they suggest a false equivalence, but a visabled legal system will adjudicate those boundaries if infringement is alleged. This can lead to further marginalization of those who cannot participate according to ableist understandings of access and suitable adaptation.

For states implementing the commercial availability clause, like the UK,[53] further hurdles arise: if the accessible format copy is commercially available on reasonable terms that provide a level of access enabling enjoyment, the exception no longer applies.[54] Those seeking access must purchase the commercially available version. Importantly, a limitation exists around profit: those who make accessible copies of in-copyright works cannot profit by selling or making them available for hire.[55] They may recoup the cost of creation and supply, but no more.[56] Importantly, if the source work is in the public domain, this restriction will not apply and a market price may be set for securing a copy.

This raises the question posed in the introduction: how will legal exceptions apply to *new* works generated by GLAMs? Here, we are faced with a Catch-22: in making the new work, copyright might be claimed in some component of the process or in the end result. Thus, how might such material be subject to the *same* legal exceptions that apply to the in-copyright works in collections? Moreover, new works in accessible formats may be sold or licensed to generate revenue, thereby satisfying the commercial availability clause in jurisdictions like the UK.

49 Kleege provides the example of using tactile sensation to depict a Degas with pictorial clarity, rather than to communicate the painting's hazier qualities. Kleege (n 7) 54.

50 Marrakesh Treaty, Art. 3(1).

51 CDPA 1988, s. 31F(5).

52 Directive 2017/1564, Art 3(2).

53 Sections 31A, 31B and Schedule 2, paragraphs 3A and 3B of the CDPA contain "commercial availability" restrictions that require the beneficiary to verify before copying that copies in the same accessible format are not already available on the market.

54 CDPA 1988, s. 31A(2)(c), s. 31B(2), s. 31B(6).

55 CDPA 1988, s. 31B(10).

56 Ibid.

This combination of ownership of the source object and the act of making and licensing the accessible format copy could mean that PVI access is both extended and restricted simultaneously. With commercial partnerships on the rise, this scenario is already playing out.

As detailed in the previous chapter, the Van Gogh Museum worked closely with Fujifilm Belgium to develop an innovative technique combining a 3D scan of a painting with a high-resolution print.[57] Nine works have been reproduced and access is extended to onsite PVI communities through the *Feeling Van Gogh* program. This multisensory experience allows groups of up to 12 people to book a two-hour tour and workshop, which includes 3D-printed paintings, as well as sound and scent elements and 3D miniature models of scenes like van Gogh's bedroom.[58] As discussed in the previous section, such access must be examined against parameters set to generate revenue. *Feeling Van Gogh* costs €120 in addition to a €19 admission ticket for each participant (carers receive free admission).[59] The 3D replicas are available in limited editions of 260[60] and can be purchased in the gift shop for around €25,000.[61] The Museum extended its business model in 2018 to offer pop-up museums with gift shops in North American shopping malls.[62] Visitors could now purchase a 3D replica at the reduced price of $17,750.[63] The *Feeling Van Gogh* experience is not offered at pop-up museums.

Generating revenue for public sustainability is imperative to support mission-driven goals. In addition to reduced public funding, sources of private funding have received increased scrutiny. Many institutions are renaming galleries and ending long-term partnerships with contentious private funders, such as the Sackler Family.[64] Indeed, in 2018, the Van Gogh Museum ended its 18-year

57 Van Gogh Museum, 'Van Gogh Museum Edition Collection' (*Van Gogh Museum*) <https://www.vangoghmuseum.nl/en/business/van-gogh-museum-edition-collection> accessed 2 April 2020.

58 'Feeling Van Gogh - Van Gogh Museum' <https://www.vangoghmuseum.nl/en/whats-on/feeling-van-gogh?v=1> accessed 2 April 2020.

59 'Blind and Partially-Sighted Visitors' (*Van Gogh Museum*) <https://www.vangoghmuseum.nl/en/plan-your-visit/accessibility/blind-and-partially-sighted-visitors> accessed 2 April 2020.

60 Van Gogh Museum (n 57).

61 Sarah Webb, 'Van Gogh Copies in 3D Look Almost Real, Cost 25,000 Euros' *Reuters* (13 September 2013) <https://uk.reuters.com/article/us-art-vangogh-copies-idUKBRE98C0QZ20130913> accessed 2 April 2020.

62 Van Gogh Museum, 'Van Gogh Museum Editions Pop-up Tour' (*Van Gogh Museum*) <https://static.vangoghmuseum.nl/en/business/van-gogh-museum-editions-pop-up-tour> accessed 2 April 2020.

63 Ibid.

64 This includes the Louvre, National Portrait Gallery, London, Tate Modern, and Metropolitan Museum of Art. See Elizabeth A Harris, 'The Louvre Took Down the Sackler Name. Here's Why Other Museums Probably Won't.' *The New York Times* (18 July 2019) <https://www.nytimes.com/2019/07/18/arts/sackler-family-museums.html> accessed 2 April 2020; Naomi Rea, 'As a Wave of UK Museums Cut Ties with the Sackler Family, One Small London Gallery May Have Led the Way' (*artnet News*, 22 March 2019) <https://news.artnet.com/art-world/south-london-gallery-rejected-sackler-money-1495687> accessed 2 April 2020.

partnership with the Royal Dutch Shell oil and gas company.[65] With reduced support, institutions must explore new business models and opportunities for income. The irony is that through copyright, accessible format copies of public domain works become a new exploitable product rather than being used to increase access and participation as envisioned by disability rights treaties. Given this approach, Bess Williamson warns institutions against presenting projects as empowering while downplaying the commercial interests in profit.[66] In our case, this includes profit from not only PVI audiences but also broader commercialization opportunities with non-PVI and non-disabled audiences made possible by accessible format copies.

Making art accessible: examining the landscape of (a more) inclusive culture

We will now turn to institutional, private, and grassroots initiatives that challenge historical assumptions about disability and access. The following projects explore facets of accessibility with varying results and provide lessons that can inform subsequent initiatives, both onsite and online. To capture that spectrum of access, it is crucial to analyze how PVI audiences have been integrated and what effect that had on project missions, functionality, and revenue generation goals. The following examples help demonstrate how inclusive design might conflict or cooperate with the role of IP in accessibility projects.

The first example demonstrates the importance of centring voices of wider communities during accessibility projects, rather than those of lawmakers or communities of practice, to upend the exclusive systems that inclusivity seeks to dismantle. In 2015, the Museum of Contemporary Art in Chicago (MCA) and Prime Access Consulting launched a project called *Coyote* to enable the MCA's new website to meet the Web Accessibility Initiative's WCAG 2.0 AAA technical standard and extend digital access of its in-copyright collection to wider communities.[67] *Coyote* aimed to make all 18,000 images of exhibitions, programs, collection artworks, and even retail items accessible to the widest possible audience through visual description.[68] Working with Sina Bahram and Prime Access Consulting, the partnership designed a workflow tool using the principles of universal design, which advances that products designed to be useful to one community are likely to benefit a variety of users, not only those with disabil-

65 Martin Bailey, 'Shell Sponsorship Deal with Amsterdam's Van Gogh Museum Ends' <http://theartnewspaper.com/news/shell-sponsorship> accessed 2 April 2020.

66 Bess Williamson, 'Access + Ability, Cooper-Hewitt National Design Museum, Smithsonian Institution, New York, USA, December 15, 2017 - September 3, 2018' (2018) 10 *Design and Culture* 223, 226.

67 Sina Bahram and Anna Chiaretta Lavatelli, 'Using Coyote to Describe the World' (*MW18: Museums and the Web 2018*) <https://mw18.mwconf.org/paper/using-coyote-to-describe-the-world/> accessed 2 April 2020.

68 Ibid. The MCA relied on copyright law provisions Section 107 (fair use as clarified by *Authors Guild v HathiTrust*) and Section 121 (the Chafee Amendment).

ities.[69] The public-facing website includes an opt-in description layer available to any visitor to show users a new way to approach artworks and images and to increase awareness of digital accessibility;[70] the software itself is open source.

Behind the scenes, *Coyote* enables users to create accounts and author descriptions for a given resource, which are sent to an administrator for approval.[71] Edits, co-authoring, and attribution are supported by *Coyote*'s functionality. And rather than nominate a single, preferred description for a work, the metadata model enables storage and retrieval of multiple descriptions to capture a "multiplicity of voices" in line with *Coyote*'s ethos.[72] During the process, the MCA learned that the core task of image description was more easily and accurately performed by non-experts than by curatorial staff.[73] This demonstrates how the lens through which we have been trained to consume art might actually define (or inhibit) our understanding of a work, area of law, or cultural concept. The MCA has embraced this realization by experimenting with poetry or rap-style descriptions for certain artworks, as well as cadence, tempo, and volume to convey a work's visual qualities.[74] Copyright will protect these and more basic descriptions. Accordingly, the open-source software includes a multilevel rights and permissions function and stores description-level rights information using Creative Commons licenses.[75] Institutions may select a default license; viewing its descriptions as metadata, the MCA uses CC0.[76]

Coyote has also enabled the Museum to revisit its onsite inclusivity approach. The MCA is now integrating new digital functionalities into its physical space: visual descriptions will be used for a number of in-gallery applications, including electronic labels and recorded audio descriptions, to support more independent audiences onsite.[77] Descriptions also were repurposed as clues for scavenger hunts in the MCA and around Chicago.[78] By bringing outside institutions onboard for the event and providing training, the MCA has increased the number of cultural organizations participating in digital accessibility and accessible experiences across Chicago.[79] Future plans involve Word Press integration, multi-

69 Ibid.

70 MCA Chicago, 'Welcome to Coyote' (*Coyote*) <http://coyote.mcachicago.org/> accessed 11 June 2019.

71 Bahram and Lavatelli (n 67).

72 Ibid.

73 Ibid. This observation is consistent with ARCHES, discussed *infra*. Jonathan Rix and Garcia Carrizosa, 'Deliverable D2.1 "Initial Recommendations and Guidelines"' (2016) *ARCHES* 12.

74 Bahram and Lavatelli (n 67).

75 Ibid.

76 Interview with Sina Bahram and Susan Chun.

77 Bahram and Lavatelli (n 67). See also Claire Voon, 'This Open Source Software Could Make Museum Websites More Accessible' (*Artsy*, 19 April 2019) <https://www.artsy.net/article/artsy-editorial-open-source-software-museum-websites-accessible> accessed 2 April 2020.

78 'Case Study: Coyote Scavenger Hunt' (*Coyote*, 3 December 2018) <https://coyote.pics/resources/case-study-coyote-scavenger-hunt/> accessed 2 April 2020.

79 Bahram and Lavatelli (n 67).

lingual capabilities, and expanding *Coyote* to the private sector to aid the ageing market of art investors.[80] By situating inclusivity at its core, the open source initiative has fed a network of innovative accessibility developments across various platforms with ongoing benefits to vast audiences.

For comparison, in 2017, the Cooper-Hewitt Museum hosted an exhibition entitled "Access + *Ability*" that featured visually appealing products designed for disabled users.[81] In her review, Bess Williamson highlights how the exhibition was organized by categories similar to those used by the medical profession – "Mobility", "Connecting", and "Daily Routines" – which echo the medical model of disability, defining it "as primarily a functional concern, instead of a cultural one".[82] As Williamson observes, this approach sustained a narrative that "does little to challenge the notion that disability needs to be treated or fixed".[83]

Similar to the previous example, the Museum hired a consultant from the disabled community, Liz Jackson, a Disability Design expert, to consult on the exhibition.[84] Later, Jackson wrote the Museum had declined a number of her recommendations, such as signaling which products were created by disabled designers and allowing disabled people to author title card descriptions.[85] Jackson wrote she also had to advocate strongly for using "by" as in "designed for and *by* disabled people".[86] While the Museum adopted its use, Jackson was ultimately disappointed, especially in the Museum's failure to embrace the word "disability", on the basis that it was perceived to be stigmatizing,[87] and opting instead for the more generalizing term "ability".[88] Both Jackson and Williamson note that the consequences of these decisions led to primarily non-disabled designers being interviewed by the press and therefore directing the narrative around the exhibition's importance.[89] Jackson tweeted about her experience and expressed disappointment with the Museum being comfortable adopting her language but without the values.[90] On a metalevel, the experience underscores the need for the program Jackson created in response called "WITH", encapsulating "how

80 Interview with Sina Bahram and Susan Chun.

81 Cooper Hewitt, 'Access+Ability' (*Cooper Hewitt, Smithsonian Design Museum*) <https://www.cooperhewitt.org/channel/access-ability/> accessed 2 April 2020.

82 Williamson (n 66) 225. By contrast, the social model of disability frames environments themselves as disabling, rather than any person's individual impairment or difference.

83 Ibid.

84 Liz Jackson, 'It Started a Year Ago When @cooperhewitt Asked Me to Consult on Their Access + Ability Exhibit. I Jumped in without Pause, as Disability Design Is My Passion.' (*@elizejackson*, 30 April 2018) <https://twitter.com/elizejackson/status/991082381535793152> accessed 2 April 2020.

85 Ibid.

86 Ibid.

87 Ibid.

88 Williamson (n 66) 226.

89 Jackson, 'It Started a Year Ago When @cooperhewitt Asked Me to Consult on Their Access + Ability Exhibit. I Jumped in without Pause, as Disability Design Is My Passion.' (n 84).

90 Ibid. Williamson (n 66).

disabled people have historically experienced the design process" via products that are often designed *for* them, but rarely *with* them.[91]

We must also critically examine the narratives embedded or left unchallenged in accessibility projects. Another initiative engaging with PVI communities includes *Touching Masterpieces*, a partnership among tech and VR collaborators NeuroDigital, the Leontinka Foundation for the blind and visually impaired, and the National Gallery of Prague.[92] The physical exhibition was accessible for PVI and non-PVI audiences. Visitors were invited to "view" statues through haptic feedback provided by patented gloves sensitive enough to convey the difference between rough, smooth, and textured materials.[93] The experience sought to remedy "relief aids and tactile pictures that far from accurately reflect reality".[94]

Currently, the series includes three works selected for their value to art history: the Venus de Milo (Louvre, Paris), David (Galleria dell'Accademia, Florence), and the Nefertiti Bust (Neues Museum, Berlin).[95] Yet a moment occurs in video documentation that suggests visabled communities might rethink how selection proceeds to avoid perpetuating the values of mainstream (*i.e.*, Western) art history. As one visitor feels the space around Venus's shoulders and midsection, he asks: "How about the arms?" There is a pregnant pause as those present realize they must explain a visual given and one of her most valuable features for visabled audiences: "It doesn't have arms".[96] Reproduction enables PVI audiences to engage with works valued by – and thereby participate in – dominant discourses within the authorized heritage discourse.[97] However, new technologies enable us to challenge power dynamics embedded in this heritage by considering how we might prioritize reproduction within the values of historically excluded audiences, thereby educating non-disabled audiences of the excluded or oppressed values systems of othered communities.

Various components of these projects might support greater digital accessibility online, whether using existing data online or when generating new data. Indeed, *Touching Masterpieces* explores a different way of "feeling art" that could be generated using the same raw data produced during 3D scans. But what happens to institutions' raw data? Who should own it? And how might it be used in other ways? It is unclear how the *Touching Masterpieces* procured or generated its data.[98] For the works selected, access to the source is unnecessary. A number

91 Liz Jackson, 'WITH' (*NYCxDESIGN*) <https://www.nycxdesign.com/events/with/> accessed 2 April 2020.

92 Touching Masterpieces, 'Presenting the Unthinkable' (*Touching Masterpieces*) <http://touchingmasterpieces.com> accessed 2 April 2020.

93 Ibid.

94 Ibid.

95 Ibid.

96 00:56 to 01:10, "How It Works," ibid.

97 Laurajane Smith, *Uses of Heritage* (Routledge 2006).

98 3D expert Cosmo Wenman was able to trace the source of David (david.blend, 10.5 MB) to TurboSquid and match the Venus file (venus.blend, 31.5 MB) to the SMK Denmark's public

of high-quality and large-scale copies are held among various institutions, commercial platforms, or, as in the case of Nefertiti, high-quality public domain data are available online.[99]

Unlike touch exhibitions of the past, *Touching Masterpieces* considers how access might be extended to non-local audiences. While the website is not web-accessible, it includes downloadable machine-readable PDFs for PVI visitors.[100] The PDF includes basic instructions to install the experience, which is presumably contingent upon access to patented technologies developed by the project.[101] It remains unclear how the files are licensed: no copyright policy is provided online and/or embedded in the metadata.

Yet technological sophistication at this level is not necessary. In fact, already-existing technologies could be repurposed for disability art access so long as institutions release openly-licensed data. For example, *Touch Mapper* is a website created by a sighted person after learning the challenges faced by PVIs travelling independently.[102] The website uses Open Street Map data, rather than commercial data sources (e.g., Google Maps) that prohibit commercial use.[103] Users are able to enter an address, adjust the map area, and create a file that can be downloaded and sent to almost any 3D printer, as well as a link for placing online orders. The software is open source, permitting further development, for example, to translate digital surrogates of artworks.

Imagine a similar online tool designed for enriched learning experiences: upload a high-quality image to the website that interprets the visual data and renders a file to be printed at home or commercially, or even modified, remixed, and sold. *Unseen Art* attempted to raise funds for a platform where users could contribute and download files for free, but the Indiegogo campaign was unsuccessful in reaching its £24,000 goal.[104] While such translations could be used for various audiences worldwide, the majority of GLAMs prohibit the type of access required,[105] and those with open policies rarely release data at the quality

---

domain scan based on the triangle number (274, 243). Nefertiti (nefertiti.fbx, 6.7 MB) is more difficult to read, but seems to be a reduced resolution version of The Other Nefertiti (*supra*, n. 99). Upon closer inspection, the digital files appear difficult to translate to a haptic system and lack provenance and metadata. Correspondence with Cosmo Wenman (9–11 August 2019), on file with the author.

99 Jan Nikolai Nelles and Nora Al-Badri, 'Nefertiti Hack' (*The Other Nefertiti*) <http://nefertitihack.alloversky.com/> accessed 2 April 2020.

100 However, the PDF includes hyphenated words and other visual elements that disrupt the machine-readable experience.

101 Gloves are available for €1,500. 'Avatar VR' (*NeuroDigital Technologies*) <https://avatarvr.es/product/avatarvr/> accessed 2 April 2020.

102 See Samuli Kärkkäinen, 'Tactile Maps Easily | Touch Mapper' (*Touch Mapper - Tactile Maps for the Visually Impaired*) <https://touch-mapper.org/> accessed 2 April 2020.

103 This provides a cautionary tale against adopting non-commercial licenses.

104 Marc Dillon, 'Unseen Art: Experiencing Art for the First Time' (*Indiegogo*) <https://www.indiegogo.com/projects/unseen-art-experiencing-art-for-the-first-time#/> accessed 2 April 2020. Notably, art does not need to be seen, or even touched, in order to be experienced.

105 See Wallace and Deazley (n 31).

necessary for such a tool.[106] Revisiting an issue discussed earlier, how might someone request a high-resolution digital surrogate from a closed institution in order to translate the image from 2D to 3D? Institutions will arguably charge for this type of reuse despite whether the copyright is valid or whether there is a clear copyright exception. Some users have turned to Freedom of Information legislation or filed public lawsuits to secure access to institutions' digital materials.[107] But releasing high-resolution digital surrogates and data around public domain artworks would enable the relevant communities to design their own initiatives, which have value to wider communities for a number of purposes.

Multifaceted communities have been integrated during initiatives like ARCHES, a Horizon 2020 funded project that developed gesture-controlled multi-sensory technology for accessing heritage artefacts and resources.[108] ARCHES values echo Jackson's: its principles of participation stress the "intention of all those involved must be to do "research with" rather than "research on" the participatory research group members".[109] ARCHES's delivery method, designed *with* the relevant communities, simultaneously engages different senses as "analogues for vision" by using low-cost depth cameras that operate directly on relief surfaces to produce an interactive experience with location-dependent, verbal, captioned, and image-supported descriptions as the artefact is explored by the visitor.[110] And, similar to *Coyote*, the project produced an open source data management platform that can be freely downloaded, customized, and extended to meet individual needs.[111] Online, informational videos include British Sign Language interpreters, closed captioning, and downloadable machine-readable descriptions and PDFs in multiple languages.[112]

Key questions underlying these examples are as follows. What role might technology play to invite alternative uses of public domain works that advance marginalized voices and facilitate more inclusive discussions around copyright, culture, and digital media accessibility? And how might GLAMs help clear the way for disability communities to explore and design their own solutions? As discussed in the first section, funding sources or partners might determine the final shape and format taken by accessibility projects. But besides funding, the IP rights claimed in newly accessible works raise one of the biggest barriers to

106 See McCarthy and Wallace (n 5).

107 Cosmo Wenman, 'Rodin's Thinker 3D Scan Access Effort' (*Cosmo Wenman*, 25 April 2018) <https://cosmowenman.com/bmamuseerodinthinker3dscan/> accessed 2 April 2020.

108 ARCHES, 'Accessible Resources for Cultural Heritage EcoSystems | Projects | H2020' (*CORDIS | European Commission*) <https://cordis.europa.eu/project/rcn/204798_en.html> accessed 2 April 2020.

109 Rix and Carrizosa (n 73) 17.

110 ARCHES, 'Arches Project Cultural Heritage Inventory and Management Software' (*Arches Project*) <https://www.archesproject.org/> accessed 2 April 2020.

111 Ibid.

112 'ARCHES, Accessible Resources for Cultural Heritage EcoSystems' <https://www.arches-project.eu/> accessed 2 April 2020.

accessibility. Accordingly, this final section considers how GLAM open access and IP policies might be (re)designed for inclusivity.

Moving away from visabled exclusivity and control

The current framework of copyright is unequipped to handle the potential of technology during the translation of works from 2D to 3D for accessibility. Not only does it underestimate the potential of accessibility, but its economic incentives encourage business models that secure exclusivity and control in order to maximize potential revenue generation. But the necessary reform cannot proceed via visabled communities alone. Society's understanding of this area must be adaptable and continually enriched by listening, learning, and working *with* communities that have long been invested in accessibility and inclusive design.[113] Considering the history of accessibility, a reflective and reiterative process is necessary.[114] Accordingly, this chapter recommends embracing the work of many who call for broadly integrating the principles of universal inclusive design into policy and practice and making space for disabled communities to become wholly embedded in the fabric of our cultural and legal institutions.[115] Only then can our cultural and legal measures begin to reflect the needs of a more inclusive society.

Liz Jackson advocates for an equitable and mutual framework of "mutuality", which she defines as "a radical act by an individual or group of individuals intended to create space for sustainable participation within a system or institution that benefits from representing or serving them".[116] Jackson distinguishes mutuality from empathy, which she explains is "more focused on the gesture than the impact" and can lead to situations of "pathological altruism" that worsen the conditions for the people they are intended to benefit.[117] By contrast, mutuality allows us to reconsider access and reflect on problematic areas in IP and heritage management, in general, through interdependence – and, importantly, it aligns with Article 30 of the UNCRPD. We must therefore consider the structural changes necessary to support mutuality.

On a legislative level, this requires sustainable investment and copyright reform. Governments must reconsider policies impacting the GLAM sector ranging from public funding to revenue-generating obligations to allow for greater inclusivity. As Georgina Kleege stresses, accessibility must "cease to be random

113 Jackson, 'WITH' (n 91). See also Bess Williamson, *Accessible America: A History of Disability and Design* (First edition, NYU Press 2019); Elizabeth DePoy and Stephen Gilson, *Rethinking Disability: Principles for Professional and Social Change* (Wadsworth 2004).

114 Williamson (n 113); DePoy and Gilson (n 113).

115 This list is far too long to include here. This chapter highlights: Sina Bahram, Fiona Campbell, Fiona Candlin, Elizabeth Depoy, Elizabeth Ellcessor, Stephen Gilson, Paul Hapur, Liz Jackson, Georgia Kleege, Bess Williamson.

116 Liz Jackson, 'Empathy Reifies Disability Stigmas' (Interaction19, 24 February 2019) <https://vimeo.com/319388683> accessed 2 April 2020.

117 Ibid; Barbara Oakley and others (eds), *Pathological Altruism* (Oxford University Press 2011).

acts of charity and become a way to enlarge cultural understanding of art".[118] Practically, this requires a serious commitment to increased funding for the cultural sector and, specifically, for disability projects. Such funding must be accompanied by obligations to adopt open-access policies to the greatest (appropriate) extent around project data and outputs.

Copyright has much to learn from inclusive design. To begin with, disability challenges whether ableist assumptions in the law even serve the purposes they have been designed to serve for the dominant culture.[119] Meanwhile, the pervasiveness of ableism in copyright reinforces prevailing prejudices against disability. These legal measures historically designed *for* visabled societies perpetuate repressive norms of access and reuse.[120] Exceptions to these norms must recognize the continuum of visual impairments to ensure that equity, not only equality, is reached through different iterations of a work according to need. We must critically examine what an "accessible format copy" is in an age of rapidly developing technologies and consider the pressing need to adapt inflexible legal measures as technologies blend and progress to better reflect the messiness of reality. Lawmakers must revisit copyright through the lens of ableism and challenge ocular-centric cultural and legal practices that protect a rightsholder in opposition with the spirit of disability rights law. As Elizabeth Ellcessor argues, this process must better consider alternate uses, marginalized voices, and collaborative innovations in disabled accessibility to rethink digital media accessibility.[121] This same process must encompass copyright reform.

Practically, reframing copyright through inclusive design may prove challenging. But we must begin by critically examining the visabled structure of the copyright regime, especially by confronting the general bias underlying legislation that precludes "any changes to the work which are not necessary to overcome the problems *suffered by* the disabled persons for whom the accessible copy is intended".[122] Such ableist language and mindsets must be eliminated from legal framework and its framing of access to culture and perceptions around engagement.

On an institutional level, this requires a revision of access and operational policies and a commitment to gradated treatment of materials generated during accessibility initiatives. Institutions may not be bound by soft law, but GLAMs should embrace the 2006 UNCRPD similar to the 1970 UNESCO Convention in order to enable disability communities to digitally engage with accessibility projects protected by IP rights.

118 Kleege (n 7) 11.
119 See, e.g., Thomas Hehir, 'Eliminating Ableism in Education' (2002) 72 *Harvard Educational Review* 1.
120 The Marrakesh Treaty marks an important advancement in the 'Nothing about us without us' mantra for more inclusive legal reform.
121 Elizabeth Ellcessor, *Restricted Access: Media, Disability, and the Politics of Participation* (NYU Press 2016).
122 CDPA 1988, s. 31F(5)(b). (emphasis added).

Operationally, institutions can work *with* disabled artists and communities to make onsite and online spaces more accessible.[123] Onsite, this must extend to creating sustainable employment positions for disabled persons within cultural institutions. Online, institutions must acknowledge digital disability communities through website policies and web accessibility and stop using overbroad language to claim rights in all digital materials.

As reproduction and accessibility projects become more complex, different components may – or may not – attract IP protection in addition to the output that becomes the accessible format copy. Rights management will naturally become more complicated as wider audiences and perspectives are incorporated during production. But not all components of these initiatives should be exploited. A climate already exists where IP's economic incentives can outweigh cultural obligations, thereby reducing disability to a market for which the law must design an exception. Research shows this negatively impacts competition and consumers, especially when multiple forms of protection, like copyright and patent, are secured for the same creation.[124] In the context of *this* market, GLAMs should consider *who* will lose out when reserving all rights for commercial exploitation and how licensing and reuse terms might be designed to enable greater access for disabled audiences, especially the new audiences made possible by the digital realm.

Importantly, this does not require an all-or-nothing release of new IP. In fact, releasing non-original and less innovative materials, like raw data and digital surrogates of public domain works, from commercialization goals helps justify the exploitation of IP generated during more complex initiatives and desired by third parties. During contract negotiations, institutions must advocate for releasing these basic outputs for public reuse. Doing so will enable disability communities to design accessible works for themselves and enrich our creative industries.

The Open GLAM Movement could also adopt accessibility as a central tenet. Open GLAM recognizes technology's potential to free source objects from physical locations and conservation concerns, and it challenges efforts to conserve territory and authority around cultural heritage. Similar to accessibility,[125] Open GLAM embraces the potential for hybrid knowledge generation. As Kleege advocates, we must depart from initiatives that require PVI audiences to rely on others' interpretations and reconsider how art engagement might "expand beyond segregated accommodation to create a more inclusive culture".[126]

123 This work is already ongoing. See also Liz Jackson's, 'The Disabled List' (*The Disabled List*) <https://www.disabledlist.org/> accessed 2 April 2020.

124 Buccafusco, Lemley, and Masur explore the social costs of IP rights in functional aspects of creations in Christopher Buccafusco, Mark A Lemley, and Jonathan S Masur, 'Intelligent Design' (2018) 68 *Duke Law Journal* 75.

125 Fiona Candlin, 'Don't Touch! Hands Off! Art, Blindness and the Conservation of Expertise' (2004) 10 *Body & Society* 71; Hetherington (n 16).

126 Kleege (n 7) 99.

Open GLAM is ideally situated to promote this endeavor. This will lead to more inclusive environments onsite and online for people with perception, memory, cognition, and communication impairments as well as people with physical disabilities.

Conclusion

There is no shortage of culture to translate for accessibility. However, as demonstrated, a real risk exists of copyright erecting unintended barriers around GLAM-generated material to expand access and enable new knowledge generation by PVI and other disabled audiences. Without clearer guidance on these pressing issues, desires to exploit low-hanging IP could prevent plural narratives from developing and contributing to a more inclusive society.

At the same time, it is imperative to acknowledge costs and design sustainable business models to support digital strategies that can adapt to each inevitable advancement in technology. Institutions must balance public-facing missions against desires for exclusive exploitation when deciding whether a work's value and its various components are best suited for commercialization or open access. In reality, gradated treatment of IP in digital media will better enable current and future generations to access, participate in, and innovate using our cultural heritage in the public domain. Otherwise, with each technological advancement, reproductions of public domain works will continue to be restricted by a monolithic view of art and art history, commercial goals will prevail, and access will be granted to only the few able to afford fees.

New technologies enable GLAMs to explore and invite alternative uses of public domain and in-copyright works that advance marginalized voices and facilitate more inclusive discussions around copyright, culture, and digital media accessibility. GLAMs are ideally placed to bargain for openly-licensing certain outputs at the outset of digital initiatives and establish meaningful standards around inclusivity during third-party partnerships. However, this necessitates an unequivocal commitment to adopting a more inclusive philosophy around open access. Indeed, accessibility enables us all to reevaluate not only *what* open access means, but to *whom*, in a visabled and ableist culture. Advancing accessibility will enable lawmakers, GLAMs, and the plural public to more accurately represent and consider diverse voices when designing projects, policies, and the law to better reflect the richly diverse society in which we live.

4 3D printing in arts and heritage

Renegotiating relationships between the original and the replica

Vivian van Saaze

Introduction

In 1935, the German cultural critic Walter Benjamin published his now canonical essay about the status of the work of art in modern mass culture. In 'The Work of Art in the Age of Mechanical Reproduction', Benjamin expressed great concerns about the drawbacks of reproduction technologies such as film and photography, as the aura – 'the unique aesthetic authority' – was lost in the process of mechanical reproduction. According to Benjamin, although mechanical reproduction brought about new possibilities for collective experience, it also resulted in a decline of the original, and thus a loss of the aura of art. More than 80 years later, Walter Benjamin's seminal essay can be reconsidered in light of the even greater reproducibility of works of art in the digital age fostered by 3D technologies.

Over the last few years, the access, ease and thus popularity of 3D printing have increased as a result of the drop in the costs of 3D modelling software and printers. 3D printing has become popular in many different industries, from product design, food and the medical industry, to civil construction. The technology has also found its way into museums and other cultural institutions. Koller et al. have identified an article by Leo Biek on stereovideo presented at the Annual Conference of Computer and Quantitative Methods in Archaeology in 1985 as the first major article on 3D capturing in the cultural realm.[1] Since then, the number of applications has grown substantially, and as with any technological surge, the digital imperative comes with many promises. Already in 2014, Neumüller et al. predicted that '3D Printing' will not only become vital in the field of reconstruction of objects, but also for the research, documentation, preservation and educational purposes, and has the potential to serve these

1 Koller, D., Frischer, B., & Humphreys, G. (2009). Research Challenges for Digital Archives of 3D Cultural Heritage Models. *ACM Journal on Computing and Cultural Heritage*, 2(3), DOI: 10.1145/1658346.1658347. For an early overview of 3D reproductions or so-called virtual heritage, see Forte, M. & Siliotti, A. (1997). *Virtual Archaeology*. New York: Abrams. For a more recent overview, see: Münster, S., Pfarr-Harfst, M., Kuroczynski, P., & Ionnides, M. (eds.) (2016). *3D Research Challenges in Cultural Heritage II*. New York: Springer.

purposes in an accessible and all-inclusive way.[2] Indeed, artists, designers and cultural institutions recognised the potential of replicas to increase access to and engagement with cultural artefacts – many of which, given their historical importance and fragility, cannot be touched and are exhibited in glass displays or stored in inaccessible repositories. For tech companies and computer programmers, cultural institutes and heritage sites were perceived as exciting test beds for 3D scanning and technological advancement.

This chapter takes stock of 3D technology applications in cultural institutions, and asks the following question: How is 3D printing being used in arts and heritage today? While inventorying the different user practices, the chapter also explores how 3D reproductions influence the appreciation for – and interaction with – 'the original' object. In doing so, it will assess the complex relationships between originals and reproductions and the impact of digitalisation on cultural values of authenticity, uniqueness and aura.

Unlike most contributions to this volume, the chapter will not talk from a legal perspective. Instead, it traces the shifting definitions of authenticity and explores how – in different user practices – 3D reproductions renegotiate relationships between the original and the replica. Before addressing the different usages of 3D printing in arts and heritage, and the complex relationships between originals and reproductions, the chapter first provides a brief discussion of the changing attitudes towards the authentic and the inauthentic in the arts and heritage.

Redefining the relationship between replica's and authenticity

'The presence of the original is the prerequisite to the concept of authenticity.'[3]

In 'The Work of Art in the Age of Mechanical Reproduction' (1935), Walter Benjamin expressed great concerns about the drawbacks of reproduction technologies such as film and photography, as the aura – 'the unique aesthetic authority' – was lost in the process of mechanical reproduction. For Benjamin, mechanical reproduction threatened authenticity and resulted in a decline of the original. Unlike original artworks, reproductions lack what Benjamin called the artwork's 'aura', the unique presence in time and space. Mechanical reproduction is thus equivalent to a loss of the aura and the artwork's uniqueness.

2 Neumüller, M., Reininger, A., Rist, F., & Kern, C. (2014). '3D Printing for Cultural Heritage: Preservation, Accessibility, Research and Education' in Ionnides, M. & Quack, E. (eds.) *3D Research Challenges in Cultural Heritage. A Roadmap in Digital Heritage Preservation*. New York: Springer, pp. 119–134. (p. 119)

3 Benjamin cited in Gumbrecht, H-U., Marrinan, M. (2003). *Mapping Benjamin. The Work of Art in the Digital Age*. Stanford: Stanford University Press, p. 125.

His canonical work had a tremendous impact on the thinking about the complex relationships between the original and the copy, and strengthened the still dominant proposition that any copy is a weak counterfeit of the original.[4]

In their essay with the provocative title 'How to make mistakes on so many things at once and become famous for it', sociologists of technology Antoine Hennion and Bruno Latour criticise Benjamin's legacy and claim that the success and lasting appeal of his essay is due to the mistakes and confusions it entails.[5] They argue against Benjamin's observation that any multiplication is an impoverishment of the original by countering one among many of Benjamin's claims that 'the main function of technique is to reproduce mechanically an original'.[6]

In a more recent article, Latour revisits Benjamin's essay, this time with Adam Lowe, founder of Factum Arte, one of the largest companies dedicated to digital mediation of art and heritage. Instead of mourning over a loss of the aura, the authors argue that the original work benefits from the existence of reproductions. Against the dichotomy of original versus facsimiles, Latour and Lowe place Kopytoff's notion of the object's biography (1986). The notion of biography indicates that a work of art has a life history with different stages of segments of a trajectory. As such, it allows us to rethink the relationships between the so-called originals and reproductions, as they all belong to the object's biography. According to the authors, our quest for the original version stems from the availability of better copies. Instead of diminishing the value of the reproduction, the authors claim that 'facsimiles, especially those relying on complex (digital) techniques, are the most fruitful way to explore the original and even to help re-define what originality actually is' (n.p.).

Latour and Lowe belong to the growing number of authors who acknowledge a shift in thinking about authenticity and the relationship between originals and copies, and the increasing acceptance of the inauthentic. In their essay 'The migration of the aura or how to explore the original through its facsimiles', Latour and Lowe suggest moving from the question 'Is it an original or merely a copy?' to another one that they take to be decisive, especially at the time of digital reproduction: 'Is it well or badly reproduced?'

While it is a relevant question to ask how we can distinguish bad from good reproductions, this chapter takes a different focus by asking: 'What kind of experience is enabled by the replica?'

4 Benjamin, W. (1986/1936). *The Work of Art in the Age of Mechanical Reproduction*. London: Random House.

5 Latour, B. & Lowe, A. (2011). 'The Migration of the Aura, or How to Explore the Original through Its Facsimiles' in Bartscherer, T. & Coover. R. (eds.) *Switching Codes: Thinking through Digital Technology in the Humanities and the Arts*. Chicago: Chicago University Press, pp. 275–298.

6 Hennion, A. & Latour, B. (2003). 'How to Make Mistakes on So Many Things at Once and Become Famous for It' in Gumbrecht, H-U., Marrinan, M. (eds.) *Mapping Benjamin. The Work of Art in the Digital Age*. Stanford: Stanford University Press, pp. 91–97. (p. 93)

User practices of 3D printing in arts and heritage

The proliferation of reproduction technologies has challenged well-established understandings of authenticity. Copying is not new, but our attitudes towards authenticity have changed with the introduction of each new technology. What sets three-dimensional, digitally produced replicas apart from previous technologies is the accuracy that can be achieved. 3D prints can be exceptionally faithful and accurate in terms of 'look and feel'. While it is often claimed that current 3D reproductions can hardly be distinguished from the original, this is usually followed by a disclaimer along the lines of: 'No replica can ever take the place of an original painting crafted by an artist's hands'. Advocates of digitally fabricated replicas are thus careful in making claims that could be perceived as a threat to the original.

As already mentioned, the use of 3D technology in arts and heritage is manifold. In order to provide more insight in the diverse applications, I will categorise and discuss them under the following headings:

- Public outreach and education
  - Catering to specific needs of diverse audiences
  - Offering richer, multi-sensorial experiences
  - Dissemination
- Preservation
  - Documentation and monitoring change
  - Protecting endangered heritage

In what follows, I will outline the different applications and the motivations behind them. For each of the particular usages, I will address the kind of experience the facsimile allows to produce, thereby shedding light on the relationships between the original and the replica. Particularly, the first category, produced to serve specific needs of diverse audiences, is immediately of interest to the context of 3D reproductions of 2D works of art for the benefit of persons with visual impairment (PVI). All examples mentioned later illustrate a shift in thinking and the emergence of a larger playing field for exploring different relationships between the original and the 3D replica. As such, the categories provide a framework that may enhance the further development of 3D printing of 2D works of art for the benefit of differently abled people.

Public outreach: catering to specific needs of diverse audiences

One of the most often mentioned advantages of 3D reproductions of cultural objects is the affordance of touch. While the default mode of enjoying objects of value in museums is limited to a visual experience, 3D printing allows audience members to touch the reproduction and experience its texture, its shape and its weight in a hands-on manner, offering a multi-sensorial and material-learning experience. An example of an application that puts emphasis on the multi-sensorial experience of 3D replicas is the reproduction of Van Gogh's *Sunflowers* painting by the Van Gogh Museum in Amsterdam, The Netherlands. This reproduction is part of the Feeling Van Gogh Programme, and taps into the potential of custom-made replicas to engage diverse audiences. While the permanent display is accessible to all visitors of the museum, its prominent target group consists of PVI who can participate in an interactive tour and a workshop. As part of this workshop, audience members can touch the replicas and models on display, smell the scent of wet grass and listen to Van Gogh, thereby engaging in a museum experience. In its marketing and communication materials, the museum is careful not to confuse this particular multi-sensory experience with a regular museum experience in which the visual is usually dominant. For a better understanding of the interactions between the visitors and the replicas, and the kind of museum experience it offers, more in-depth visitor research would be paramount.

Qualitative research into visitors' experiences and interactions with 3D printed artefacts is still in its infancy, but it is increasingly considered to be of importance, especially since a shift towards 'the prevalence of the inauthentic' is observed in the museum context.[7] Hede and Thyne explore how a literary heritage museum facilitated visitors to engage with replicas – in their words, 'how one museum assists visitors to negotiate the inauthentic' (p. 701) – and arrive at a set of recommendations for museum marketing and exhibition displays to overcome the informants' expressed feelings of dissonance when confronted with the inauthentic.

Hede and Thynes' observations that cultural institutions need to develop strategies allowing enhanced visitor experiences that involve inauthentic artefacts are confirmed in a blog by Samaroudi and Rodriguez Echavarria. They report on their research into visitor interactions with 3D printed artefacts at the Archaeology Gallery of the Brighton Museum. The researchers reveal that:

> ...we observed that visitors were hesitant to touch replicas or try hands-on activities with replicas. Interestingly, it seems that some of the "no-touch" qualities of the original artefacts have been inherited by the replicas. In these cases, clear guidance, thoughtful design and audience motivation should make the replicas and the environments in which they are displayed as inviting as possible for visitors to interact with.[8]

7 Hede, A-M. & Thyne, M. (2010). A Journey to the Authentic: Museum Visitors and Their Negotiation of the Inauthentic. *Journal of Marketing Management*, 26(7–8), pp. 686–705 (p. 690), DOI: 10.1080/02672571003780106.

8 http://theconversation.com/how-3d-printing-is-transforming-our-relationship-with-cultural-heritage-112642, accessed 27 October 2019.

Public outreach: offering richer, multi-sensorial experiences

Another example of an application that puts emphasis on the multi-sensorial experience of 3D reproductions can be found in the work of the Dutch designer Maaike Roozenburg. Whereas the Van Gogh project, mentioned earlier, focuses on 3D reproductions of 2D works of art, Roozenburg concentrates on 3D reproductions of 3D objects of heritage.

Roozenburg's Smart Replica Project[9] was launched in 2012. It explores how 3D prototyping can encourage the actual use of heritage and how augmented reality can enhance the use-object by adding augmented reality. The 3D replica can not only be touched, but also be acquired, brought home and used. The Smart Replica Project thus aspires to 'contribute to the accessibility of museum objects while also increasing our knowledge of the objects'.[10] It does so by regaining the original function of ordinary objects beyond their museum life and beyond the museum walls. Through augmented reality, an extra layer of data is added which can be accessed using mobile devices. The term 'smart' refers to 'intelligent', indicating that these are not just copies, but replicas enriched through innovative technologies adding data about, for instance, the history of the original object.

The first object to be reproduced by Studio Maaike Roozenburg was a seventeenth-century teacup in the collection of the Boijmans Van Beuningen Museum in Rotterdam, The Netherlands. Several CT scans were made of the original teacup and translated into a 3D computer model to produce a mould. The mould was then used to make a new teacup out of porcelain. The historical object carried a wealth of information about its travels, places of fabrication and use, paintings representing the owner of the teacup and so forth. These narratives can be accessed on a tablet or smartphone as they are linked to the new cup by means of a 'smart tag'. Whilst the original teacup remains 'untouched' in the collection of the Boijmans Van Beuningen Museum, its facsimile can be acquired in the museum shop to be taken home and used. This extension of the object's biography is an important aspect of the project. On the museum website, it reads:

> This combination of innovative techniques brings objects from the past back to life. An object that has lost its original function now that it is part of a museum collection gets a second life outside the museum's galleries and repository. Modern technology makes the replicas 'smarter' than their pre-industrial predecessors – and they can be put to use again.[11]

9 The Smart Replica Project is a collaboration between Studio Maaike Roozenburg, Museum Boijmans Van Beuningen in Rotterdam, Delft University of Technology, Erfgoed Delft, the AR(Lab) of the Koninklijke Academie Den Haag and LikeFriends.

10 http://smartreplicas.blogspot.com/2013/, accessed 10 October 2019.

11 https://www.boijmans.nl/en/exhibitions/design-column-4-the-circle-is-round, accessed 10 October 2019.

The quote suggests that the smart replica offers a richer form of engagement with cultural heritage. The object gets a second life and allows a sensorial and tactile experience that would not be possible without the replica. While these 'smart objects' renegotiate the relationship between the original and its replica in their own specific ways, it is important to mention that Roozenburg does not aim to produce exact copies of the original object. Instead, the designs are used to make new designs. In this sense, the replica does not come to stand in the place of the original; it offers a different – perhaps richer – experience, but it is not competing with the original. While the 3D 'smart replicas' are not developed with the visually deprived in mind, the objects could cater to their specific needs by providing access to artworks through touch and audio data added.

Public outreach: dissemination

In 2018, the Van Gogh Museum engaged in another public outreach project involving three-dimensional replicas of Van Gogh's original paintings, for which replicas of nine works from its collection were created. The exhibited pieces, all faithful reproductions duplicating the size, color and texture of the originals, were part of a year-long travelling exhibition touring around several shopping malls in the United States. The works are produced in a limited-edition of 260 replicas for each of the nine iconic Van Gogh's paintings and are being sold (at the cost of $17,750 each) as the so-called 'museum editions', carefully distinguishing the original from its replica. On the museum's website, its motivations are described as follows:

> How can Van Gogh's heritage be made available globally, without endangering the collection? Most of the masterpieces are so delicate that moving them around is hazardous, yet not everyone is able to visit the museum in Amsterdam. With the *Van Gogh Museum Editions Pop-up tour* the Van Gogh Museum is exploring new ways and techniques to share Vincent's work with people from all over the world.[12]

Less than a decade ago, such an application by a major museum would have been unthinkable. Not so much because of the technology required, but because dominant museum discourse did not allow such bold reproduction and dissemination of replicas by a reputed museum. In the nineteenth and twentieth centuries, being truthful to material authenticity prevailed in museum discourse.[13] The pop-up museum illustrates a shift in thinking and the emergence of a larger playing field for exploring different relationships between the original and the

12 https://static.vangoghmuseum.nl/en/business/van-gogh-museum-editions-pop-up-tour?v=1, accessed 27 October 2019.

13 Saaze, V. van. (2013). Authenticity and Artist's Intent: Key-Concepts and Stumbling Blocks. *Installation Art and the Museum. Presentation and Preservation of Changing Artworks*. Amsterdam: Amsterdam University Press, pp. 48–57.

replica, between the authentic and the inauthentic – as long as the latter is authorised and monitored by the collecting institute.

Preservation: documentation and monitoring change

Besides serving goals of public outreach and increasing access, over recent years, 3D scanning has also become part of a non-contact approach to the documentation of cultural heritage sites and museum objects, and their long-term preservation. The scanning technology is considered non-invasive and thus does not inflict damages to the original object or site. High-resolution 3D recordings of sites, monuments and artefacts are, for instance, created to monitor material change. By producing a zero-measurement and comparing this with 3D recordings of a later date, physical changes to the object can be perceived and monitored. With the goal to preserve the original material object, unwanted change is measured and monitored, and preservation measures that prevent such change are inflicted.[14] Such reproductions are subordinated to the original, and they are created to serve the long-term preservation of the cultural artefact in its material state. The 3D recordings are used and valued for their documentation purposes.

Preservation: protecting endangered heritage

Finally, the application of 3D scanning and printing in the arts and heritage sector is spurred by increased destruction of heritage sites caused by mass tourism, wars and natural disasters. A well-known example of this type of user practice is the replica of Tutankhamun's tomb in the Valley of the Kings in Egypt. This particular application again mobilises another relationship between the original and the replica (or 'facsimile' as Factum Arte, the company behind the reproduction, denotes), as it concerns an 'exact replica' of the burial site. The replica is considered a solution for mass tourism, since it allows tourists to experience the tomb without damaging the original. An additional value of the facsimile is the inclusion of information about the history of the tomb, thereby also fostering the learning experience. Adam Lowe, owner of Factum Arte and the author of the aforementioned article with Bruno Latour, sees a great future for such applications of 3D technology as an important step towards sustainable tourism.[15] Here too, one could imagine that this type of 3D replicas of 3D heritage might provide PVI with greater access to heritage. The replicas can be entered and touched, while audio can be added to enhance the learning experience.

14 Jung, T.H. & tom Dieck, M.C. (2017). Augmented Reality, Virtual Reality and 3D Printing for Co-Creation of Value for Visitor Experience at Cultural Heritage Places. *Journal of Place Management and Development*, 10(2), pp. 140–151, DOI: 10.1108/JPMD-07-2016-0045.

15 Lowe cited in Kingsley, P. (2014). Exact replica of Tutankhamun's tomb unveiled in Egypt. *The Guardian*. https://www.theguardian.com/world/2014/may/01/exact-replica-tutankhamun-tomb-egypt, accessed 2 October 2019.

Conclusion

Against the backdrop of shifting definitions of authenticity, this chapter explored how 3D reproductions of 2D and 3D works of art and heritage influence the appreciation for – and interaction with – 'the original' object and its replica. The aim of the chapter was to shed light on the complex relationship between the original and reproductions in light of the emergence of 3D printing technologies.

The chapter revealed diverse motivations and strategies of user practices and demonstrates how different 3D applications mobilise different relationships between the original and the replica. The chapter argued that the shift towards a greater recognition of the value of reproductions may encourage 3D printing of 2D works for the benefit of differently abled people. Following Latour and Lowe, it argued that replicas are increasingly recognised as enhancing – rather than diminishing – the original. The examples illustrate a shift in thinking and the emergence of a larger playing field for exploring new applications of 3D reproductions of 2D and 3D works of art and heritage objects and sites that would allow a greater access to a more diverse audience.

Considering the diversity of applications and the proliferation of technology, it is of vital importance to expand current research into visitors' engagement and interactions with replicas. On the one hand, visitor research should focus on analysing the engagement of PVI with such replicas to identify and cater to their needs. More generally speaking, visitor research would be beneficial to gain a better understanding of how these technologies impact the understandings of authenticity and contribute to an increased acceptance and recognition of the value of the inauthentic.

5 Art accessibility

Advantages and prospects given by new technologies

Fernando Torrente

An inalienable right

In this chapter, I shall try to emphasize some fundamental points to be taken into account in order to achieve the goal of providing real access to cultural, museum and artistic heritage to the visually impaired (PVI) and, I would like to add, to disabled persons in general. At all events, it is clear that in this context I will essentially focus on the issues concerning PVI.

Furthermore, I am going to talk about the complex issue of translating painting (paintings, frescoes and other two-dimensional shapes, such as mosaics) into three-dimensional objects (low reliefs, relief drawings, other experimental items, etc.). I will expand on the translation aspect relating to new technologies, for example, digital technology and 3D printing. I will also highlight the importance of using different technologies to make the experience of museum and cultural site visits increasingly accessible and interesting for PVI.

In addition, I will underline that the use of different technologies must be part of a system, combining their potential with human presence, which is always essential and required.

Clearly, I will have to dwell on some aspects concerning haptic perception, without presuming to be exhaustive on any of the matters debated.

Furthermore, I will focus on the possibility of using/enjoying a certain type of contemporary art that can be defined 'immersive', to put it simply. I will end this chapter with some suggestions I deem useful to make the artistic heritage accessible to PVI.

Foreword

Today, museums, archaeological sites, cultural institutions and so forth are increasingly aware of the value of making the art/historical/cultural heritage they were entrusted with more accessible to PVI and to disabled persons in general.

It should be stressed out that this attention to persons with disabilities should not be construed as a kind concession, but rather as an obligation, an inalienable right that PVI and their associations have always claimed, and that is crucial for them.

Most importantly, this right is recognized by the Universal Declaration of Human Rights, approved by the UN General Assembly on December 1948, and specifically by Article 27, which guarantees the right to enjoy the cultural, artistic and scientific heritage to anyone, without exclusions. This right is reaffirmed and strengthened in the UN Convention on the Rights of Persons with Disabilities (UNCRPD) (hereinafter referred to as *The Convention*) approved by the UN in 2006, specifically in Article 9[1] and in Article 30, 'Participation in cultural life, recreation, leisure and sport'. The latter reads:

1 States Parties recognize the right of persons with disabilities to take part on an equal basis with others in cultural life, and shall take all appropriate measures to ensure that persons with disabilities:

   a Enjoy access to cultural materials in accessible formats;
   b Enjoy access to television programmes, films, theatre and other cultural activities, in accessible formats;
   c Enjoy access to places for cultural performances or services, such as theatres, museums, cinemas, libraries and tourism services, and, as far as possible, enjoy access to monuments and sites of national cultural importance.

2 States Parties shall take appropriate measures to enable persons with disabilities to have the opportunity to develop and utilize their creative, artistic and intellectual potential, not only for their own benefit but also for the enrichment of society.
3 States Parties shall take all appropriate steps, in accordance with international law, to ensure that laws protecting intellectual property rights do not constitute an unreasonable or discriminatory barrier to access to cultural materials by persons with disabilities.
4 Persons with disabilities shall be entitled, on an equal basis with others, to recognition and support of their specific cultural and linguistic identity, including sign languages and deaf culture.
5 With a view to enabling persons with disabilities to participate on an equal basis with others in recreational, leisure and sporting activities, States Parties shall take appropriate measures:

   a To encourage and promote the participation, to the fullest extent possible, of persons with disabilities in mainstream sporting activities at all levels;
   b To ensure that persons with disabilities have an opportunity to organize, develop and participate in disability-specific sporting and recreational activities and, to this end, encourage the provision, on an equal basis with others, of appropriate instruction, training and resources;

1 See annex.

c To ensure that persons with disabilities have access to sporting, recreational and tourism venues;
d To ensure that children with disabilities have equal access as other children to participation in play, recreation and leisure and sporting activities, including those activities in the school system;
e To ensure that persons with disabilities have access to services from those involved in the organization of recreational, tourism, leisure and sporting activities.

In our opinion, in order to achieve these goals, the involvement of PVI, their associations and the experts designated by them is essential when designing an accessible path. This involvement should occur at the early stages of planning to avoid any initiatives that – although well intentioned – end up creating questionable products, from the perspective of accessibility and usability by disabled persons. I think we can effectively encapsulate this concept in the following catchphrase: '*Nothing About Us Without Us*', at the foundation of the Convention. Although the Convention does not add any new rights to those already present in the convention approved in 1948 and in other further treaties, it affirms a new cultural standpoint, highlighting how often disabilities are the product of a non-inclusive society, and therefore of a discriminating attitude towards those who are different.

Making physical access to cultural, museum and artistic heritage and temporary exhibitions possible, and being concerned that the disabled visitor is properly welcomed, are certainly essential preconditions, but they cannot and should not overlook the fact that the main reason someone visits a museum or an archaeological site is to actually enjoy the cultural heritage exhibited in the best way possible, and more and more according to the principles of *Design for All.*

A very important point to be highlighted in order to achieve real access to the cultural and artistic heritage that museums, archaeological sites and so forth must take into account is to have internal staff trained to welcome disabled visitors in order to provide high-quality service when guiding them, especially when it comes to the haptic exploration of pictorial masterpieces translated into low reliefs, because – as we shall see – this translation entails some issues that should be tackled in the best way possible, without improvising.

We know very well that a museum is a complex machine, a living and evolving body; we also know that a visit by a PVI in complete autonomy is no easy task, and that you should not work on the museum contents only but also on the way those contents are displayed, which should have accessibility as its objective.

I would like to conclude this foreword with a fundamental principle contained in the guidelines issued on July 2018 by the Italian Minister of Cultural Heritage,[2] stating that museums must clearly justify why an artwork cannot be ex-

2 See point 16.6, paragraph 16 Museum Routes, Annex 1 PEBA. http://musei.beniculturali.it/wp-content/uploads/2019/06/Linee-Guida-PEBA-ALLEGATO-1_Piano-strategico.pdf (Accessed: 11 October 2019).

plored in a haptic way. This principle overturns the universally accepted 'No touching' principle.

This principle – that we hope will not remain just a statement written on paper – overcomes both a concrete obstacle and a psychological/cultural hindrance.

Indeed, it states that artworks can be enjoyed in other ways other than visually, allowing visitors to relate to the matter and retrieving the relationship between the artist and the materials selected and handled to create his/her artwork.

I also think that these considerations should inspire a debate aimed at creating a new relationship between art and touch, and between art and non-visual exploration in general.

Translating two-dimensional artworks (paintings, frescoes, mosaics) into three-dimensional objects

A brief word on haptic and visual perception and on their differences

This is not the main focus of this chapter; however, I think that a brief word on this topic is essential.

This quick and unpretentious glance is indispensable for anyone wanting to reproduce two-dimensional artworks (hereinafter, '2D artworks') into three-dimensional objects (hereinafter, '3D objects'), and for those guiding disabled persons in the exploration/discovery of these objects.[3]

Our tactile organ is the skin, the largest sensory organ of all. It extends for about 2,500 cm^2 in newborns and for 18,000 cm^2 in adults, and it accounts for 20% of the total weight in newborns and 18% in adults. It is characterized by a high density of receptors: 50 every 100 square millimetres.[4] In summary, we could say that skin is the organ that filters the outside world and reacts to it.

On the one hand, the sense of touch is attributed to a specific and well-localized organ: our hands; in contrast, it relates to our entire body's perception and presence. In other words, the sense of touch is a complex sensory system, torn between two polarities: a widespread and extensive polarity – usually called somaesthetic perception – and a focused and local polarity – called haptic perception.

It is precisely through the haptic mode that the sense of touch can perceive shapes in an accessible way; therefore, we can explore objects in their concrete and simultaneous three-dimensionality only through our hands.

It is through haptic exploration, combined with kinaesthetic exploration, that we can grasp many of the characteristics of an object:

3 Cf., to read more, Marco Mazzeo, *Tatto e linguaggio Il corpo delle parole*, Editori Riuniti, Rome, 2003; Yvette Hatwell, *Il tatto e l'accesso manuale ai beni culturali*, in *L'arte a portata di Mano*, Armando Editore, Rome, 2006; Aldo Grassini, *Per un'estetica della tattilità. Ma esistono davvero arti visive?*, Armando, Rome, 2015.

4 Cf. Didier Anzieu, *Le Moi-peau*, Edizioni Borla S.r.l., Rome, 1995.

1 its texture, by rubbing our fingers on the object we want to explore,
2 its consistency, by pressing down on the object,
3 its temperature, by simply touching the object,
4 its weight (only if we can lift it),
5 its immediate (stereoplastic) shape, if the object is small enough to wrap our fingers around it and hold it in our hands,
6 its shape, by following its contour, through haptic exploration and movement, if the object is too big and it cannot be explored by simply widening our arms.

Obviously, colour cannot be explored with the sense of touch, just as temperature cannot be explored visually.

That being said, it should be taken into account that the tactile system has a very limited perceptive field, and it can hardly compensate the effects of visual sensory deprivation completely: it is ill-suited to explore very large or moving objects, the environmental context where the movement takes place and, in general, the spatial consequences of the driving forces at play.

Haptic exploration always starts from the analytical perception of the object, and then rebuilds it as a whole, to create a synthetic mental image of the object explored by the user. Instead, the sense of sight starts from a global vision of the object, and then captures each single detail; maybe, in this second step, we could say it becomes similar to haptic exploration.

It is important to stress out that exploring an object that cannot be held in one hand, due to its large size, requires a combination of touch (haptic exploration) and kinaesthetic: it is a dynamic operation.

Says Loretta Secchi:

> We can talk about "dynamic act" in both experiences. In tactile perception, coordinate motion has a great influence, manifested in the action of experiencing the appearance of a shape. The exercise of kinaesthetic prepares for tactile perception in all its completeness.[5]

In any case, we must take into account that the sense of touch has a lower perceptive capacity than the sense of sight; therefore, we must consider the relief thresholds that can be perceived tactically.[6]

I would like to conclude this short note – without the assumption of exhausting such a vast subject – by quoting Johann Gottfried Herder, who in 1778 wrote:

5 Loretta Secchi, *L'educazione estetica per l'integrazione*, ed. Carocci, Rome, 2004, p. 25.

6 To read more on the issues of perceivable tactile thresholds: Paola Bucciarelli, *Ci.Vis. Città Visibili. Strumenti, metodi e tecniche per la realizzazione di mappe visuo-tattili architettoniche, urbane e urbanistiche*, Istituto dei Ciechi F. Cavazza, Bologna, 2004.

> We believe we see something when we should just listen; in the end, we see so much and so quickly, that we cannot hear anything anymore, and therefore we cannot feel anything, because the latter is always the foundation and guarantor of the former. In all those cases, sight is just a shortened version of touch. [...] Sight gives us dreams, touch gives us truth.[7]

We believe Johann Gottfried Herder's intuition is even more important nowadays, because we live in a society dominated by image, by rapid information, by a 'contraction' of the time required to enjoy artworks and to reflect.

Issues concerning the translation of 2D artworks into 3D artworks

The translation or transduction of a painting (2D) into a 3D object should be guided by an accurate interpretation and adaptation to the potential of haptic perception, while considering the limitations of this sensory channel concerning, for instance, objects and elements arranged on different levels, transducing the chromatic, quantitative and qualitative effects of every detail, their volume, mutual relationships and their main content. These artworks are the result of an interpretation that seeks a tactile value in the aesthetic equivalent of the optical value, in order to faithfully replicate the plastic, prospective and detailed characteristics of a painting that can be portrayed via the sense of touch.

This must be carefully analysed, through a deep knowledge of the artwork to be translated, the author's style and also the aspects of tactile and kinaesthetic perception. As previously seen, it is clear how haptic perception allows exploring an object in depth, but it is also clear that the sense of touch has a lower perceptive capacity compared to the sense of sight.

Therefore, to enable somebody to 'see with the hands', it is essential to understand that a reproduction must enhance haptic perception. It should not be a mere instrument of knowledge – surely an important aspect – but it should be an evocative tool that allows for aesthetic enjoyment, which is probably the most difficult result to achieve, and also the one confirming the method's validity. Because of the interpretation work that the translation (transduction) of 2D artwork into 3D artwork requires, it should in no way be considered an exact copy of the original, and we think that the regulations should take this aspect – which will be further explored in the conclusion – into account.

Translating 2D artwork into 3D artwork means understanding and highlighting what should be the (essential) strengths to be underlined, and the details that must be left out in order to prevent the reproduction from being overly complex and too difficult to comprehend, especially when it comes to tactile drawings.

There are different methods for reproducing a 2D artwork in 3D. Here are some examples:

7 Johann Gottfried Herder, *Plastica*, Aesthetica, 1994, p. 33.

- silkscreen printing,
- goffrage/embossing,
- capsule system (Minolta)
- low relief.

It is essential to also keep in mind the importance of describing the tactile reproduction orally (this applies also to the exploration of original artwork) in an evocative way to enrich the experience of those discovering it.

I would like to add just a few basic observations for partially sighted persons that can combine the visual experience with the haptic experience.

In these cases, it is important to take into account the chromatic contrasts and the need for large print drawings/pictures; as we shall see in the following paragraphs, new technologies can offer some very interesting solutions in this sense.

I would like to conclude this section by underlining how important it is to educate PVI in understanding artworks from a very early age and to give value to this subject in school curricula; however, this topic would require a separate chapter, and the available literature is quite extensive.

Using 3D printers

When tackling the issue of the use of new technologies, we always have to keep in mind their speed of development; therefore, there is always a risk that some statements may become obsolete in the blink of an eye.

One of the advantages of using digital technologies is their reproduction capability. It is possible to use digital technology and 3D printing to create low reliefs, maquettes and so forth. We can say that this technology has a great benefit: escaping the prototype logic, that is, escaping the single-piece logic, allowing, in perspective, for lower costs and increased production speed.

Another important aspect of the study on the use of 3D printers is the search for new materials. Experimentation with these new technologies had led to the discovery of new materials that accurately simulate some of the tactile qualities of real materials (marble, wood, bronze).

Using these materials allows us to obtain accurate replicas from a shape, texture, surface and weight standpoint.

Some examples:

- Ceramic objects can be reproduced with mixtures of different type, texture and colour, depending on the object's shape and size, and on the replica's end use.
- Marble objects can be reproduced using synthetic marble, which gives the printed object a surface finishing very similar to authentic marble, both from a visual and a tactile standpoint.
- Stone objects can be reproduced using synthetic gypsum that, if suitably coloured, can simulate stone very well, both from a visual and a tactile standpoint.

Until a few years ago, 3D printers only used plastic materials which were not always pleasant to touch.

There is no one-size-fits-all technology: depending on the object to be reproduced and on the related purposes, the best technology must be selected. There are several 3D printing technologies, and their main differences concern the way the layers are formed. Some methods use materials that are melted, sintered or softened with heat (in general, generated by electromagnetic radiations or by an electron beam) to produce the layers, such as SLS (selective laser sintering) and FDM (fused deposition modelling), while other methods use liquid materials hardened with different technologies. Lamination-based systems produce thin layers cut according to the final shape and then joined to one another.

Apart from reproducing 2D artwork in 3D, 3D printers are also used for archaeological finds, sculptures, architectural elements, building and monument maquettes and so forth.

Behind a 3D print, there is an accurate computer-developed work, for example, a 'digital' object. This object created by a digital modeller is indeed the most complex part. The 3D model to be printed is created on a PC using CAD (computer-sided design) software. Alternatively, 3D scanner solutions can be used to replicate the object that needs to be printed. After this step, the model is saved in stl format and loaded in a special software, called Slicer. There are different versions, both open-source and proprietary. This software allows setting all the 3D printers data, and many printing parameters, such as the layer thickness, infill and printing speed. After all parameters are set, the object can be printed by saving the file in a special format that can be read by the 3D printer.

Based on my experience, after printing the object with the 3D printer, it still needs to be manually perfected, to improve the results, remove any protuberances (excess material) and so forth. In any case, these issues could be overcome once technology develops further.

Thanks to the digital prototype, we can transform our object into something we can share with others, by making it available, for instance, in 3D model-sharing tutorials.

In summary, like every technology, it makes a lot of sense to study it, especially given the fact that it could potentially lead to the generation of a global heritage, a 'library of digital objects' that can be reproduced and made available to the entire community. Many universities and companies continue to study and develop new methods to improve these technologies, which are also used in fields other than this one, such as in the medical field.

The importance of using different technologies

Today, technology provides us with a series of opportunities to make our museum, monument or archaeological site visits increasingly interesting. It allows us to easily access a massive quantity of information independently. In addition, the use of different technologies allows us to continue experimenting and understanding which ones are the most suitable.

Furthermore, in my opinion, it is essential that new technologies are supported by traditional aids, such as orientation and mobility maps, Braille and large print plates.

For example, using QR codes (quick response codes) and NFC (near-field communication) tags located on accessible (reproduced and original) artwork allows us to obtain more information on that work on our smartphone in audio, large print format. These apps – that obviously should be developed with the required criteria to make them accessible to PVI – are not necessarily designed for a limited audience: they can be used also by people with normal vision, or, for instance, they could include some videos with sign language for the hearing impaired.

In summary, we believe these technologies, when developed and used correctly, to be fully compliant with the *Design for All* development principles.

An immersive contemporary art experience

In this paragraph, I want to highlight the possibility of enjoying contemporary artistic installations that go beyond the haptic perception, and that – through evocative sounds, olfactory effects, spatial arrangements that arouse sensations evoking some feelings in the visitor's mind – make the artwork enjoyable, from an aesthetic standpoint, even by PVI, without being framed within a specific category such as tactile or visual art.

In order to do this, I will share with you one of my many personal experiences in visiting contemporary artistic installations. The first experience dates back to the summer of 1997, in Bologna, at the Contemporary Art Gallery that hosted an exhibition of Boltanski's works. The exhibition was set in different rooms, unfolding through a path of the guilt and horrors of the Holocaust and the 'Repentance', where also the 'banality of evil' and the casualty that often determines human attitude and life in general were highlighted.

Moving through the different rooms, the visitor was immersed in a series of stimulations, facts and evocations aimed at arousing sensations, memories and feelings, in a sort of rebound between intimate feelings and external events. In order to recreate these sensations, the artist used images, lights, sounds, scents and the space layout itself.

Obviously, here I will focus only on some of the aspects that seem especially interesting to our subject matter. I want to clarify that it was not possible for a visually impaired visitor to visit all the rooms independently: the exhibition was not designed for a visually impaired audience or to be visited in the dark. I will focus on three different rooms of the exhibition: *Les regards*, *Les grands tombeaux* and *Les lenges.*

Les regards

In a very large room, some posters fluttering in the wind were hanging on the walls. They portrayed faces taken from anonymous photos of missing persons and/or war victims.

When walking into this large and barren room, with the increasing riffling sound of the posters in the air, the visitor felt like being amidst leaves lost in the wind, without any time reference.

In addition, knowing what the images portrayed and the exhibition's topic, one had the clear sensation that those leaves lost forever were souls swept away by their destiny.

It is clear that, in order to perceive all these sensations, the visitor had to be prepared and know the artist's poetics in general; also, it is clear how the sound of the wind, the paper fluttering and all those non-visual stimuli were essential to build the poetic essence of the operation rather than the informative one.

Les grands tombeaux

In another exhibition environment, space was used differently: the vastness of the first environment was opposed to the sense of anguish, of being squashed in a very tiny space, overwhelming the visitor.

The room housed a series of iron structures, some of them slightly taller than a man, some of them shorter, with crates on top. The visitor had to move by passing underneath these crates, or in the narrow space between them, when the structures were too low.

This use of the space gave visually impaired visitors the sense of dramatic force of the whole, and the sensation of being subjected to a great and relentless external pressure that they felt physically; this sensation was amplified when I learned from the seeing person that accompanied me that the crates above me, burdening down on me, were coffins (I did not recognize them, because I wasn't able to touch them in their entirety).

This time too, it was a mere information, adding to the somehow complete sensation I had already perceived, probably the same intended by the artist.

Les lenges

The floor of another room was strewn with hundreds of flowers, and the sweet smell of their rot, combined with the perceivable sensation of their consistency under my feet and of their mutation under the action of the steps of all the visitors who passed by, created a very special atmosphere, where the sensation of time that passes and transforms/deteriorates everything was intertwined with the vital action of visitors, who, by moving through the room, continuously transformed its structure.

This exquisitely Proustian operation – based on the activation of the involuntary memory of all these solicitations – evoked many different sensations and references to personal experiences, thoughts, readings, situations and memories in the visitor. In summary, inner past experiences were intertwined with the artistic event in which the visitor was participating, mainly by using non-visual stimulations.

I mentioned this example to prove that in some contemporary artworks, non-visual elements are equally important, without removing or hiding the visual elements, and yet without them becoming secondary or designed solely for visually impaired visitors.

This topic too could be discussed in a separate chapter/essay, deepening all the related questions, and including the many artworks that involve visitors in an immersive way, relating to all their senses.

Conclusions

I would like to conclude by adding some other considerations and an omen.

In some of the previous paragraphs, we talked about the importance of new technologies both when creating artwork reproductions/transductions and when we want to obtain information on them, on the places we want to visit and on the original artworks we can explore and discover in a haptic way. In any case, in my opinion, it is essential that museums, archaeological areas and so forth. always have suitably trained staff to welcome and accompany visually impaired visitors in discovering the heritage that the institution has made available to them. The staff must be capable of explaining the artwork that the disabled visitor is exploring in a haptic way, and also be trained on how to guide this exploration, that is, on the potential of haptic exploration.

In my opinion, the presence of this kind of suitably trained and constantly updated personnel is still essential, despite the increasing importance of the use of technology; this is especially true in educational/workshop areas that are now offered in the majority of museums.

I would also like to reiterate the importance of the principle that the 'No touching' dogma must be replaced with the concept that we need to justify why an original artwork should not and must not touched. We are clearly aware that artworks must be protected and their integrity safeguarded, but this requirement cannot be used to justify the 'No touching' dogma in all occasions.

I would also like to highlight that the haptic experience also enriches seeing visitors. Indeed, my experience has taught me that exploring a reproduced relief artwork haptically can be very interesting and educational even for a seeing audience, and for students especially, in order to learn the importance of touch – something that is often downplayed by the invasion of images in our society – and, at the same time, to learn that there are different ways to perceive something and that an object can be 'seen' from many different angles.

From a regulatory standpoint, I hope we will reach an harmonization of the different regulations (along the lines of the Marrakesh VIP Treaty, for published works) authorizing the free creation of low reliefs, relief drawings and maquette reproductions to be used in museums, exhibitions, archaeological sites and specific museums dedicated to PVI (such as the 'Omero' Tactile Museum in Ancona, the 'Anteros' Ancient and Modern Painting Tactile Museum at the Francesco Cavazza Institute in Bologna, the ONCE Typhlological Museum in

Madrid), to allow PVI to enjoy the enormous artistic heritage produced by man over the centuries and contribute to the realization of the principles set out by the Convention.

This must be said also in view of the fact that they are not profit-making products or faithful reproductions of the original, since, as mentioned, the 3D translation of a 2D painting, drawing or artwork requires processing and adaptation for the haptic perception to be effective. When creating a 3D copy, the digital modeller transduces and, in a certain way, reworks the original artwork.

Lastly, I also hope that more and more original artworks can be made available to PVI for haptic exploration, without jeopardizing their integrity, of course.

Incidentally, since this topic lies outside the scope of this chapter – and it would probably require a separate chapter – we need to take into account that accessibility to cultural heritage starts before reaching the destination we want to visit: it is important to have websites made according to the WCAG guidelines in order for them to be easily accessible and navigable with the reading tools used by PVI (screen readers, magnifiers). Exhibition venues should be easily reachable, and their entrance signalled (acoustic signalling devices, tactile-plantar routes, etc.), but these topics cannot be covered in depth herein.

In conclusion, we can say that the time is now ripe– both on the PVI side and on the museum staff side – to tackle the matter of accessibility in the spirit of *Design for All*, even though there is still a lot to do. We can also affirm that there are many technologies available, and we must start using them, studying them and further developing them to solve some of the current issues, as seen in the chapter.

Annex

Article 9 Accessibility

1 To enable persons with disabilities to live independently and participate fully in all aspects of life, States Parties shall take appropriate measures to ensure, to persons with disabilities, access, on an equal basis with others, to the physical environment, to transportation, to information and communications, including information and communications technologies and systems and to other facilities and services open or provided to the public, both in urban and in rural areas These measures, which shall include the identification and elimination of obstacles and barriers to accessibility, shall apply to, inter alias:

   a Buildings, roads, transportation and other indoor and outdoor facilities, including schools, housing, medical facilities and workplaces;
   b Information, communications and other services, including electronic services and emergency services.

2 States Parties shall also take appropriate measures:

   a To develop, promulgate and monitor the implementation of minimum standards and guidelines for the accessibility of facilities and services open or provided to the public;
   b To ensure that private entities that offer facilities and services which are open or provided to the public take into account all aspects of accessibility for persons with disabilities;
   c To provide training for stakeholders on accessibility issues facing persons with disabilities;
   d To provide signage in Braille in buildings and other facilities open to the public, and in easy-to-read and understand forms;
   e To provide forms of live assistance and intermediaries, including guides, readers and professional sign language interpreters, to facilitate accessibility to buildings and other facilities open to the public;
   f To promote other appropriate forms of assistance and support to persons with disabilities to ensure their access to information;
   g To promote access for persons with disabilities to new information and communications technologies and systems, including the Internet;
   h To promote the design, development, production and distribution of accessible information and communications technologies and systems at an early stage, so that these technologies and systems become accessible at minimum costs.

Source https://www.un.org/development/desa/disabilities/convention-on-the-rights-of-persons-with-disabilities.html

6 Sensory art from a 3D printer's perspective

The deployment of 3D printing to produce artworks

Noël Daemen

Introduction

3D printing is a relatively new (but highly accessible) manufacturing technology to produce objects. This means that works of art can be made or reproduced in a new way. Due to the easy access, relatively low costs and the ability to reproduce objects, 3D printing can be used to produce physical 3D artworks for people with visual impairments ("PVI"). Reproduction of existing artworks is easily done through 3D scanning. The digital file resulting from the scan is converted into a 3D model which can be 3D printed. The 3D scanning does no harm to the scanned object and the process can be done on-site (where the artwork is located). Another possibility is to take all measurements of the object and make a new 3D drawing of the piece of art. This latter option does not require a 3D scanner.

When using a digital production method like 3D printing, the digital files of the artwork can be distributed digitally, via the Internet, across the globe. The physical artwork can then be 3D printed locally.

This chapter aims to provide an overview of the technical features of 3D printing. For that purpose, first it is explained what 3D printing is and how the 3D printing process works. As there are different 3D printing technologies, I will briefly describe the features of some of the most commonly used ones. I will then give an overview of the opportunities that 3D printing offers for 3D printing artistic works for the benefit of PVI.

The 3D printing process at a glance

3D printing is a relatively new production technology. It is being used to make all kinds of objects, ranging from technological parts to creative pieces of art and medical instruments. Many different materials can be used, of which plastic and metal are the most common. The size of the objects that can be printed range from nano-level to complete wings of aircrafts.

3D printing has become widely known and popular because many patents relating to the technology expired around 2010. For example, the patent on the Fused Deposition Modeling printing process expired in 2009. Likewise, patents for liquid-based, powder-based and metal-based printing processes also expired. This allowed brands like Ultimaker and MakerBot to start producing cheap, consumer-friendly 3D printers. 3D printing technologies thus became widely accessible, also aided by the fact that some of the necessary software is open source. Moreover, people from all over the world started to work collaboratively online. One of such collaborations resulted in the creation, about ten years ago, of the first low-cost 3D printer that could be used at home. As a result of these developments, anyone is currently able to make things on their own. 3D printing can be done on a self-owned 3D printer or by a professional 3D printing service.

It takes a 3D file, software, a 3D printer and raw material to make objects on your own. The 3D file is a digital 3D model, also called a computer-aided design model (a CAD-model). The file is created either by scanning a physical object (with the use of a 3D scanner) or by drawing the digital model directly, through the use of appropriate software. The scanner does not produce a file which can immediately be 3D printed. It takes a specific software to process the file obtained from the scanner and turn it into a 3D printing-usable file. Namely, the scan often needs to be corrected for inaccuracies and converted into a .PLY or .OBJ file format.

The object is then 3D printed in a machine called a 3D printer. A main feature of the majority of 3D printing processes is that layers of material are melted together. The 3D printer successively adds layers of material, which are melted on top of each other with high precision. This is done in a pattern that is determined according to the mentioned 3D file. The additive characteristic is what gave 3D printing the industrial term "additive manufacturing." Both terms ("3D printing" and "additive manufacturing") are used interchangeably. We will use 3D printing as it is more known to the public.

There are over 20 different 3D printing technologies, which can be categorized by the materials (feedstock) used. Examples of materials are plastic, metal, ceramics, concrete, bio-materials, food ingredients and combinations thereof.

Relevant 3D printing technologies

Some 3D printing technologies are more relevant than others as manufacturing processes for producing art. Criteria to select a certain technology include the desired material of the final object, costs, accessibility to 3D print in-house versus the need to rely on external suppliers and the required expertise level.

The most accessible and therefore most used technology is called Fused Filament Fabrication (FFF). The technology offers an affordable production solution. A plastic wire called filament is melted in a nozzle, extruded and cooled down. One can compare it with a glue gun. Each layer is extruded on top of the other. Many kinds of plastic in all types of colours can be used. Combinations of plastic with other materials are also available. For example, it is possible to 3D print using wood-like material, which is dust-shredded from wood, combined with binding material that holds the substance together in the shape of the filament. Other possibilities are filament with copper, brass or metallic particles.

These are a combination of plastic, metal powder and binding material. It is also possible to combine colours or make multi-coloured objects. Moreover, the 3D printed object can be post-finished to get a certain look, like a metallic shine or the look of an ancient statue. Methods for doing this are polishing, coating, chroming, dying, electroplating and/or vapour-smoothing.[1] In any case, more often than not and independently of the specific 3D printing technology used, post-processing steps are required after 3D printing, because 3D printed objects have a rough surface structure when they come out of the 3D printer.

Moreover, in terms of sustainability, this technology allows for the use of waste material. PET-G (polyethylene terephthalate glycol) filament, for instance, can be made almost completely from collected and reused material. Even sewage sludge can be used to make PLA/PHA filament (a thermoplastic aliphatic biodegradable plastic derived from renewable resources), which can be used for 3D print.

FFF 3D printers are available in a broad price range. Their capacity also varies widely, from 10 × 10 × 10 cm-sized platforms upon which the 3D print is made, up to large-scale building systems. In sum, FFF technology works with many different kinds of materials (which are widely available), displays low entry and production costs and requires only moderate expertise level.

Stereo Lithography Apparatus (SLA) is one of the oldest 3D printing technologies. It works with resin and uses a tray which is dimensionally polymerized in a very precise way. This occurs when a photo-initiator is activated by UV light via laser or LED beaming. There is a selection of commercially available stereolithographic 3D printers, with performance according to the size and the detail of parts they can build. The printed objects can be very small (to a micrometre detail) or up to meter-high parts with very sharp details. In the post-production phase, the objects need to be rinsed and cleaned to remove the excess of resin. Many resins also need to be post-cured to increase the crosslink density in the object, resulting in improved stiffness. The 3D printer ought to be kept clean, and professional expertise is needed to get 3D printed products of high quality. It is possible to use different kinds of materials with the SLA technology, many of which are widely available. The technology displays moderate to high entry and production costs and requires skilled expertise level.

Selective laser sintering (SLS) is a powder bed fusion technology. It works by spreading powder across a build platform into a layer. Each layer of the SLS process begins with recoating the build platform with a layer of powdered polymer. A laser heats selective areas into layers. This is consecutively done layer by layer to build an object. Materials used are, for example, thermoplastics, ceramics and

1 See, for example, the Horse of Selene, 3D printed and post-finished by Cosmo Wenman, at https://cosmowenman.com/2013/10/27/3d-printshow-collection-londonparis-2013/2013-parthenon-head-of-a-horse-of-selene-3d-printed-and-finished-in-patinated-brass-by-cosmo-wenman/ (Accessed: 14 October 2019). Other examples can be found in the Dallas Lighthouse of the Nasher Center in Dallas, which creates 3D printed art replicas for PVI: https://www.dallaslighthouse.org/ (Accessed: 14 October 2019).

composite materials like nylon combined with clay, glass fibres or carbon fibre. The production process involves cleaning the 3D printed parts after 3D printing in order to remove the extra powder. In addition to the 3D printer, extra drying equipment is needed to ensure the powder is dry and consistent enough. Equipment for post-processing and cleaning of the printed parts is also needed.

Multi-jet fusion (MJF) is a technology similar to SLS. In this method, infrared radiation absorbing material is deposited onto areas of the powder bed that need to be fused. The material reacts to an infrared lamp which is passed over the whole built area. Only the areas that have the material that absorbs the infrared radiation become hot enough to melt the polymer powders and form the object. The MJF process is faster than SLS and less sensitive to failures in quality. Moreover, in MJF, a second material can be used (for example, in order to add colour so that a coloured object can be created).

It is possible to use different kinds of materials with both the SLS and the MJF technologies. However, these technologies display high entry and production costs and require a highly skilled expertise level.

For metal 3D printing, there are also some relevant technologies worth mentioning, such as the selective laser melting (SLM), which is a powder bed process as well. The technology allows for the printing of metal objects with complex geometries in a wide variety of alloys. The technology requires additional types of material to support the first material at certain levels of overhang. Support is made from the same material as the object itself. The SLM has very high entry and production costs and requires a skilled expertise level.

3D printing artistic works for PVI

3D printing offers unprecedented and innovative opportunities

Artworks are traditionally made with methods like painting, sculpting or carving. But 3D printing is a production method that can also be used to produce artworks and which has several key advantages to it.

First, it easily reproduces objects without the need for a mould. For example, with regard to sculptures, an artist using a traditional method would start by making a single piece of art. To make a copy of it, he or she would need to put a plastic or silicone cover over the object to get a mould. With this mould, a second piece could be produced. With 3D printing, the production starts with a 3D drawing, a CAD model. The 3D printer builds an object according to this model, which can be made on a computer or by scanning the original object, as explained earlier. Scanning the artwork is safer than traditional methods, as the artwork will not be touched by any silicone or similar product.[2] Another impor-

2 It is also possible to 3D print the mould, which could decrease moulding costs substantially, as some moulds (e.g., the ones made in metal using CNC technology, also called machining) can be quite expensive, depending on shape and size.

tant fact is that objects can be 3D scanned wherever they are placed – they don't need to be touched or removed. Already many existing sculptures or paintings have been reproduced this way.[3]

Second, reproducing or manufacturing art with 3D printing needs only a relatively low investment. Very realistic pieces of art can be made in an affordable way with the FFF-3D technology. For instance, copies of 3D scanned statues can be printed locally, either in real size or in different sizes. Material costs are low. The main cost factor to make the first artwork is producing a usable, correct 3D scan or drawing the CAD file, due to the labour hours needed for engineering and designing. Moreover, 3D printing with technologies other than FFF will, in general, be costlier, because the equipment (both the 3D printers and the post-processing equipment) is more expensive (and so are the other materials used by other technologies). However, it should be noted that, regardless of the particular 3D printing technology used, once the first artwork is correctly 3D printed, the costs of (re)producing a second or even more pieces do not increase exponentially. Small series can thus be made cheaply and at fixed costs.

Third, 3D printing accommodates a high level of design freedom and creativity. This means also that the design of a copied piece of art can be changed in the digital 3D model. Moreover, because complexity in 3D printing is made at almost no extra costs, it is possible to come up with completely new designs. 3D printing makes it possible to produce new kinds of artwork with very complex shapes. Connected to design freedom is also the ability to digitally copy a 3D file, or scale it to different sizes, which allows for easy redistribution of copies of originals in the desired size. Likewise, 3D printing enables 2D artworks such as photos or paintings to be scanned and then transformed into 3D artworks by adding a vertical z-axis. But it also allows for customization (a reproduced artwork can be customized with, for example, an added stamp or additional design from the museum which allowed the object to be reproduced) and personalization (which could amount to, for example, 3D print in each object an individual name).

Looking ahead – challenges from the industry perspective

3D printing is just one step in the process of digitization of the production of artworks for PVI. When using a digital production method like 3D printing, the digital files of the artwork can be distributed digitally via the Internet. The physical artwork can be 3D printed locally, which is convenient and also contributes to a more sustainable way of making products with respect to shipping goods around the world. Moreover, from a sustainability point of view, there are already recycled materials available which can be used in order to prevent single use of materials, but a future challenge will be to increase such use.

3 See e.g., the work of Cosmo Wenman https://cosmowenman.com/ or Océ https://www.oce.com/the-genius-of-the-great-masters-at-your-fingertips/ (Accessed: 15 October 2019).

From a technological standpoint, there are hardly any thresholds or limitations when deploying 3D printing to produce artworks. The applicable technologies are widely available and relatively cheap depending on the particular 3D printing system. The main problem resides in the expertise needed to 3D print and post-finish objects when making high-quality artworks, as skilled workers can sometimes be difficult to find. Still, around the globe, there are a number of 3D printing "artists" who have presented experiments, showcases or specifically 3D printed artwork. Well-known names are Cosmo Wenman, Morehshin Allahyari, Greco, Gentileschi and José de Ribera.[4]

Several companies within this industry have already contributed to making or reproducing artworks, be it for marketing purposes or merely to experiment with new technological features for specific applications. It is foreseeable that the 3D printing industry will respond positively when asked to contribute to the 3D printing of artworks, once this can be done legally. However, most companies are led by technical people who do not want to get involved in issues with respect to intellectual property infringement, which might have a chilling effect on widespread practices of 3D printing works of art. Therefore, it would be desirable to clarify the legal questions that arise. A common doubt of 3D printing service bureaus relates to knowing who infringes the copyright in protected art when printing a copy: the customer who delivers the file or the service bureau who 3D prints it. These bureaus try to rule out any responsibilities in their terms and conditions of service provision, but currently there's still uncertainty about whether it is that simple.

4 Several artists can also be found on this website: https://www.marcomahler.com/3d-printing-artist-sculpture-art/ (Accessed: 15 October 2019). Furthermore, a good overview of artworks and 3D printing can be found in this article: https://all3dp.com/2/3d-printed-art-how-3d-printing-makes-way-into-creativity/ (Accessed: 15 October 2019).

Part 2

International framework for disability rights and exceptions

7 Paradigm shifting to a point

Disability human rights, copyright protection, and access to visual art in international law

Joseph Lelliott and Paul Harpur

Introduction

The *Convention on the Rights of Persons with Disabilities* ('*CRPD*') introduced a new disability human rights paradigm.[1] The rights of persons with disabilities are now expressly articulated and delineated in international law, with obligations on state parties to take positive steps towards achieving equality between persons with and without disabilities. The normative force of these rights is strengthened by the *CRPD's* rapid and widespread acceptance by the international community, with 181 states having ratified the Convention.[2]

While the *CRPD* has shifted how international law constructs disability and how the rights of persons with disabilities are recognised, attaining substantive equality for such persons remains frustratingly remote. One significant barrier to equality is the conflict between copyright law and disability rights. Protection of property rights holders' interests in copyrighted materials impacts the rights of persons with disabilities in a number of respects, including their right to access cultural materials in accessible formats.[3] This chapter explores this tension and outlines how, and the extent to which, the new disability human rights paradigm introduced by the *CRPD* alters the balance between the protection of disability and copyright. It observes that changes to this balance have manifested primarily in the context of international copyright protections, which have traditionally precluded persons with a visual impairment from accessing not only the vast majority of the world's written works[4] but also visual art and films.

Part 1 of this chapter explains constructions of disability and copyright in international law and the real medical conditions and information on which they

1 *Convention on the Rights of Persons with Disabilities*, opened for signature on 30 March 2007, UN Doc A/RES/61/106 (entered into force 3 April 2008).

2 United Nations, *Convention on the Rights of Persons with Disabilities (CRPD)* <https://www.un.org/development/desa/disabilities/convention-on-the-rights-of-persons-with-disabilities.html>.

3 *CRPD*, art 30(1)(a).

4 This phenomenon is often referred to as the 'book famine'. See, e.g., World Intellectual Property Organization, 'The Marrakesh Treaty – Helping to End the Global Book Famine' (Factsheet, 2016) <http://www.wipo.int/edocs/pubdocs/en/wipo_pub_marrakesh_overview.pdf>.

are based. Printed books, visual art, and films are all real, while intellectual property is a concept that restricts the use of information associated with these cultural materials. Similarly, medical conditions are real and may impair certain abilities, but it is society that transforms a particular range of abilities into a disability. Part 1 briefly maps the evolution of the construction of 'disability', from medical to social and critical models. It then explains how the *CRPD* has drawn on these models to transform the concept of disability in international law and thus introduce a new disability human rights paradigm.

Part 2 illustrates how this human rights paradigm has affected the interaction between the rights of persons with disabilities and copyright. It analyses the commonly disabling consequences of international copyright laws, as illustrated by the Three-Step Test in the *Berne Convention for the Protection of Literary and Artistic Works* ('*Berne Convention*'), before demonstrating how the positive obligations in the *CRPD* provide the foundation for a paradigm shift from the current exception-based approach to disability access to copyrighted cultural materials. Part 2 then turns to the operation of the *Treaty to Facilitate Access to Published Works for Persons Who Are Blind, Visually Impaired, or Otherwise Print Disabled* ('*Marrakesh Treaty*').[5] It explains that, despite the change brought about by the *Marrakesh Treaty* with regard to persons with visual impairments' access to literary works, the Treaty mostly fails to address such persons' access to visual art.

This chapter concludes that the *CRPD* represents a normative paradigm shift in how disability is constructed in international law and how the rights of persons with disabilities are protected. It is a valuable resource for those arguing for greater access to copyright-protected cultural materials. It observes, however, that the new human rights paradigm the *CRPD* introduces has only had a limited impact on the balance between persons with disabilities' rights and copyright protection. This, together with the limited reach of the *Marrakesh Treaty*, means that disability rights advocates will likely need to identify new strategies outside the current international legal framework to advance the struggle for equality of access to visual art.

Part 1. Disability and copyright in international law

The legal construct of copyright

As a legal concept, copyright is not concerned with physical property that suffers from scarcity, but instead constructs particularised concepts, information, and knowledge as goods capable of protection.[6] To encourage continuing invention,

5 *Treaty to Facilitate Access to Published Works for Persons Who Are Blind, Visually Impaired, or Otherwise Print Disabled*, opened for signature 28 June 2013, VIP/DC/8 (entered into force 30 September 2016).

6 Niva Elkin-Koren and Eli M Salzberger, *The Law and Economics of Intellectual Property in the Digital Age* (2013) Routledge, 44–45.

copyright protects the creative and production costs associated with copyright subject matter. This reward for effort is achieved through granting rights holders monopolies over their property for specified periods.[7]

Copyright is not properly construed as a human right; it has a broad range of purposes including, but not limited to, protecting the economic interests of owners. These economic interests often conflict with human rights. For example, ownership of copyright entitles rights holders (often creators) to restrict the use of information for which they own the rights, such as books, visual art, or computer software programmes. On the one hand, this incentivises people to create cultural and other works; on the other hand, it prevents many people from accessing the information, particularly those who cannot compensate the owner. International laws protecting copyright are extensive and permit only limited exceptions to the monopoly of owners. Copyright protection is also included within the mandate of the World Trade Organisation and benefits from it strong enforcement mechanisms.

The construction of disability prior to the CRPD

Disability as a concept has been subject to substantial and continuing change. The definition of disability is fundamentally mutable, subject to social, political, and scientific views on what it means to be 'able-bodied' or what constitutes an 'impairment'. As Irina Metzler notes, 'bodies are never just physical objects, to be described in a neutral, "scientific" way, but are objects whose understanding is determined by the intellectual culture of the day'.[8] Various models and theories of disability have influenced how society interacts with persons with certain abilities, particularly where they fall outside traditional notions of 'normalcy'.

The medical model has proved one of the most enduring approaches towards defining and categorising disability. Medical criteria have been developed to classify certain types of abilities as disabilities. Being categorised as disabled has resulted in the determination of whether or not a person should be euthanised or sterilised;[9] be able to access justice on the same basis as others;[10] enjoy liberty

7 William M Landes and Richard A Posner, 'An Economic Analysis of Copyright Law' (1989) 18 *Journal of Legal Studies* 325, 326.

8 Irina Metzler, *Disability in Medieval Europe: Thinking about Physical Impairment during the High Middle Ages, c.1100–1400* (2006) Routledge, 38.

9 Kerstin Braun, '"Nothing About Us Without Us": The Legal Disenfranchisement of Voters with Disabilities in Germany and Its Compliance with International Human Rights Standards on Disabilities' (2015) 30 *American University International Law Review* 315; Willie V Bryan, *The Social Perspectives and Political History of Disabilities and Rehabilitation in the United States* (2010) Charles C Thomas Ltd; Thomas Lemke, *Perspectives on Genetic Discrimination* (2013) Routledge, 71–72; Marius Turda, *Modernism and Eugenics* (2010) Macmillan, 84–85.

10 Nandini Devi, 'Supported Decision-Making and Personal Autonomy for Persons with Intellectual Disabilities: Article 12 of the UN Convention on the Rights of Persons with Disabilities' (2013) 41(4) *Journal of Law, Medicine & Ethics* 792; Kathryn D DeMarco, 'Disabled by Solitude: The Convention on the Rights of Persons with Disabilities and Its Impact on the Use of

of movement on an equal basis;[11] live independently and be included in the community;[12] and enjoy respect for home and family.[13] The label of disability has been, and continues to be, associated with substantial denials of human rights and policies that have been equated with a social apartheid.[14]

A purely medical approach to defining disability resulted in public policies that denied persons with disabilities their human rights. Under the medical model approach, the policy focus is upon the personal issue of impairment rather than on attempting to critique the social processes and policies that cause disablement.[15] The limitations of the medical model are highlighted in situations where there is limited or no current means of 'curing' the impairment. Under the model, supporters argue that until medicine can 'cure' them, persons with disabilities are regarded as imperfect specimens who are unable to reach 'their human potential given their insufferable condition[s]'.[16] In this context, persons with disabilities are not discussed in terms of equality or rights, but rather they are regarded as people who must be cured or institutionalised. The medical model portrays the cause of persons with disabilities' oppression as their impairment itself, which is held to define them as people who are 'abnormal, deserving of pity and care'.[17]

Supermax Solitary Confinement' (2012) 66 *University of Miami Law Review* 523; Robert D Dinerstein, 'Human Rights and the Protection of Persons with Disabilities: Implementing Legal Capacity Under Article 12 of the UN *Convention on the Rights of Persons with Disabilities*: The Difficult Road From Guardianship to Supported Decision-Making' (2012) 19(2) *Human Rights Brief* 8; Frances Gibson, 'Article 13 of the *Convention on the Rights of Persons with Disabilities* - A Right to Legal Aid?' (2010) 15(2) *Australian Journal of Human Rights* 123; Piers Gooding, 'Navigating the "Flashing Amber Lights" of the Right to Legal Capacity in the United Nations *Convention on the Rights of Persons with Disabilities*: Responding to Major Concerns' (2015) 15(1) *Human Rights Law Review* 45.

11 Vandana Peterson, 'Understanding Disability Under the Convention *on the Rights of Persons with Disabilities* and Its Impact on International Refugee and Asylum Law' (2014) 42 *Georgia Journal of International and Comparative Law* 687; Michael Ashley Stein and Janet E Lord, 'Enabling Refugee and IDP Law and Policy: Implications of the UN *Convention on the Rights of Persons With Disabilities*' (2011) 28 *Arizona Journal of International and Comparative Law* 401.

12 Camilla Parker and Luke Clements, 'The UN *Convention on the Rights of Persons with Disabilities*: A New Right to Independent Living?' (2008) 13(4) *European Human Rights Law Review* 508; Nell Munro, 'Define Acceptable: How Can We Ensure that Treatment for Mental Disorder in Detention Is Consistent with the UN Convention on the Rights of Persons with Disabilities?' (2012) 16(6) *International Journal of Human Rights* 902.

13 Lindsey Coffey, 'A Rights-Based Claim to Surrogacy: Article 23 of the *Convention on the Rights of Persons with Disabilities*' (2011) 20 *Michigan State University Journal of International Law* 259; Bret Shaffer, 'The Right to Life, the *Convention on the Rights of Persons with Disabilities*, and Abortion' (2009) 28 *Penn State International Law Review* 265.

14 Gerard Goggin and Christopher Newell, *Disability in Australia: Exposing a Social Apartheid* (2003) University of New South Wales Press.

15 Simi Linton, *Claiming Disability: Knowledge and Identity* (1998) New York University Press, 11.

16 Kaley Maureen Roosen, 'From Tragedy to "Crip" to Human: The Need for Multiple Understandings of Disability in Psychotherapy' (2009) 1 *Critical Disability Discourse* 1, 2–3.

17 Neil Rees, Simon Rice and Dominique Allen, *Australian Anti-Discrimination Law*, 2nd Edition (2014) Federation Press, [6.3.2.1].

Since the 1980s, advocates interested in improving the lives of persons with disabilities have resisted the medicalisation of impairment, focusing instead on the social causes of disablement.[18] If impairments are constructed as the cause of disablement, this, arguably, reduces the social consciousness concerning the role society plays in disabling people who fall outside the 'normal' range of abilities.[19] Social model scholars reject the notion that disability is caused by impairment and focus on the external sources of disablement.[20] The social model turns the focus away from impairment itself and concentrates on disabling barriers, whether these be attitudinal, physical, or political.[21] Critical disability studies scholarship has built on this approach, recognising the complexity and variability of disability, and the interaction between individual and structural factors.[22] Sir Thomas Shakespeare explains that disability is understood by medical, psychological, environmental, economic, and political factors.[23] As will be seen in the next section, this intersectional approach to constructing disability is reflected to a significant degree in the duties under the *CRPD* that are placed on the state parties to it.

How the CRPD *constructs disability*

While the medical aspects of impairments are ontologically real – many people cannot see or walk – the determination of when, and which, impairments should be regarded as 'disabling' is the result of shifting social constructions and identities.[24] The *CRPD* reflects this ever-shifting debate over how disability should be defined.[25] Following the trend set by the World Health Organization and World Bank,[26] the *CRPD* emphasises the role society has on constructing 'disability'. This position is articulated in the Preamble of the *CRPD*, which recognises in paragraph (e) 'that disability is an evolving concept and that disability results from the interaction between persons with impairments and attitudinal and

18 Samuel Bagenstos, *Law and the Contradictions of the Disability Rights Movement* (2009) Yale University Press, 7–13.

19 Michael Oliver, *Understanding Disability: From Theory to Practice* (1996) Palgrave Macmillan, 37.

20 Michael Oliver, *The Politics of Disablement* (1990) Macmillan, 11.

21 Sandra Fredman, *Discrimination Law*, 2nd Edition (2011) Oxford University Press, 171–173.

22 Sir Thomas Shakespeare, *Disability Rights and Wrongs Revisited*, 2nd Edition (2014) Routledge, 74–75.

23 Ibid. 83.

24 Fiona Campbell 'Stalking Ableism: Using Disability to Expose "Abled" Narcissism' in D Goodley, B Hughes and L Davis (eds), *Disability and Social Theory: New Developments and Directions*, (2012) Palgrave Macmillan; Sir Thomas Shakespeare, *Disability Rights and Wrongs Revisited*, 2nd Edition (2014) Routledge, 60.

25 Paul Harpur, 'Embracing the New Disability Rights Paradigm: The Importance of the Convention on the Rights of Persons with Disabilities' (2012) 27(1) *Disability and Society* 1.

26 The WHO and WB adopt a bio-psycho-social model of disability which acknowledges 'the negative aspects of the interaction between an individual (with a health condition) and that individual's contextual factors (environmental and personal factors)': World Health Organization and World Bank, *World Report on Disabilities* (2011) 3.

environmental barriers that hinders their full and effective participation in society on an equal basis with others'. Reflecting social and critical studies scholarship, the *CRPD* Preamble explains that a key cause of disablement is the barriers in society. As explained during the seventh session of the Ad Hoc Committee on a Comprehensive and Integral International Convention on the Protection and Promotion of the Rights and Dignity of Persons with Disabilities, the approach to disability in the *CRPD* 'incorporates three elements: impairment, which is the physiological function, disability, which recognises the interaction of disability with the environment, and the notion of handicap, which refers to the disadvantage created by the impairment or disability'.[27] Accordingly, the notion of disablement requires a focus on a range of factors including barriers in society.

The *CRPD* considers a wide range of factors when conceptualising disablement, including health care, habilitation and rehabilitation, poverty and economic exclusion,[28] and the impact of intersecting attributes, such as race, colour, sex, language, religion, political or other opinion, national, ethnic, indigenous or social origin, property, birth, age, or other status.[29] Importantly for this chapter, the *CRPD* recognises the role that intellectual property has in causing disability and takes steps to reduce its disabling impact.[30]

The rights protected in the *CRPD* are comprehensive,[31] reflecting an extremely broad human rights agenda.[32] The *CRPD* preamble builds on existing human rights conventions including the *Universal Declaration of Human Rights*, the *International Covenant on Economic, Social and Cultural Rights*, the *International Covenant on Civil and Political Rights*, the *International Convention on the Elimination of All Forms of Racial Discrimination*, the *Convention on the Elimination of All Forms of Discrimination against Women*, the *Convention against Torture and Other Cruel, Inhuman or Degrading Treatment or Punishment*, the *Convention on the Rights of the Child*, and the *International Convention on the Protection of the Rights of All Migrant Workers and Members of Their Families*.[33] Beyond these existing instruments, which only apply to persons with

27 Comments by Australia: Summaries of the Seventh Session of the Ad Hoc Committee on a Comprehensive and Integral International Convention on Protection and Promotion of the Rights and Dignity of Persons with Disabilities, daily summary of discussion at the seventh session, 31 January 2006 <http://www.un.org/esa/socdev/enable/rights/ahc7sum31jan.htm>.

28 *CRPD*, Preamble (m).

29 *CRPD*, Preamble (p).

30 See in particular the discussion of *CRPD*, art 30(3) below in this chapter.

31 Jill Stavert, 'United Nations *Convention on the Rights of Persons with Disabilities*: Possible Implications for Scotland for Persons with Mental Disorder' (2009) 49 *Scottish Human Rights Journal* 2.

32 Janet E Lord, Deepti S Raja, and Peter Blanck, 'Law and People with Disabilities' in James D Wright (ed), *International Encyclopaedia of the Social and Behavioural Sciences*, 2nd Edition (2015) Elsevier, 497.

33 *Universal Declaration of Human Rights*, UN Doc A/810 (12 December 1948); *International Covenant on Civil and Political Rights*, opened for signature 16 December 1966, 999 UNTS 171 (entered into force 23 March 1976); *International Covenant on Economic, Social and Cultural Rights*, 16 December 1966, 993 UNTS 3 (entered into force 3 January 1976); *International*

disabilities implicitly, the *CRPD* specifically attributes rights to persons with disabilities. For example, the *Universal Declaration on Human Rights* states that 'everyone' is entitled to the rights and freedoms set forth in the declaration.[34] While persons with disabilities fall within the description of 'everyone', it is significant that disabilities are not included in a list of specific classes in need of protection from human rights violations.[35]

The *CRPD* promotes inclusion and equal accessibility in society as a fundamental human right and rejects the notion that persons with disabilities should have their rights discounted due to ability differences.[36] Under this human rights-based approach, the notion of ability equality is not a privilege, but a human right that the state must help realise.[37] The *CRPD* preamble focuses on achieving 'equalization of opportunities', mainstreaming disability protections for persons requiring intensive support or less support, actively involves persons with disabilities in policy developments, and recognises that action is required to redress past discrimination which has resulted in poverty.[38]

The new disability human rights paradigm

The human rights agenda of the *CRPD* substantially transforms how international human rights law approaches persons with disabilities.[39] Professors Janet Lord and Michael Stein explain that:

Convention on the Elimination of All Forms of Racial Discrimination, opened for signature 21 December 1965, 660 UNTS 195 (entered into force on 4 January 1969); the *Convention on the Elimination of All Forms of Discrimination against Women*, opened for signature 1 March 1980, 1249 UNTS 13 (entered into force 3 September 1981); *Convention against Torture and Other Cruel, Inhuman or Degrading Treatment or Punishment*, opened for signature 10 December 1984, UNTS 1465 (entered into force 26 June 1987); *Convention on the Rights of the Child*, opened for signature 20 November 1989, 1577 UNTS 3 (entered into force 2 September 1990); *International Convention on the Protection of the Rights of All Migrant Workers and Members of their Families*, opened for signature 18 December 1990, UNTS 2220 (entered into force 1 July 2003).

34 *Universal Declaration on Human Rights*, art 2.

35 The non-exhaustive list of categories requiring attention include 'race, colour, sex, language, religion, political or other opinion, national or social origin, property, birth or other status'.

36 Anna Lawson, 'Accessibility Obligations in the UN *Convention on the Rights of Persons with Disabilities*: *Nyusti and Takacs v Hungary*' (2014) 30(2) *South African Journal on Human Rights* 380.

37 Arlene S Kanter, *The Development of Disability Rights Under International Law: From Charity to Human Rights* (2015) Routledge, 31.

38 *CRPD*, Preamble (f), (g), (j), (o), (p), (t) and (v).

39 Heiner Bielefeldt, 'New Inspiration for the Human Rights Debate: The *Convention on the Rights of Persons with Disabilities*' (2007) 25(3) *Netherlands Quarterly of Human Rights* 397; Camilla Parker and Luke Clements, 'The UN *Convention on the Rights of Persons with Disabilities*: A New Right to Independent Living?' (2008) 4 *European Human Rights Law Review* 508; Nell Munro, 'Define Acceptable: How Can We Ensure that Treatment for Mental Disorder in Detention is Consistent with the UN *Convention on the Rights of Persons with Disabilities*?' (2012) 16(6) *International Journal of Human Rights* 902; Michael Waterstone, 'The Significance of the United

> The *CRPD* advances social rights in a way that may profoundly affect the development of emergent social rights jurisprudence and advance human rights advocacy. Its comprehensive rights catalogue allows direct invocation of social rights claims, eliminating the need to fit such claims within the framework of more established civil or political rights.[40]

Professor Gerard Quinn heralds the *CRPD* as the 'Declaration of Independence' for persons with disabilities.[41] For the first time in history, persons with disabilities are regarded by international law as full and equal citizens.[42] State signatories are required to comply with the provisions of the *CRPD*, with its sweeping human rights agenda ideally driving domestic law and policy reforms. The *CRPD* requires states to take immediate, effective, and appropriate measures

a To raise awareness throughout society, including at the family level, regarding persons with disabilities and to foster respect for the rights and dignity of persons with disabilities;
b Combat stereotypes, prejudices, and harmful practices relating to persons with disabilities, including those based on sex and age, in all areas of life;
c Promote awareness of the capabilities and contributions of persons with disabilities.[43]

Effectively, the *CRPD* requires states to take positive steps to promote a sweeping disability rights-based agenda.[44] The interventions are not just limited to changing laws but include wider community education and the promotion of organisations of persons with disabilities.[45] Importantly, this new disability

Nations *Convention on the Rights of Persons with Disabilities*' (2010) 33 *Loyola International and Comparative Law Review* 1.

40 Janet E Lord and Michael Ashley Stein, 'Social Rights and the Relational Value of the Rights to Participate in Sport, Recreation, and Play' (2009) 27 *Boston University International Law Journal* 249, 251.

41 Gerard Quinn, 'Closing: Next Steps - Towards a United Nations Treaty on the Rights of Persons with Disabilities' in Peter Blanck (ed), *Disability Rights* (2005) Ashgate, 519, 541.

42 Michael Waterstone, 'The Significance of the United Nations *Convention on the Rights of Persons with Disabilities*' (2010) 33 *Loyola International and Comparative Law Review* 1, 2.

43 *CRPD*, art 8.

44 Eilionóir Flynn, 'Ireland's Compliance with the *Convention on the Rights of Persons with Disabilities*: Towards A Rights-Based Approach for Legal Reform?' (2009) 31(1) *Dublin University Law Journal* 357; Piers Gooding, 'Navigating the "Flashing Amber Lights" of the Right to Legal Capacity in the United Nations *Convention on the Rights of Persons with Disabilities*: Responding to Major Concerns' (2015) 15(1) *Human Rights Law Review* 45; Kelley Johnson 'The UN *Convention on the Rights of Persons with Disabilities*: A Framework for Ethical and Inclusive Practice?' (2013) 7(3) *Ethics and Social Welfare* 218; Janet Lord, Deepti Samant Raja, and Peter Blanck, 'Beyond the Orthodoxy of Rule of Law and Justice Sector Reform: A Framework for Legal Empowerment and Innovation through the *Convention on the Rights of Persons with Disabilities*' (2013) 4 *World Bank Legal Review* 45.

45 *CRPD*, art 29.

rights paradigm has significant implications for the balance between the rights of persons with disabilities and the protection of intellectual property.

Part 2. Copyright and persons with disabilities' right to access cultural materials

Advances in technology during the twentieth and twenty-first centuries, from audio recordings to 3D printing, have brought about new ways for persons with visual impairments to experience the world's visual art, much of which was previously difficult or impossible for them to experience. Combined with greater awareness of persons with disabilities and a desire to increase inclusivity, museums, art galleries, and other custodians and creators of visual art have developed innovative ways for persons with visual impairments to understand and interact with all forms of visual art, from paintings, photographs, and book illustrations, to statues, sculptures, and architectural designs. These methods may supplement, or in some cases replace, simple audio descriptions.

Indeed, while most museums and galleries continue to display visual artworks in traditional ways, they are increasingly creating unique installations, rearranging exhibits, and finding new methods to present their collections in ways that can be enjoyed by persons with visual impairments, as well as adding to the experiences of sighted persons. One particularly popular method is the use of tactile art. The Musée du Louvre, for example, has maintained a 'touch gallery' containing casts of the museum's artworks.[46] The Prado in Madrid created a display of 3D artworks by taking high-resolution images of paintings and then working with persons with visual impairments to identify details that could be accentuated to increase engagement with the work.[47] Grants given to the Art Institute of Chicago allowed the Institute to experiment with 3D printing and create 1:1 scale models of some pieces in its collection. In an interview, an assistant director at the Institute stated that the technology had proved 'an extremely resourceful and legitimate way of making these works of art accessible to people with blindness and low vision'.[48]

Of course, the majority of the world's visual art exists outside of museums and art galleries and is not accessible to persons with visual impairments. This includes representations of objects on television or in movies, or illustrations in books. 3D printing offers an increasingly cost-effective avenue for these works to be made accessible. However, copyright protection often stands in the way of creating 3D models, such as when HBO prevented the creation of a model of the

46 Musée du Louvre, 'The Touch Gallery' <https://www.louvre.fr/en/touch-gallery>.

47 David Hewitt, 'Please Touch the Art: 3-D Printing Helps Visually Impaired Appreciate Paintings' *Smithsonian.com* (online), 26 February 2015 <https://www.smithsonianmag.com/innovation/please-touch-art-3-d-printing-helps-visually-impaired-appreciate-paintings-180954420/>.

48 Paulette Beete, 'Touch and See: Accessibility Programs for People with Vision Impairments at the Art Institute of Chicago' *NEA Arts Magazine* (online), 2015 <https://www.arts.gov/NEARTS/2015v1-challenging-notions-accessibility-and-arts/touch-and-see>.

'Iron Throne' from its drama 'Game of Thrones'.[49] Copyright may also attach to 3D data files themselves, preventing printing without the rights holder's permission. It is, of course, understandable that rights holders are concerned that their works will be copied and distributed in breach of copyright; estimates of the impact of 3D printing on intellectual property run into many billions of dollars.[50]

A balance needs to be struck between, on the one hand, rights holders' interests in preventing unauthorised copying of their works through 3D printing and, on the other hand, the genuine benefits of 3D printing to persons with visual impairments.

The exception paradigm and the Berne Convention

Traditionally, international human rights laws strongly supported intellectual property interests including copyright, with disability rights peripheral to the protection of such property. An example is Article 15 of the *International Covenant on Economic, Social and Cultural Rights*, which recognises in 15(1)(a) and (b) that all people have a right 'to take part in cultural life' and 'to enjoy the benefits of scientific progress and its applications'.[51] Nonetheless, article 15(1)(c) limits the right of people to access scientific, literary, or artistic productions by a right of individuals 'to benefit from the protection of the moral and material interests resulting from' creating such works. Thus, Article 15 of the Covenant creates a tension between access to artistic, cultural, and scientific works and the right of people to restrict access for exploitative purposes. This is illustrative of how human rights laws have often accepted the notion that rights holders should be entitled to set the terms on which people exercise their right to access cultural materials.

The prioritisation of rights holders' interests manifests through the exception-based model for exercising the right to access copyrighted works, articulated in international agreements such as the *Berne Convention for the Protection of Literary and Artistic Works* ('*Berne Convention*').[52] The *Berne Convention*, which applies to 'every production in the literary, scientific and artistic domain' and deals with the rights of authors and protection of their works,[53] sets out minimum standards of protection for works and authors' rights. This includes the right to make reproductions in any manner or form, and the moral right of authors to prevent any modification or deformation of their work that would be prejudicial to their honour or reputation.[54] Importantly, the *Berne Convention* does not

49 Sarah Craig, 'Protection for Printing: An Analysis of Copyright Protection for 3D Printing' (2017) 1 *U Ill L Rev* 307, 308–309.

50 See, e.g., 'Gartner Reveals Top Predictions for IT Organizations and Users for 2014 and Beyond', Gartner (8 October 2013) <http://www.gartner.com/newsroom/id/2603215>.

51 *International Covenant on Economic, Social and Cultural Rights*, art 15(1)(a) and (b).

52 Opened for signature 9 September 1886, 1161 UNTS 30 (entered into force 5 December 1887).

53 Art 2(1).

54 Arts 6(1) and 9(1).

place duties on owners of copyright to make works accessible, instead placing restrictions on those trying to make copyrighted works available to persons with visual impairments. Such persons must satisfy exemptions in the Convention before dealing with works without obtaining permission from the rights holder.[55]

Exemptions permitting persons to make reproductions of works without authorisation or payment of compensation flow from Article 9(2) of the *Berne Convention*. This provision, commonly referred to as the 'Three-Step Test', has been in operation since 1967.[56] The Test has been incorporated into subsequent copyright treaties, a number of free-trade agreements, and EU law.[57] The Three-Step Test constructs non-standard uses of copyright works as exceptions and permits such uses where three factors are satisfied:

1 There is a 'certain special case' or use;
2 That does not 'conflict with a normal exploitation of a work'; and
3 That does not 'unreasonably prejudice the legitimate interests of the author'.

The exceptions in the Test are tailored narrowly and generally construed as such, effectively deterring social measures aimed at increasing access to works in contravention of the rights and economic interests of copyright holders.[58] Even allowing for a wide interpretation of the Test, the exemption model places the burden of converting works into accessible formats on those using the Test. This means that, in practice, persons with visual impairment and persons and organisations assisting them are left to do all the heavy lifting. Under the exception paradigm, disability advocates must argue for limited deviations from the status quo of strong monopoly rights and market-based solutions. The exception model is reflected in the laws of most Western states, which generally permit the digitisation and copying of copyrighted works for the specific benefit of persons with visual impairments. The difficulties with the Three-Step Test are clearly demonstrated in the case of books, where the gap between the number of published works and those available in formats accessible to persons with visual

55 Bashar H Malkawi, 'A Long "TRIP" Home: How the *Berne Convention*, *TRIPS Agreement*, and Other Instruments Complement the International Copyright System' (2013) 35(2) *European Intellectual Property Review* 93, 94.

56 Christophe Geiger, Daniel Gervais, and Martin Senftleben, 'The Three-Step Test Revisited: How to Use the Test's Flexibility in National Copyright Law' (2014) 29 *American University International Law Review* 583, 583.

57 See, e.g., *Marrakesh Agreement Establishing the World Trade Organization*, opened for signature 15 April 1994, 1867 UNTS 3 (entered into force 1 January 1995), Annex 1C ('*Agreement on Trade-Related Aspects of Intellectual Property Rights*') art 1; *Australia-United States Free Trade Agreement*, Australia-United States, signed 18 May 2004, [2005] ATS 1 (entered into force 1 January 2005) art 17.4(10); *North American Free Trade Agreement*, United States-Mexico-Canada, signed 17 December 1992, 32 ILS 612 (entered into force 1 January 1994) art 17.05(5); *Directive 2001/29/EC of the European Parliament and Council* [2001] OJ L 167/10, art 5(3)(b).

58 Henning Grosse Ruse-Khan, 'Time for a Paradigm Shift - Exploring Maximum Standards in International Intellectual Property Protection' (2009) 1 *Trade, Law and Development* 56.

impairments has grown since the Test's development.[59] The exception model operates in a similar way with respect to 3D printing and access to visual art, limiting the extent to which accessible copies of versions of such works can be made available to persons with visual impairments.

The CRPD *and the human rights paradigm*

The new disability human rights paradigm introduced by the *CRPD* realigns the interaction between copyright and persons with disabilities right to access cultural materials in international law. The *CRPD* adopts a transformational approach to the interaction between intellectual property and the human rights of persons with disabilities.[60] In Article 30, the *CRPD* directly addresses the right to participate in culture, recreation, and leisure. Article 30(1) entitles persons with disabilities to 'take part on an equal basis with others in cultural life' and requires that member states 'shall take all appropriate measures to ensure that persons with disabilities … [e]njoy access to cultural materials in accessible formats'.[61]

The duty in the *CRPD* to provide persons with disabilities access to cultural materials creates situations where copyright interests are impacted. 'Cultural material' is defined broadly, encompassing literature, artefacts, radio, screen and television productions, performance, and visual arts.[62] Of course, providing persons with disabilities access to cultural materials will almost certainly require dealing with copyright protected works in ways that the copyright owner may resist. Article 30(3) specifically considers how the potential conflicts between access to culture and intellectual property should be resolved:

> States Parties shall take all appropriate steps, in accordance with international law, to ensure that laws protecting intellectual property rights do not constitute an unreasonable or discriminatory barrier to access by persons with disabilities to cultural materials.

It is notable that Article 30(3) refers to 'intellectual property' and not just 'copyright'. During the sessions of the Ad Hoc Committee on a Comprehensive

59 Brian Watermeyer, 'Freedom to Read: A Personal Account of the "Book Famine"' (2014) 3(1) *African Journal of Disability* 144; Kaya Koklu, 'The Marrakesh Treaty: Time to End the Book Famine for Visually Impaired Persons Worldwide' (2014) 45(7) *International Review of Intellectual Property and Competition Law* 737.

60 Paul Harpur and Nicolas Suzor, 'The Paradigm Shift in Realising the Right to Read: How Ebook Libraries are Enabling in the University Sector' (2014) 29(10) *Disability and Society* 1658.

61 *CRPD*, art 30(1).

62 The concept of cultural material is broadly defined in a range of international agreements. For example: *Convention for the Safeguarding of Intangible Cultural Heritage*, opened for signature 17 October 2003, 2368 UNTS 3 (entered into force 20 April 2006); *Hague Convention for the Protection of Cultural Property in the Event of Armed Conflict*, opened for signature 14 May 1954, 249 UNTS 3511 (entered into force 7 August 1956).

and Integral International Convention on the Protection and Promotion of the Rights and Dignity of Persons with Disabilities, the wording of Article 30(3) was discussed. During the sixth session, although the proposal to replace 'intellectual property rights' with 'copyright' received strong support, there was no general agreement.[63] The idea of limiting Article 30(3) to copyright came up again during the seventh session. Interestingly, the leading voice on promoting intellectual property, WIPO, did not participate in the seventh session or any of the other seven sessions.[64] Importantly, there were no reservations in relation to Article 30(3) of the *CRPD*.[65]

Article 30(3) is most relevant to the conflict between copyright and disability access to cultural materials, given that there are very few situations where there would be a conflict between disability access to cultural materials and types of intellectual property other than copyright. In this context, Article 30(3) marks a shift from the construction of disability rights as exceptions to copyright, instead of placing a ceiling on the extent of property rights conferred by intellectual property.[66] The *CRPD* provides that copyright can exist up to the point at which it creates a conflict with persons with disabilities' access to cultural materials. While the exception paradigm demarcates minimum standards for copyright protection, the human rights paradigm sets out maximum limits. Article 30 imposes a strong positive obligation on member states to ensure that persons with disabilities enjoy access to culture and knowledge on an equal basis, including to material protected by copyright.

The human rights paradigm, the Marrakesh Treaty, *and the visual arts Lacuna*

The *CRPD*, and the disability human rights paradigm it introduced, have led to further significant shifts in the balance between disability rights and copyright. In particular, disability rights advocates have used the *CRPD* to justify altering international copyright laws to increase persons with visual impairments' right to access written works.[67] To this end, a significant achievement has been the adoption of the *Marrakesh Treaty*, which creates mandatory exceptions to copyright

63 UN General Assembly, Ad Hoc Committee on a Comprehensive and Integral International Convention on the Protection and Promotion of the Rights and Dignity of Persons with Disabilities, *Report of the Ad Hoc Committee on a Comprehensive and Integral International Convention on the Protection and Promotion of the Rights and Dignity of Persons with Disabilities on Its Sixth Session*, UN Doc A/60/266 (17 August 2005) 139.

64 List of NGO representatives registered at the Seventh Session <http://www.un.org/esa/socdev/enable/rights/ahc7ngorepslist.htm>.

65 United Nations - Treaty Collection on the Internet <https://treaties.un.org/Pages/ViewDetails.aspx?src=IND&mtdsg_no=IV-15&chapter=4&lang=en>.

66 Henning Grosse Ruse-Khan, 'Time for a Paradigm Shift - Exploring Maximum Standards in International Intellectual Property Protection' (2009) 1 *Trade, Law and Development* 56, 62.

67 Paul Harpur and Nic Suzor, 'Copyright Protections and Disability Rights: Turning the Page to a New International Paradigm' (2013) 36(3) *University of New South Wales Law Journal* 745.

protection.[68] The Treaty was adopted in the face of sustained pressure and objections from publishing groups.[69] The United States Copyright Industries, for example, argued that

> [b]y requiring the recognition of a specific, detailed exception to copyright protection, the draft treaty would break the mould of every previous treaty instrument that forms part of the long-standing global framework of copyright norms.[70]

Criticism during the drafting process for the *Marrakesh Treaty* was reflective of the tension between the dominant exception-based paradigm in global copyright politics and the human rights paradigm introduced by the *CRPD*. The Preamble of the Treaty acknowledges the dual objectives of 'effective protection of the rights of authors' and ensuring 'effective and timely access to works for the benefit of persons with visual impairments'.

The main goal of the *Marrakesh Treaty* was to enhance persons with visual impairments' right to read, and, to this end, the Treaty increases such persons' access to books by reducing, in limited and prescribed ways, the restrictive operation of copyright.[71] Under the Treaty, it is mandatory for state signatories to adopt copyright exceptions for the non-profit creation and distribution of accessible versions of works for the benefit of persons with visual impairments.[72] The *Marrakesh Treaty* is remarkable insofar as it makes exceptions to mandate, rather than permit, exceptions to copyright's exclusive rights, thus imposing a ceiling on the strength of copyright interests. The Treaty also contains provisions facilitating the international exchange of books and publications in accessible formats, requiring WIPO to establish information sharing procedures to enhance cooperation between member states, and mandating that states allow

68 Opened for signature 28 June 2013, WIPO Doc VIP/DC/8 (entered into force 30 September 2016).

69 For example, see e-mails from the Publishers Association to the UK Intellectual Property Office, 28 March 2012 <http://www.scribd.com/doc/140886790/Redacted-UK-IP-Office-Pub-Assoc-Emails-digitized-searchable-versio>; James Love, 'UK IPO Office Releases Emails that Show Close Collaboration with Publishers on WIPO Treaty for the Blind' *Knowledge Ecology International* (11 May 2013) <http://keionline.org/node/1719>; James Love, 'Disney, Viacom and Other MPAA Members Join Book Publishers to Weaken a Treaty for the Blind' *Huff Post Politics* (23 April 2013) <http://www.huffingtonpost.com/james-love/disney-viacom-and-other-m_b_3137653.html>; Jim Fruchterman, 'Poisoning the Treaty for the Blind' *Huff Post Politics* (7 May 2013) <http://www.huffingtonpost.com/jim-fruchterman/poisoning-the-treaty-for-_b_3225181.html>.

70 Steven J Metalitz, Submission No 19 to US Copyright Office, *Notice of Inquiry and Request for Comments: Facilitating Access for the Blind or Other Persons with Disabilities* (13 November 2009) 3.

71 Jingyi Li, 'Reconciling the Enforcement of Copyright with the Upholding of Human Rights: A Consideration of the *Marrakesh Treaty to Facilitate Access to Published Works for the Blind, Visually Impaired and Print Disabled*' (2014) 36(10) *European Intellectual Property Review* 653.

72 *Marrakesh Treaty*, art 4.

circumvention of digital locks placed on e-books and other works.[73] Among other things, these provisions reduce the marked inefficiency of the current system under the Three-Step Test, which requires institutions in each country to digitise their own accessible copies of works.[74] This change is having a profound impact in the Global South, where resources are more limited.[75] Importantly, nothing in the *Berne Convention* or other international instruments prevents any of the measures introduced by the *Marrakesh Treaty.*

Nonetheless, while the *Marrakesh Treaty* makes an important contribution to improving persons with visual impairments' access to books, there are important limitations to its scope. One such limitation is its focus on written work; Pursuant to Article 2(a), it applies to literary or artistic works 'in the form of text, notation and/or related illustrations, whether published or otherwise made publicly available'. The Treaty does not apply to other types of 'literary or artistic works' as defined under the under 2(1) of the *Berne Convention*, which includes, inter alia, 'works of drawing, painting, architecture, sculpture, engraving and lithography; photographic works ... maps, plans, [and] sketches'. Thus, the *Marrakesh Treaty* only increases persons with visual impairments' access to visual art if that art comprises illustrations in published or publicly available written works.

The *Marrakesh Treaty* sends a strong normative message that persons with visual impairments should be able to fully take part in cultural life and, furthermore, signifies a successful intrusion of human rights into international intellectual property politics, but stops short of facilitating access to a broader range of cultural works. While the requirement in Article 30, the *CRPD* – that persons with disabilities must have access to all cultural materials, without discrimination – applies broadly, it lacks the practical force of the *Marrakesh Treaty.* Further work must be done before the human rights paradigm can substantively alter persons with visual impairments' access to visual art.

A pertinent question follows: should this work be done at the international level through law making? Although an additional treaty, or perhaps expansion of the *Marrakesh Treaty* through a Protocol, to address persons with visual impairments' access to visual art is not untenable, it would likely run into the same concerted resistance as the *Marrakesh Treaty* did.[76] Access to visual art

73 *Marrakesh Treaty*, arts 5, 6, 7 and 9.

74 See generally Judith Sullivan, 'WIPO Study on Copyright Limitations and Exceptions for the Visually Impaired' WIPO SCCR 15/7 (February 2007); Paul Harpur and Nic Suzor, 'Copyright Protections and Disability Rights: Turning the Page to a New International Paradigm' (2013) 36(3) *University of New South Wales Law Journal* 745; Simonetta Vezzoso, 'The Marrakesh Spirit - A Ghost in Three Steps?' (2014) 45(7) *International Review of Intellectual Property and Competition Law* 796.

75 Paul Harpur and Michael Ashley Stein, 'The Relevance of the CRPD and Marrakesh Treaty to the Global South' in Michael Ashley Stein and Jonathan Lazar (eds), *Accessible Technology and the Developing World* (2020) Oxford University Press.

76 Representatives of the US copyright industry expressed fear that the Treaty would be a 'wedge... driven into the long-standing structure of global copyright norms': Steven J Metalitz, Submission No 19 to US Copyright Office, *Facilitating Access to Copyrighted Works for the Blind or Other Persons with Disabilities: Notice of Inquiry and Request for Comments* (13 November 2009).

(the copyright in which is usually retained by the creator) may raise different issues than access to published literary works (the exploitation of which is usually undertaken by assignees or licensees). However, the interests of copyright protection, and the historically strong and complex policy and legal frameworks that reinforce them, may still vigorously resist any further limitation on international copyright norms. More immediate avenues may be usefully explored at the domestic level where, ultimately, the tension between the human rights paradigm and copyright interests plays out at a practical level. Indeed, as this book illustrates, a number of states have already adopted copyright exceptions facilitating disability access to visual art, often in the name of the *Marrakesh Treaty*. Building on the human rights paradigm introduced by the *CRPD*, and the example of the *Marrakesh Treaty*, advocates for persons with visual impairments should highlight the benefits of engaging with visual art, methods (like 3D printing) that may facilitate more meaningful access, and the barriers that copyright protections pose to this access.

Conclusion

The *CRPD* represents a fundamental shift in how international law frames and protects the rights of persons with disabilities. The new human rights paradigm introduced by the *CRPD* recognises the underlying causes of disablement for persons with disabilities and imposes positive obligations on state parties to take steps towards achieving substantive equality. In some cases, these steps may involve conflict between the rights of persons with disabilities and persons with copyright interests. The *CRPD* explicitly acknowledges this conflict in the context of cultural materials, providing that copyright should not erect unreasonable or discriminatory barriers to persons with disabilities' right to access to materials.

The *CRPD* introduces a potential paradigm shift from the exception model, which permits limited deviations from monopoly rights of copyright owners, towards a human rights model, where copyright protection is circumscribed by persons with disabilities' right to access cultural materials. This new paradigm is reflected in the *Marrakesh Treaty*, the first international instrument to mandate, rather than permit, exceptions to copyrighted material.

Nonetheless, persons with visual impairments' access to visual art has, to date, received much less attention than access to print materials. The *Marrakesh Treaty* does not address visual art, aside from the limited exception of book illustrations. This belies the significant barriers persons with visual impairments face in trying to access ways of better engaging with visual art works. While technological innovations, such as 3D printing, offer potentially life-changing ways for persons with visual impairments to access visual art, copyright interests are likely to stand in the way of broader uptake. Solutions must be found to these issues, whether at the international level or through advocacy and law reform domestically. The potential for the disability human rights paradigm to shift the balance between human rights and copyright in this context remains to be seen.

Part 3

The EU framework for disability rights and exceptions

8 The EU disability exceptions

Ana Ramalho

Introduction

This chapter analyses the European Union (EU) legal framework governing 3D printing of 2D artistic works to facilitate access to persons with a visual impairment (PVI). While focusing on this specific application, the discussion is relevant to disability access more generally. As made evident from previous chapters, the act of 3D printing a copyright protected work might involve exclusive rights of the copyright owner. These include, chiefly, the right of reproduction (when scanning the 2D work and/or when printing the file containing the scanned work), as well as, possibly, the right of adaptation (if the file containing the 2D work is changed, either for aesthetic reasons or for technical reasons of readjusting the 2D image into a 3D object). The act of 3D printing the 2D artistic work may also infringe the moral right of integrity (depending on the concrete alterations made to the work). However, the EU harmonisation programme in copyright has left several non-harmonised gaps, including a (general) right of adaptation and moral rights. Both are issues that are dealt with at national level and in very different ways.[1]

The present contribution concerns only the EU harmonised landscape. The reason is twofold: on the one hand, it is useful to scrutinise the law at a supranational level; on the other hand, detailing the differences between (still) 28 Member States would be an unsurmountable task for just one chapter.

The following section will thus elaborate on the exclusive economic rights implied in the act of 3D printing, with a specific focus on the rights harmonised at the EU level (without prejudice to referring to non-harmonised rights where necessary). Next, I will scrutinise exceptions or limitations at the EU level that might exempt from infringement the act of 3D printing 2D artistic works

1 For example, the moral right of integrity might pose extra obstacles to 3D printing of 2D artistic works, depending on the Member State concerned. In France, for instance, the moral right of integrity is quite broad (Article L121-1 of the Intellectual Property Code states simply that the author has a right to "respect for his work"). According to Sundara Rajan, M 2011, *Moral rights*, Oxford University Press, Oxford, p. 66, this means that any modification of the work is to be considered a violation of the right of integrity.

to promote disability access. I will show that the present situation is both non-harmonised and insufficient to fulfil the needs of PVIs, which paves the way to the section that follows: an exploration of the normative basis to introduce a broader disability exception at the EU level. In the last section of the chapter, I will present some conclusions.

The exclusive rights

Central to the act of 3D printing 2D artworks is the right of reproduction, which has been harmonised in the EU and is part of all national copyright laws. The general reproduction right is formulated in Article 2 of the Information Society Directive[2] in very broad terms ("Member States shall provide for the exclusive right to authorise or prohibit direct or indirect, temporary or permanent reproduction by any means and in any form, in whole or in part(...)"). The broad interpretation of the reproduction right is further supported by Recital 21 of the Directive.[3] The Directive does not specifically define acts of reproduction. The expression "by any means and in *any form*" might indicate that technical modifications that do not substantially change the essence of the work still amount to a reproduction, even though the line between such reproductive modifications and an adaptation or alteration of the work is hard to draw.[4]

Case law from the Court of Justice of the European Union (CJEU) has confirmed that the reproduction right is to be broadly interpreted.[5] In particular, in *Allposters*, a case which concerned the physical transformation of the medium of the work from posters into canvasses, the CJEU ruled that both the posters and the canvasses contained the image of a protected artistic work, and thus that practice amounted to a reproduction.[6] The process of transferring the work from posters to canvasses involved applying a synthetic coating to the poster and then

2 Directive 2001/29/EC of the European Parliament and of the Council of 22 May 2001 on the harmonisation of certain aspects of copyright and related rights in the information society, O.J. L167, 22.6.2001, pp. 10–19. Other Directives also grant a reproduction right specifically in respect of computer programmes and databases – see Article 4 of Directive 2009/24/EC of the European Parliament and of the Council of 23 April 2009 on the legal protection of computer programmes (Codified version), O.J. L111, 5.5.2009, pp. 16–22 ("Software Directive") and Article 5 of Directive 96/9/EC of the European Parliament and of the Council of 11 March 1996 on the legal protection of databases, O.J. L77, 23.3.1996, pp. 20–28 ("Database Directive").

3 Recital 21:

> This Directive should define the scope of the acts covered by the reproduction right with regard to the different beneficiaries. This should be done in conformity with the acquis communautaire. A broad definition of these acts is needed to ensure legal certainty within the internal market.

4 Discussing this point, see Depreeuw, S 2014, *The variable scope of the exclusive economic rights in copyright*, Kluwer Law International, Alphen aan den Rijn, p. 200.

5 See e.g. Case C-5/08 *Infopaq*, ECLI:EU:C:2009:465, paras. 39–43; Joined Cases C-403/08 & C-429/08 *Premier League*, ECLI:EU:C:2011:631, para. 159;

6 C-419/13 *Allposters*, ECLI:EU:C:2015:27, paras. 27 and 43.

transferring the image to the canvas by means of a chemical process.[7] Although the final outcome is different, this process is arguably similar to transferring the image of a 2D medium into a 3D medium, in the sense that an image – the copyright work – is transferred to a different support. If that is the case, then the reproduction right would be at stake.

However, it may be too far-fetched to consider the transformation of 2D into 3D as a reproduction. Indeed, in some instances – namely, where it is necessary to adjust the file containing the 2D work, thus modifying the original work – the act might constitute an adaptation rather than a reproduction. The right of adaptation is not harmonised at the EU level, except in relation to software[8] and databases.[9] Most Member States have a separate adaptation right in their catalogue of exclusive rights, but in some countries (e.g. the Netherlands, Belgium and Sweden), adaptation is devised as part of a broad reproduction right.[10]

In any case, the act of 3D printing 2D artistic works would amount to an exclusive right of the copyright owner. It is, however, possible that such act is exempted from a claim of copyright infringement, should an exception or limitation be applicable. The next section will analyse whether the EU copyright framework comprises any relevant exception in this regard.

The exceptions

The Information Society Directive contains 21 exceptions to the rights of reproduction and/or communication to the public,[11] but only the temporary copies exception, in Article 5 paragraph 1 of the Directive, is mandatory. Relevant to this chapter, Article 5 paragraph 3(b) exempts "uses, for the benefit of people with a disability, which are directly related to the disability and of a non-commercial nature, to the extent required by the specific disability (…)" ("the disability exception"). Recital 43 urges Member States to adopt "all necessary measures to facilitate access to works by persons suffering from a disability which constitutes an obstacle to the use of the works themselves, and to pay particular attention to accessible formats."

While Member States were not obliged to implement the disability exception, all of them did. In theory, the scope of the exception should be the same in all Member States, as their freedom to determine the scope of the exceptions is curtailed by internal market objectives (as per *Deckmyn*)[12] and by the high level

7 *Allposters*, para. 15.

8 Article 4 paragraph 1(b) of the Software Directive.

9 Article 5(b) of the Database Directive.

10 van Eechoud et al. 2009, *Harmonizing European copyright law. The challenges of better lawmaking*, Kluwer Law International, Alphen aan den Rijn, pp. 83–84.

11 With the possibility to further extend the exception to the distribution right, under Article 5 paragraph 4 of the Directive.

12 Case C-201/13 *Deckmyn*, ECLI:EU:C:2014:2132, para. 16.

of protection that EU legislation affords authors.[13] Member States' discretion was also limited by the three-step test included in Article 5 paragraph 5, of the Information Society Directive, which makes the implementation of an exception or limitation subject to three conditions: that it is applied only in certain special cases, that it does not conflict with a normal exploitation of the work and that it does not unreasonably prejudice the legitimate interests of the copyright holder[14] ("the three step test"). However, both *Deckmyn* and Opinion 3/15 came after the implementation of the Information Society Directive at the national level.[15] Moreover, neither Article 5 paragraph 3(b) nor Recital 43 gives any indication as to the type of works, disabilities or beneficiaries that come under the scope of the exception. Arguably, this was due to the European legislator seeing the disability exception as one of limited economic importance. Instead, the objective was to set out the minimum conditions for the application of the exception, and then let Member States detail the limits of its use within the limits established by the Directive.[16] In practice, the failure to define key concepts led to different implementations throughout the Member States. National solutions vary in terms of the works in relation to which the exception applies (for instance, in some countries, the exception applies to all types of works, whereas in others, it only applies to "published works"), the beneficiaries entitled to make use of the exception (either only the end-beneficiary, or a third party on their behalf or both) and the definition and types of disabilities (all types of disabilities or particular ones).[17] Some countries have also inserted additional conditions and restrictions in their laws, such as the need to provide compensation for the use, or the restriction of the exception to a private consultation of the work by the person with a disability.[18]

13 Opinion 3/15 of the Court (Grand Chamber), ECLI:EU:C:2017:114, para. 124.

14 Opinion 3/15, para. 125. Note, however, that the role and addressees of this test have been discussed extensively in literature, with no consensus in sight – see *inter alia* Senftleben, M 2004, *Copyright, limitations and the three-step test: an analysis of the three-step test in international and EC copyright law*, Kluwer Law International, The Hague; Jacques, S 2019, *The parody exception in copyright law*, Oxford University Press, Oxford, pp. 46–55. Moreover, and according to the latter author, the CJEU has not issued a definitive interpretation of this matter, but it has at least been consistent in affirming that the three step test does not broaden the scope of the exceptions (Jacques, *op. cit.*, pp. 48–49).

15 In addition, previous to *Deckmyn*, some authors also held the opinion that some of the exceptions are prototypes and that therefore there was some flexibility when implementing them in national law – Hugenholtz, B & Senftleben, M 2011, *Fair use in Europe. In search of flexibilities.* Available at https://www.ivir.nl/publicaties/download/Fair%20Use%20Report%20PUB.pdf (Accessed: 17 September 2019).

16 European Commission, *Proposal for a European parliament and council directive on the harmonisation of certain aspects of copyright and related rights in the information society*, Brussels 10.12.1997, COM (1997) 628 final, p. 32.

17 Triaille, J-P et al. 2013, *Study on the application of Directive 2001/29/EC on copyright and related rights in the information society.* Available at http://www.culturaydeporte.gob.es/planes-nacionales/dam/jcr:b15ddad4-6800-41d8-8b66-96c6d12029fb/131216-study-en.pdf (Accessed: 1 October 2019).

18 Ibid.

Conceptually, national implementations of Article 5 paragraph 3(b) can roughly be divided into three categories: those having the same scope as the Directive's provision, those that are more restrictive and those that have a wider scope than the Directive's.

National laws that have the same scope as the Directive's disability exception usually implement the provision exactly in the same terms as it appears in the Directive. This is the case of, for example, Portugal,[19] Estonia[20]or the Czech Republic.[21] Similarly to the Directive, these provisions do not restrict the type of work involved. They could therefore be interpreted as covering acts of reproduction, communication to the public and, in some cases, distribution of artistic works for disability access purposes.

Examples of narrower disability exceptions at the national level include those, for instance, making the exception additionally subject to the three-step test (Belgium),[22] covering only the exclusive right of reproduction (Greece,[23] Bulgaria,[24] Luxembourg),[25] mandating that the use be personal (Italy,[26] United Kindgom),[27] making the exception subject to the payment of fair compensation (the Netherlands)[28] or equitable remuneration (Germany)[29] or adding certain requirements to the exception, such as the need for the reproduction to be carried out by legal persons and certain cultural establishments for the purposes of a strictly private consultation of the work by people with visual or other impediments (France).[30]

19 Article 75 paragraph 2(i) of Portuguese Copyright Law. Available at https://wipolex.wipo.int/en/text/451732 (Accessed: 10 September 2019).

20 Section 19 paragraph 6 of Estonian Copyright Law. Available at https://wipolex.wipo.int/en/text/510478 (Accessed: 10 September 2019).

21 Article 38 of Czech Copyright Law. Available at https://wipolex.wipo.int/en/text/186403 (Accessed: 10 September 2019).

22 Article 190-15° of the Belgian Code of Economic Law, Book XI. Available at https://wipolex.wipo.int/en/text/490517 (Accessed: 12 September 2019).

23 Article 28A of Greek Copyright Law. Available at https://wipolex.wipo.int/en/text/480968 (Accessed: 12 September 2019).

24 Article 24 paragraph 10 of Bulgarian Copyright Law. Available at https://wipolex.wipo.int/en/text/477765 (Accessed: 12 September 2019).

25 Section 10.14 of Luxembourgian Copyright Law. Available at https://wipolex.wipo.int/en/text/128652 (Accessed: 12 September 2019).

26 Article 71bis of Italian Copyright Law. Available at https://wipolex.wipo.int/en/text/477618 (accessed: 12 September 2019).

27 Section 31A of the Copyright, Designs and Patents Act. Available at http://www.legislation.gov.uk/ukpga/1988/48/section/31A (Accessed: 12 September 2019).

28 Article 15i of Dutch Copyright Law. Unofficial translation. Available at https://www.ivir.nl/syscontent/pdfs/119.pdf (Accessed: 12 September 2019).

29 Article 45a paragraph 2 of German Copyright Law. Available at https://www.gesetze-im-internet.de/englisch_urhg/englisch_urhg.html (Accessed: 12 September 2019). The provision, however, makes clear that "production solely of individual copies shall be exempted."

30 Article L122-5 paragraph 7 of the Intellectual Property Code. Available at https://www.legifrance.gouv.fr/affichCode.do?cidTexte=LEGITEXT000006069414 (Accessed: 12 September 2019).

Examples of national provisions that have a scope wider than Article 5 paragraph 3(b) are, for instance, Section 17 of Finish Copyright Law,[31] Articles 2 and 9 paragraph 1(i) of Maltese Copyright Law[32] and Article 15(i) of the Dutch Copyright Act, all specifically including within the scope of the disability exception artistic works. Croatia[33] and Poland[34] both exempt "uses" of works without referring to the exclusive right(s) in relation to which the exception applies. Therefore, presumably, the disability exception works also in the framework of adaptations (making it thus broader than its EU version). Lithuania expressly allows for the disability exception to apply to adaptations.[35]

Some countries have implemented the disability exception with conditions that both restrict and widen its scope. For example, the Netherlands expressly includes artistic works within the scope of the disability exception, but also adds the requirement that fair compensation be paid to the right holder.[36]Another example is Ireland, where the disability exception does not apply if there is a licensing scheme in place, and the beneficiary knew or ought to have been aware of that licensing scheme;[37] however, the scope of permitted acts is wider by exempting the act of copying the work "for the purpose of modifying the copy," as well as supplying the modified copy to beneficiaries.[38] Sweden makes express reference to visual works, but subjects the exception to the payment of remuneration to the author when libraries and organisations distribute or communicate copies of works to persons with a disability in such a way that those persons may keep a copy of the work, or when anyone transfers more than a few copies to persons with a disability.[39]

The result of this mosaic legal landscape is that the act of 3D printing 2D artworks for the benefit of PVIs would not be exempted from copyright infringement in all Member States of the EU, or at least would not be exempted with any certainty. An exemption from infringement would depend on the extent of modification of the original work and, in some cases, on whether a particular

31 Finish Copyright Law. Available at https://wipolex.wipo.int/en/text/466938 (Accessed: 12 September 2019).

32 Maltese Copyright Law. Available at https://wipolex.wipo.int/en/text/447070 (Accessed: 12 September 2019).

33 Article 86 of Croatian Copyright Law. Available at https://wipolex.wipo.int/en/text/478413 (Accessed: 10 September 2019).

34 Article 33.1 of Polish Copyright Law. Available at https://wipolex.wipo.int/en/text/408585 (Accessed: 12 September 2019).

35 Article 25 paragraph 2 of Lithuanian Copyright Law. Available at https://wipolex.wipo.int/en/text/496613 (Accessed: 12 September 2019).

36 Article 15i of Dutch Copyright Law. Unofficial translation. Available at https://www.ivir.nl/syscontent/pdfs/119.pdf (Accessed: 12 September 2019).

37 Section 104A of Irish Copyright Law. Available at https://wipolex.wipo.int/en/text/526053 (Accessed: 12 September 2019).

38 Section 104 paragraph 1 of Irish Copyright Law.

39 Article 17e of Swedish Copyright Law. Available at https://wipolex.wipo.int/en/text/495847 (Accessed: 12 September 2019).

country applies the disability exception to acts of adaptation,[40] the beneficiary that carries out the scanning and 3D printing (and on whether that beneficiary, their agents or third parties are covered by national law), the types of works that are covered by the national exception, additional conditions that must be satisfied such as remuneration and so on. In the EU, the legal status of 3D printing of 2D artistic works is thus shrouded in uncertainty.

Directive 2017/1564 on certain permitted uses of works for the benefit of PVIs[41] amends the Information Society Directive and implements the Marrakesh Treaty[42] in the EU. The Directive establishes a mandatory exception benefitting specifically PVI, but, following the Treaty that it seeks to implement, it only applies to works "in the form of a book, journal, newspaper, magazine or other kind of writing, notation, including sheet music, *and related illustrations*" (Article 2(1)), emphasis added). It therefore only applies to a limited number of artistic works "related" to the listed works. A Regulation further provides for a copyright exception to allow the cross-border exchange of accessible format copies between the EU and third countries that are parties to the Marrakesh Treaty, for the benefit of PVIs.[43] However, the scope of the Regulation is the same as the Directive, that is, it only covers "related illustrations."

A source of possible restrictions to the disability exception is Article 6 of the Information Society Directive, which instructs Member States to protect technological protection measures (TPM). This could be especially relevant for artistic works in digital form that are protected with a TPM.[44] As per Article 6 paragraph 1, Member States are obliged to provide adequate legal protection

40 The disability exception only relates to the rights in the Information Society Directive. It does not, thus, apply to the adaptation right. This is especially relevant because, as mentioned earlier, the act of 3D printing the 2D artistic work may, in some cases, amount to an adaptation. In cases where it does, this situation, and the possible applicability of a disability exception, will be solely up to national laws.

41 Directive (EU) 2017/1564 of the European Parliament and of the Council of 13 September 2017 on certain permitted uses of certain works and other subject matter protected by copyright and related rights for the benefit of persons who are blind, visually impaired or otherwise print-disabled, and amending Directive 2001/29/EC on the harmonisation of certain aspects of copyright and related rights in the information society, O.J. L242, 20.9.2017, pp. 6–13.

42 Marrakesh Treaty to Facilitate Access to Published Works for Persons Who Are Blind, Visually Impaired, or Otherwise Print Disabled, adopted by the Diplomatic Conference to Conclude a Treaty to Facilitate Access to Published Works by Visually Impaired Persons and Persons with Print Disabilities in Marrakesh, on June 27, 2013.

43 Regulation (EU) 2017/1563 of the European Parliament and of the Council of 13 September 2017 on the cross-border exchange between the Union and third countries of accessible format copies of certain works and other subject matter protected by copyright and related rights for the benefit of persons who are blind, visually impaired or otherwise print-disabled, O.J. L242, 20.9.2017, pp. 1–5.

44 Article 6 paragraph 3 clarifies that a TPM will be

> any technology, device or component that, in the normal course of its operation, is designed to prevent or restrict acts, in respect of works or other subject-matter, which are not authorised by the rightholder of any copyright or any right related to copyright as provided for by law or the sui generis right provided for in Chapter III of Directive 96/9/EC.

against the circumvention of TPM. However, TPM might restrict uses of the work made legitimate under an exception. Under paragraph 4, first subparagraph of the provision, Member States shall – in the absence of voluntary measures taken by right holders – take appropriate measures to ensure that right holders make available to the beneficiaries, under Article 5(3)(b) (and other selected exceptions), the means to benefit from the disability exception, to the extent necessary and provided that the beneficiary has legal access to the subject matter concerned. Recital 51 of the Directive further clarifies that the aim was to "accommodate achieving the objectives of certain exceptions or limitations." These "certain" exceptions and limitations are those few selected exceptions considered important enough to the public interest to merit a special standing vis-à-vis TPM.[45] Not surprisingly, then, Directive 2017/1564 states that Article 6 paragraph 4 subparagraph 1 applies to the Marrakesh exception.

Member States have implemented Article 6 paragraph 4 subparagraph 1 in many different ways in what concerns the definition of "beneficiaries" (individual beneficiaries versus collective beneficiaries or interest groups) or the specific way in which beneficiaries will be entitled to make use of the exception (with only a couple of Member States going as far as granting beneficiaries the right to circumvent TPM, under certain conditions).[46] The legal landscape in this regard is thus also quite unharmonised and, in most instances, not really favourable to beneficiaries of the disability exception, as most Member States do not foresee the possibility of lawful circumvention of TPM by the beneficiary.

Normative basis for the introduction of a broader disability exception

As the previous sections have shown, the legal framework in the EU regarding a disability exception in relation to artistic works is diverse and inconsistent. While the Information Society Directive left enough room for Member States to accommodate artistic works in such an exception, only a few countries have expressly included them in the scope of their exceptions. Further, the design

45 See also Shapiro, T 2019, 'Directive 2001/29/EC on copyright in the information society', in B Lindner & T Shapiro (eds.), *Copyright in the information society. A guide to national implementation of the European Directive*, second edition, Edward Elgar, Cheltenham, p. 112.

46 It is the case of Denmark and, to some extent, Slovakia. See Guibault et al. 2007, *Study on the implementation and effect in member states' laws of directive 2001/29/EC on the harmonisation of certain aspects of copyright and related rights in the information society.* Available at https://www.ivir.nl/publicaties/download/Infosoc_report_2007.pdf (Accessed: 6 September 2019), p. 106; Schønning, P 2019, 'Denmark', in B Lindner & T Shapiro (eds.), *Copyright in the information society. A guide to national implementation of the European Directive*, second edition, Edward Elgar, Cheltenham, pp. 309–310; Olsovsky, S & Jost, J, 'Slovak republic', in B Lindner & T Shapiro (eds.), *Copyright in the information society. A guide to national implementation of the European Directive*, second edition, Edward Elgar, Cheltenham, p. 843. For an overview of the different national solutions, see also Walter M & von Lewinski, S 2010, *European copyright law. A commentary*, Oxford University Press, Oxford, pp. 1070–1073.

and content of the exception vary widely throughout the EU. The Directive and Regulation that implement the Marrakesh Treaty in the EU added additional exceptions that benefit PVIs, but artistic works are only partially covered in the form of illustrations related to literary works.

This reality is part of the broader issue of balance between exclusive rights and exceptions or limitations. At the EU level, even though the legislator has mentioned the need to strike a fair balance between rights holders and users of protected subject matter,[47] several commentators have pointed out that no such balance has been achieved.[48] Importantly, well-crafted exceptions or limitations are an essential tool in achieving such balance.[49]

This begs the question as to whether the introduction of a more encompassing disability exception is feasible, and, if so, what should its normative basis be. Recital 18 of Directive 2017/1564 states that

> With the adoption of this Directive, the Union aims to ensure that beneficiary persons have access to books and other printed material in accessible formats across the internal market. Accordingly, *this Directive is an essential first step in improving access to works for persons with disabilities.*
>
> (emphasis added)

From a policy perspective, this wording seems to leave the door open to further legislative intervention; in fact, not only is the Directive seen as a "first step," but also the final goal is to improve access to works by PVIs, regardless of the nature of those works. Further, Recital 19 of the same Directive mandates the Commission to

> assess the situation regarding the availability in accessible formats of works and other subject matter *other than those covered by this Directive*, as well as the availability of works and other subject matter in accessible formats for persons with other disabilities.
>
> (emphasis added)

47 Recital 31 Information Society Directive.

48 See, for instance, Geiger, C 2010, 'The future of copyright in Europe: striking a fair balance between protection and access to information', *IPQ*, 1, pp. 1–14; Dreier, T 2010, 'Limitations: the centerpiece of copyright in distress', *JIPITEC*, 1(2), pp. 50–54 Gervais, D 2017, *(Re)structuring copyright. A comprehensive path to international copyright reform*, Edward Elgar, Cheltenham, pp. 176–185.

49 See on this point, Hugenholtz, B 1997, *Fierce creatures, copyright exemptions: towards extinction?* Available at https://www.ivir.nl/publicaties/download/PBH-FierceCreatures.pdf (Accessed: 9 September 2019), p. 5; Geiger, C & Schönherr, F 2012, 'Defining the scope of protection of copyright in the EU: the need to reconsider the acquis regarding limitations and exceptions', in T Synodinou (ed.), *Codification of European copyright law. Challenges and perspectives*, Kluwer Law International, Alphen aan de Rijn, pp. 132–167.

The same Recital urges the Commission to review the situation "closely" and admits that changes to the scope of the Directive could be considered on the basis of a report to be presented by the Commission. Such report, according to Article 9 of the Directive, should be presented by 11 October 2020, and is to take into account relevant technological developments, as well as contain an assessment of the appropriateness of broadening the scope of the Directive in order to improve access to other types of works. As other chapters of this book have demonstrated, some institutions are already carrying out 3D reproductions of 2D artworks, and that practice is likely to become both more perfected and increasingly common. Taking into account those technological developments, then, it is envisaged that broadening the exception to encompass all types of artistic works would be a natural and appropriate way forward.

Moreover, since both the Marrakesh exception and the disability exception in the Information Society Directive have at its core the rights of people with disabilities,[50] broadening the scope of existing exceptions arguably fosters constitutionally protected rights. Exceptions or limitations in general aim to either mediate potential conflicts between copyright owners and users of protected works, or foster a specific public policy.[51] The disability exceptions in particular find their justification in the principle of non-discrimination of people with disabilities, enshrined both in Article 10 of the Treaty on the Functioning of the European Union (TFEU)[52] and in Article 21 of the Charter of Fundamental Rights of the European Union (hereinafter, "Charter").[53] In addition, Article 26 of the Charter furthers the integration of people with disabilities by recognising their right to benefit from measures designed to ensure their independence, integration and participation in the life of the community.

At the legislative level, nothing prevents the legislature from broadening the scope of existing exceptions as a way to achieve a balance between the rights of copyright owners and other interests. The EU legislator is empowered to harmonise national copyright laws based on Article 114 TFEU. As I have argued elsewhere,[54] Article 114 is devoid of normative content, but it is clearly arguable that the case law of the CJEU and the norms of the Treaties (as well as the Charter)[55] do, and should, form a sound normative basis for copyright

50 See Preamble of the Marrakesh Treaty; Helfer, L et al. 2017, *The World Blind Union guide to the Marrakesh Treaty: facilitating access to books for print-disable individuals*, Oxford University Press, Oxford, p. 10; European Commission, *Communication on copyright in the knowledge economy*, Brussels, 19.10.2009, COM(2009) 532 final, pp. 7–8.

51 Guibault, L 2002, *Copyright limitations and contracts. An analysis of the contractual overridability of limitations on copyright*, doctoral thesis, University of Amsterdam, Amsterdam, p. 27.

52 Treaty on the Functioning of the European Union (consolidated version), O.J. C 326, 26.10.2012, pp. 47–390.

53 Charter of Fundamental Rights of the European Union, O.J. C326, 26.10.2012, pp. 391–407.

54 Ramalho, A 2016, *The competence of the European Union in copyright lawmaking. A normative perspective of EU powers for copyright harmonization*, Springer, Switzerland.

55 The Charter has the same legal value of the Treaties via Article 6 paragraph 1 of the Treaty on European Union, O.J. C326, 26.10.2012, pp. 13–390, which states:

lawmaking. Specifically, achieving a balance of private interests should be one of the components of the normative basis – both the case law of the CJEU and the norms of the Treaties call for the protection of creators, but also of end users.[56] The protection of the latter can be achieved through well-crafted exceptions or by expanding on existing ones.

At the judicial level, while it is true that exceptions to copyright are, in principle, to be interpreted restrictively,[57] the CJEU has, in some instances, taken into account the rights of beneficiaries of exceptions. In Case C-201/13 *Deckmyn*, which concerned the parody exception of Article 5(3)(k) of the Information Society Directive, the Court ruled that exceptions "seek to achieve a 'fair balance' between, in particular, the rights and interests of authors on the one hand, and the *rights of users* of protected subject-matter on the other"[58] (emphasis added). This might signal that in some cases – chiefly, where "greater human rights values" underlie the exceptions[59] – the latter could be considered on par with exclusive rights.

In case C-117/13 *Ulmer*, which concerned Article 5(3)(n) of the Information Society Directive,[60] the Court ruled that publicly accessible libraries had not only the *right* of communication of works under that provision but also an ancillary *right* to digitise the works in question pursuant to Article 5(2)(c) of the same Directive (which is also part of the list of exceptions and limitations).[61] The Court does not elaborate further on the nature of these "rights" of users, and on whether such rights could be considered subjective rights. Some commentators are inclined to a negative answer, as users lack certain prerogatives that holders of subjective rights enjoy, such as the exclusive power to freely dispose of the object of the right.[62] They point out, however, that exceptions or limitations to copyright could be seen as "objective rights," which are not attributed to specific individuals and do not entail an individual right to legal redress, but which still

> The Union recognises the rights, freedoms and principles set out in the Charter of Fundamental Rights of the European Union of 7 December 2000, as adapted at Strasbourg, on 12 December 2007, which shall have the same legal value as the Treaties.

56 Ramalho 2016, pp. 135–143.

57 See e.g. *Infopaq*, paras. 56–57; Case C-145/10 *Painer*, ECLI:EU:C:2011:798, para. 109; Case C-277/10 *Luksan*, ECLI:EU:C:2012:65, para. 101; Case C-201/13 *Deckmyn and Vrijheidsfonds*, ECLI:EU:C:2014:2132, para. 22;

58 *Deckmyn*, para. 26.

59 Jacques 2019, pp. 70–71.

60 Article 5(3)(n) is an exception allowing for

> use by communication or making available, for the purpose of research or private study, to individual members of the public by dedicated terminals on the premises of establishments referred to in paragraph 2(c) [publicly accessible libraries, educational establishments, museums, by archives] of works and other subject-matter not subject to purchase or licensing terms which are contained in their collections.

61 Case C-117/13 *Ulmer*, ECLI:EU:C:2014:2196, paras. 43 and 44.

62 Guibault 2002, pp. 92–93; Jacques 2019, pp. 71–72.

confer some protection to legitimate interests of users by mandating that such interests be respected and protected.[63]

Moreover, the CJEU has expressly stated that, even though exceptions should be interpreted strictly, the effectiveness of the exception should still be safeguarded and its purpose should be observed.[64] If the purpose of the disability exception is the integration of people with disabilities in the life of the community (including the cultural life), then a case could be made for a broader interpretation to allow the 3D printing of 2D artworks for the benefit of PVIs to come under the disability exception.

There is considerable normative and legal latitude, therefore, to expand the scope of the current disability exceptions. Even though exceptions and limitations might amount to objective rights, their scope is still limited to the wording of the law.[65] As mentioned, a few countries of the EU have implemented the disability exception in stricter terms than was mandated by the Information Society Directive, and the vast majority does not expressly include artistic works in the framework of the exception. The European Commission has itself recognised that national approaches to the disability exception are not harmonised and that, therefore, "a degree of legal uncertainty ensues."[66]

A positive action from the EU legislator would thus be desirable. Given the diversity of national solutions, the legislative measure could be based on Article 114 TFEU.[67] It could also find its justification on the need to combat discrimination of people with disabilities and on integrating them in the cultural life of the community beyond accessibility to literary works.[68] After all, as mentioned earlier, the disability exception in the Information Society Directive was one of the few considered relevant enough to merit special treatment vis-à-vis TPM, which signals its importance in terms of public policy. The disability exception's foundation on fundamental rights justifies making it a mandatory exception.[69]

63 Guibault 2002, pp. 95–97; Jacques 2019, p. 75.

64 *Premier League*, para. 163; *Painer*, para. 133.

65 Guibault 2002, p. 107.

66 European Commission, *Communication on copyright in the knowledge economy*, Brussels, 19.10.2009, COM(2009) 532 final, p. 8.

67 Further harmonisation of this particular exception has already been advocated by other authors, exactly on grounds of the "great diversity of national laws" – see Geiger et al. 2009, 'What limitations to copyright in the information society? A comment on the European commission's green paper 'copyright in the knowledge economy'', *IIC*, 40(4), pp. 423–424.

68 See also Guibault 2002, p. 104:

> [w]ith respect to limitations based on fundamental rights and freedoms, one can very well argue that the 'legitimate interests' of the user are judged so important under positive law that the legislator not only has the power to accommodate these interests, but also has the obligation to do so.

69 As argued as well by van Eechoud et al. 2009, *Harmonizing European copyright law. The challenges of better lawmaking*, Kluwer Law International, Alphen aan den Rijn, pp. 128–129.

Conclusion

Disability exceptions at the EU level can be found in the Information Society Directive and in the more recent Directive 2017/1564, which implements the Marrakesh Treaty in the EU legal order. The latter is limited to "related illustrations" in the framework of literary works, and therefore its scope cannot accommodate all artistic works. The disability exception in the Information Society Directive has been implemented in many different ways throughout the EU Member States, which makes the act of 3D printing 2D artistic works for the benefit of PVIs legally uncertain.

This chapter has shown that it is not only possible but also desirable to amend the current disability exceptions within the EU legal order. In fact, the legal landscape is not harmonised when it comes to these exceptions, which could justify the intervention of the EU legislator under Article 114 TFEU. The contents of such intervention should be based on the fundamental need to integrate PVIs in the cultural life of the community. A broader – and mandatory - disability exception would also further its effectiveness and purpose, in line with CJEU case law, which has also incorporated notions of users' "rights."

The concrete drafting of a broader exception could follow best practices identified in Member States, most notably including an explicit reference to artistic works or allowing for the possibility of beneficiaries being either legal or natural persons. Ideally, the exception would also relate to other relevant rights, namely, the right of adaptation (where such right exists separately in national law), given the importance of this right for certain acts of 3D printing. Admittedly, however, this particular point would be made difficult because of the lack of harmonisation of the right of adaptation in relation to works that are not computer programmes or databases. It might then be high time for the EU to consider further harmonisation of the right of adaptation as well.

9 EU disability law and policy and access to art works through 3D printing

Lisa Waddington

The EU has a long history of adopting disability law and policy across a wide range of areas. Whilst the emphasis was initially placed on using soft law, in the form of action programmes,[1] the EU's legal competence to adopt disability-specific legislation and to mainstream disability issues in general legislation has expanded over the years, and this has been reflected in an expansion of secondary legislation addressing the rights of persons with disabilities. This process has been reinforced with the conclusion (ratification), by the EU, of the UN Convention on the Rights of Persons with Disabilities (CRPD) in 2010,[2] meaning that the EU is bound by the Convention to the extent of its competences. Whilst art and culture have not been priority areas in the emerging EU disability policy, they have not remained wholly unaddressed.

This chapter examines EU disability law and policy, and considers the scope for the EU to address access to culture for persons with disabilities and the scope for addressing access to art works through 3D printing. The chapter, firstly, reflects on the relevant competences of the EU, as established through primary legislation. This is followed by a discussion of the relevance of international law, including the CRPD, which has now acquired the status of the EU law following the EU's conclusion of the Convention. Thirdly, the chapter examines existing secondary legislation and policy addressing culture and copyright and reflects on the relevance of those measures for 3D printing. The chapter concludes that while no explicit reference to using 3D printing to improve access to art for people with visual or other impairments is found in any current EU instrument, promoting such access would be in line with the current EU policy.

1 Waddington, L 2006, *From Rome to Nice in a Wheelchair, the Development of a European Disability Policy*, Europa Law Publishing.

2 Council Decision of 26 November 2009 concerning the conclusion, by the European Community, of the United Nations Convention on the Rights of Persons with Disabilities, OJ L 23, 27.1.2010, pp. 35–36.

Primary legislation

The EU Treaties[3] and the EU Charter of Fundamental Rights[4] both contain provisions which could be regarded as relevant from the perspective of access to art works and culture for people with visual impairments.

The Treaty on the Functioning of the European Union (TFEU): Articles 10 and 19

Article 10 TFEU, which was introduced in 2009 as a result of the Lisbon Treaty,[5] contains a kind of mainstreaming provision which provides that in 'defining and implementing its policies and activities, the Union shall aim to combat discrimination based on (...) disability'. This is reinforced by Article 19 TFEU, which was included in the Treaty in 1999 as a result of the Amsterdam Treaty,[6] and which gives the EU the competence to adopt legislation and take other appropriate action 'to combat discrimination based on ... disability'. The obligation to combat disability discrimination and the competence to adopt legislation with this goal in mind may not initially seem relevant to developing 3D printing to allow access to art works for people with visual impairments. However, the EU has used its competence to adopt a Directive to prohibit disability discrimination and to explicitly establish a duty to make a reasonable accommodation.[7] The potential relevance of this kind of legislation for access to art works through 3D printing is discussed further in Section 'EU secondary legislation and soft law' of this chapter.

The European Union Charter of Fundamental Rights

Under Article 6(1) Treaty of the European Union, the Charter has the same legal value as the Treaties, and the EU is obliged to comply with the Charter in all its activities, as are the Member States when they are implementing EU law. The Charter itself specifically addresses the rights of people with disabilities in a number of articles. Under Article 21, discrimination on any ground, including disability, shall be prohibited, whilst under Article 26, the Union recognises and respects the rights of persons with disabilities to benefit from measures designed to ensure their independence, social and occupational integration, and

3 Consolidated version of the Treaty on the Functioning of the European Union, OJ C 326, 26.10.2012, pp. 47–390; Consolidated version of the Treaty on European Union, OJ C 326, 26.10.2012, pp. 13–390.

4 Charter of Fundamental Rights of the European Union, OJ C 326, 26.10.2012, pp. 391–407.

5 Treaty of Lisbon amending the Treaty on European Union and the Treaty establishing the European Community, signed at Lisbon, 13 December 2007, OJ C 306, 17.12.2007, pp. 1–271.

6 Treaty of Amsterdam amending the Treaty on European Union, the Treaties establishing the European Communities and certain related acts, OJ C 340, 10.11.1997, pp. 1–144.

7 Council Directive 2000/78/EC of 27 November 2000 establishing a general framework for equal treatment in employment and occupation, OJ L 303, 2.12.2000, pp. 16–22.

participation in the life of the community. Access to culture could fall within the scope of social integration and participation in the life of the community, but this is not further specified. However, as noted later, participation in cultural life is recognised as a right under the CRPD (Article 30), and the Charter should be read in this light.

International law

This section considers the relevance of both the CRPD and the Marrakesh Treaty to Facilitate Access to Published Works for Persons Who Are Blind, Visually Impaired or Otherwise Print Disabled.

The Convention on the Rights of Persons with Disabilities

The EU became a party to the CRPD in December 2010, with the Convention coming into force for the EU a month later, in January 2011. The European Community, represented by the Commission, had been an active participant in the negotiation of the Convention, and the Community signed the Convention in 2007. Gráinne De Búrca has noted that the EU played an active and supporting role in the drafting of the CRPD, but that it 'strove mainly to promote the adoption of its own internal model of disability discrimination at the international level'.[8] The signature and conclusion of the CRPD marks a significant step forward in the protection of human rights by the EU. Whilst the EU has become a party to international treaties in the past, this is the first such accession to a human rights treaty. The CRPD explicitly addresses participation in cultural life, recreation, leisure, and sport in Article 30, which provides that

> States Parties recognize the right of persons with disabilities to take part on an equal basis with others in cultural life, and shall take all appropriate measures to ensure that persons with disabilities: (a) Enjoy access to cultural materials in accessible formats; (b) Enjoy access to television programmes, films, theatres and other cultural activities, in accessible formats;....
>
> (Article 30(1) CRPD)

Many of the international agreements that the EU enters into, including the CRPD, involve concurrent jurisdictions of both the Member States and the EU. Such 'mixed agreements' have been described as unique in international relations since they 'involve (...) a shared contractual relationship between an international organisation and its members and one or more third countries and/or international organisations'.[9] This means that in many of the fields covered

8 De Búrca, G 2010, 'The EU in the Negotiation of the UN Disability Convention', *European Law Review*, vol. 35, no. 2, pp. 174–196.

9 Verwey, D 2004, *The European Community, the European Union and the International Law of Treaties: A Comparative Legal Analysis of the Community and Union's External Treaty-Making Practice*, T.M.C. Asser Press, The Hague.

by the Convention, both the EU and the Member States have competence to act and that together they have taken on full responsibility for complying with the Convention. Consequently, responsibility does not fall on the EU alone. Nevertheless, the EU is bound to the extent of its competences, although its competences regarding art and culture are somewhat limited. While the EU has inter alia the aim to respect Europe's 'rich cultural and linguistic diversity, and [...] ensure that Europe's cultural heritage is safeguarded and enhanced' (Article 3 Treaty on European Union), its competences under Article 6 TEU in the field of culture are confined to 'carry[ing] out actions to support, co-ordinate or supplement the actions of the Member States'. Under Article 167 TFEU, the EU is to contribute to the flowering of the cultures of the Member States, while respecting their national and regional diversity and bringing the common cultural heritage to the fore. Action by the Union should encourage cooperation between Member States and support and supplement their action in improving the knowledge and dissemination of the culture and history of the European peoples, conserving and safeguarding cultural heritage of European significance, and fostering non-commercial cultural exchanges and artistic and literary creation, including in the audiovisual sector. The Union and Member States may also foster cooperation with third countries and the competent international organisations. Respect for, and promotion of the diversity of, European cultures needs to be taken into account when taking action under other provisions of the Treaty.

Like any other State Party to the CRPD, the EU is obliged to report on the steps it has taken to implement the CRPD to the related UN Committee and, following an examination, that Committee issues Concluding Observations (Article 35 CRPD). In 2015, the EU underwent its first review, and the CRPD Committee made one recommendation concerning Article 30 CRPD:

> The Committee is concerned that the European Union has not ratified the Marrakesh Treaty to Facilitate Access to Published Works for Persons Who Are Blind, Visually Impaired or Otherwise Print Disabled, which provides for access to published material by blind persons and persons with visual impairments or print disabilities.
>
> The Committee encourages the European Union to take all appropriate measures to ratify and implement the Marrakesh Treaty as soon as possible.[10]

In conclusion, the CRPD has not prompted significant developments in EU disability policy regarding culture, and the recommendations of the CRPD Committee on this point were confined to the ratification of the Marrakesh Treaty. Access to art through 3D printing is not an issue that the CRPD Committee has raised with the EU.

10 Committee on the Rights of Persons with Disabilities 2015, *Concluding Observations on the Initial Report of the European Union*, CRPD/C/EU/CO/1, paras. 70–71.

The Marrakesh Treaty to Facilitate Access to Published Works for Persons Who Are Blind, Visually Impaired, or Otherwise Print Disabled

The EU signed the Marrakesh Treaty in April 2014. In February 2018, the Council adopted a Decision approving the conclusion of the Marrakesh Treaty to Facilitate Access to Published Works for Persons Who Are Blind, Visually Impaired, or Otherwise Print Disabled.[11] In doing so, the EU complied with the recommendation that had been issued by the CRPD Committee in 2015, and ensured that the EU is bound by the Treaty.

EU secondary legislation and soft law

This section explores a number of fields in which the EU has adopted secondary legislation and soft law which are relevant to accessing art and culture by people with disabilities, including people with visual impairments.

Secondary legislation

EU legislation prohibiting disability discrimination

In 2000, the EU adopted a Directive to prohibit disability discrimination which explicitly establishes a duty to make a reasonable accommodation (the Employment Equality Directive).[12] The obligation to make a reasonable accommodation on the ground of disability is based on the recognition that, on occasions, the interaction between an individual's impairment and the physical or social environment can result in the inability to perform a particular activity or function in the conventional manner. The characteristic or impairment is relevant in that it can lead to an individual being faced with a barrier that prevents him or her from benefitting from an opportunity that is open to others who do not share that characteristic.[13] If the characteristic or impairment is ignored, it can result in denying an individual equal opportunity. In this respect, Fredman has argued:

> Characterising disability as an irrelevant characteristic removes the underlying justification for detrimental treatment, but insisting on similar treatment simply reinforces a particular norm and perpetuates disadvantage.[14]

11 Council Decision (EU) 2018/254 of 15 February 2018 on the conclusion on behalf of the European Union of the Marrakesh Treaty to Facilitate Access to Published Works for Persons who are Blind, Visually Impaired, or otherwise Print Disabled, OJ L 48, 21.2.2018, pp. 1–2.

12 Council Directive 2000/78/EC of 27 November 2000, establishing a general framework for equal treatment in employment and occupation, OJ L 303, 2.12.2000, pp. 16–22.

13 Waddington, L 2011b, 'Reasonable Accommodation – Time to Extend the Duty to Accommodate Beyond Disability?', *Nederlands Tijdschrift voor de Mensenrechten,* NJCM-Bulletin, vol. 38, no. 2, pp. 186–198.

14 Fredman, S 2005, 'Disability Equality, a Challenge to the Existing Anti-Discrimination Paradigm?', in A Lawson and C Gooding (eds.), *Disability Rights in Europe: From Theory to Practice*, Hart Publishing, Oxford, pp. 199–203.

The Employment Equality Directive establishes a duty to make a reasonable accommodation for individuals with a disability with regard to employment and vocational training.[15] In that context, the duty prohibits an employer from denying an individual with a disability an employment opportunity by failing to take account of the individual's impairment, when taking account of it – in terms of changing tasks, organisation or the physical environment of the workplace – would enable the individual to do the work.[16] Clearly, this requires an individualised analysis, both in terms of the abilities of the recipient of the accommodation and the work-related skills and activities that are required.

While secondary EU law does not currently extend the prohibition of disability discrimination beyond the broad field of employment, it is possible to envisage that a reasonable accommodation duty could also apply with regard to access to culture. National non-discrimination legislation which prohibits disability discrimination, such as the British Equality Act 2010, extends the reasonable accommodation duty beyond employment, with the British Act, for example, prohibiting discrimination with regard to provision of services, although without explicitly mentioning culture. This means that the reasonable accommodation duty – or the reasonable adjustment duty as it is called under British law – also applies to the provision of services. Moreover, the CRPD defines the reasonable accommodation duty in light of 'all human rights and fundamental freedoms' (Article 2 CRPD), which includes participation in cultural life (Article 30 CRPD). This could lead to an obligation to provide 3D printing of art works when requested by individuals with visual and other impairments, where this is needed to allow them to enjoy and experience art works. However, it should be noted that the obligation to provide a reasonable accommodation is not absolute and is subject to the requirement that making the accommodation does not result in a disproportionate or undue burden for the duty bearer. This means that issues such as feasibility and cost can be relevant in terms of removing or reducing the duty, although the duty remains fairly far-reaching.[17]

15 Article 5 of the Directive provides:

> In order to guarantee compliance with the principle of equal treatment in relation to persons with disabilities, reasonable accommodation shall be provided. This means that employers shall take appropriate measures, where needed in a particular case, to enable a person with a disability to have access to, participate in, or advance in employment, or to provide training for such a person, unless such measures would impose a disproportionate burden on the employer. When this burden is, to a sufficient extent, remedied by existing measures as an element of disability policy in the Member State, it should not be considered disproportionate.

16 Karlan PS and Rutherglen G 1996, 'Disabilities, Discrimination and Reasonable Accommodation', *Duke Law Journal*, vol. 46, no. 9, pp. 1–41.

17 Committee on the Rights of Persons with Disabilities 2018, General comment (no. 6) 2018 on equality and non-discrimination, CRPD/C/GC/6, 26 April 2016, Section V D. Recital 21 of the Employment Equality Directive provides:

> to determine whether the measures sin question give rise to a disproportionate burden, account should be taken in particular of the financial and other costs entailed, the scale and financial resources of the organisation or undertaking and the possibility of obtaining public funding or any other assistance.

It is worth noting that the Commission proposed a further equality directive in 2008[18] to supplement the Employment Equality Directive.[19] If adopted, this would establish a more far-reaching reasonable accommodation duty in favour of persons with disabilities. The proposal covers, amongst other things, access to and supply of goods and other services which are available to the public. The proposal is not explicit on the issue of access to culture or art, and it is not clear if it could potentially cover a duty to provide a reasonable accommodation in the form of 3D printing of a work of art. Moreover, at present, the proposal is stalled in the Council, and there are significant doubts as to whether it will ever be adopted.[20]

Lastly, the EU's conception of equality also allows for, but does not require, positive action. All EU equality and non-discrimination directives[21] allow Member States to adopt positive action. This is, however, subject to limitations imposed by the case law of the Court of Justice. For example, in *Kalanke*,[22] the Court of Justice held that the positive action provision in the Equal Treatment Directive[23] (Article 2(4)) had to be read restrictively and did not allow for national rules which guaranteed women absolute and unconditional priority for appointment or went beyond promoting equal opportunities. Nevertheless, if making art available through 3D prints could be regarded as a form of positive action, then the EU's permissive approach is potentially relevant – but EU equality law does not cover culture or art at the moment, so this discussion, as well as the reflections on the reasonable accommodation duty, is all rather speculative.

18 European Commission 2008, Proposal for a Council Directive on implementing the principle of equal treatment between persons irrespective of religion or belief, disability, age or sexual orientation COM(2008) 426; Waddington L 2011, 'Future Prospects for EU Equality Law. Lessons to Be Learnt from the Proposed Equal Treatment Directive', *European Law Review*, no. 2, pp. 163–184.

19 Proposal for a Council Directive on implementing the principle of equal treatment between persons irrespective of religion or belief, disability, age or sexual orientation COM(2008) 426. See also Waddington, 'Future Prospects for EU Equality Law'.

20 For an overview of the slow / lack of progress with the adoption of this instrument, see: http://www.europarl.europa.eu/legislative-train/theme-area-of-justice-and-fundamental-rights/file-anti-discrimination-directive. Last accessed 6 April 2020.

21 In addition to the Employment Equality Directive, this is provided for, for example, in Directive 2000/43/EC, implementing the principle of Equal Treatment between persons irrespective of racial or ethnic origin [2000] OJ L180, pp. 22–26; Directive 2004/113 implementing the principle of equal treatment between men and women in the access to, and supply of, goods and services [2004] OJ L373, pp. 101–107; and Directive 2006/54 on the implementation of the principle of equal opportunities and equal treatment of men and women in matters of employment and occupation (recast) [2006] OJ L204, pp. 23–36.

22 C-450/93, *Kalanke* v. *Freie Hansestadt Bremen*, ECLI:EU:C:1995:322.

23 Council Directive 76/207/EEC on the implementation of the principle of equal treatment for men and women as regards access to employment, vocational training and promotion, and working conditions, OJ L 39 14.2.1976, pp. 40–42.

EU copyright legislation and the Marrakesh Treaty

One of the potential barriers to making art works available in 3D format is copyright law. Artists or museums may own the copyright of individual art works. Their permission may be needed to produce 3D images of the work, and this may be linked to the requirement to pay a fee. This can potentially hamper access to art in adapted formats for people with (visual) impairments. The Information Society Directive[24] addresses this issue in a general way by allowing Member States to provide exceptions to the exclusive right of reproduction 'for the benefit of people with a disability, which are directly related to the disability and of a non-commercial nature, to the extent required by the specific disability'.[25] In light of the planned accession of the EU to the Marrakesh Treaty, this Directive was amended in 2017, to establish rules on the use of certain works without the authorisation of the right holder for the benefit of visually impaired persons.[26]

In parallel, a Regulation implementing the Union's obligations under the Marrakesh Treaty with respect to the exchange of accessible format copies between the Union and third countries was adopted in 2017.[27] There are therefore a number of exceptions and limitations to copyright protection, which potentially allow for art works to be produced in 3D formats or for Member States to make such allowances whilst remaining compliant with EU copyright legislation. The potential relevance of EU copyright legislation for access to art and 3D printing is explored further elsewhere in this volume.[28]

The Creative Europe Regulation

The Creative Europe Regulation[29] aims to promote European cultural and linguistic diversity and strengthen the competitiveness of European cultural and

24 Directive 2001/29/EC of the European Parliament and of the Council of 22 May 2001 on the harmonisation of certain aspects of copyright and related rights in the information society, OJ L 167, 22.6.2001, pp. 10–19.

25 Article 5(3)(b) of the Information Society Directive.

26 Directive (EU) 2017/1564 of the European Parliament and of the Council of 13 September 2017 on certain permitted uses of certain works and other subject matter protected by copyright and related rights for the benefit of persons who are blind, visually impaired, or otherwise print-disabled, and amending Directive 2001/29/EC on the harmonisation of certain aspects of copyright and related rights in the information society, OJ L 242, 20.9.2017, pp. 6–13.

27 Regulation (EU) 2017/1563 of the European Parliament and of the Council of 13 September 2017 on the cross-border exchange between the Union and third countries of accessible format copies of certain works and other subject matter protected by copyright and related rights for the benefit of persons who are blind, visually impaired, or otherwise print-disabled, OJ L 242, 20.9.2017, pp. 1–5.

28 See in this book the chapter on the EU framework by Ana Ramalho.

29 Regulation (EU) No 1295/2013 of the European Parliament and of the Council of 11 December 2013 Establishing the Creative Europe Programme (2014–2020) and Repealing Decisions No 1718/2006/EC, No 1855/2006/EC and No 1041/2009/EC,OJ L 347, 20.12.2013, pp. 221–237.

creative sectors. It establishes the Creative Europe Programme to provide support to the European cultural and creative sectors. One of its objectives is the improvement of access to cultural and creative works, particularly for people with disabilities and under-represented groups.[30] The Regulation recognises the importance of digital technology for improving accessibility of cultural and creative works, and argues that the cultural and creative sectors require greater access to finance in order to upgrade equipment, develop new production and distribution methods, and adapt their business models. Recital 13 provides inter alia:

> While the need to seek a new balance between the increasing accessibility of cultural and creative works, fair remuneration of artists and creators and the emergence of new business models is recognised, the changes resulting from the digital shift offer wide opportunities for the European cultural and creative sectors and for European society in general.

However, copyright issues and accessibility for people with visual impairments are not mentioned in the Regulation.

The European Accessibility Act

The EU has recently adopted the European Accessibility Act,[31] which is a directive designed to achieve greater accessibility within the internal market for people with disabilities. The Act regulates the accessibility of key products and services in the internal market, such as computers, smartphones, tablets, TV sets, banking ATMs and services, payment terminals, e-books and e-readers, e-commerce websites, and mobile applications and ticketing machines. The European Disability Forum, the umbrella group representing people with disabilities, hailed the Directive as 'an important step' that improves the accessibility of these kinds of products and services.[32] Commissioner Thyssen stated that the agreement showed the EU's '*firm commitment to implement the UN Convention on the Rights of Persons with Disabilities*'.[33]

However, there are significant limitations to the Act, and these have also been recognised by the European Disability Forum. The Forum described the final agreement as a 'disappointing compromise' and stated 'the Act lacks essential aspects. It excludes transport. It excludes microenterprises that provide services.

30 Regulation No 1295/2013, Article 4(b).

31 Directive (EU) 2019/882 of the European Parliament and of the Council of 17 April 2019 on the Accessibility Requirements for Products and Services, OJ L 151, 7.6.2019, pp. 70–115.

32 European Disability Forum 2019, *European Accessibility Act: A Big Step Forward on a Long Journey*, http://www.edf-feph.org/newsroom/news/european-accessibility-act-big-step-forward-long-journey. Last accessed 6 April 2020.

33 European Commission 2018, Statement – Making Key Products and Services Accessible across the EU: Statement by Commissioner Thyssen Following the Provisional Agreement between the EU Institutions, http://europa.eu/rapid/press-release_STATEMENT-18-6323_en.htm. Last accessed 6 April 2020.

It excludes household appliances. It excludes any obligation on accessible buildings and infrastructure. It excludes the real environment where people spend most of their time'.[34] The Act also does not refer to making art or culture accessible to people with disabilities, and there is no indication that this was an issue for discussion during the negotiation of the Act.

Soft law

A number of soft law initiatives also address access to art and culture for people with disabilities, although without referring to 3D printing.

The European Disability Strategy

The most important soft law instrument from a disability perspective is the European Disability Strategy 2010–2020.[35] This has the overall objective to achieve full empowerment and participation of persons with disabilities in society and to implement the CRPD. The Strategy focuses on the elimination of barriers in eight key areas. One of these areas, Participation, addresses access to art and culture for people with disabilities. The Strategy identifies full access to culture as a fundamental right and notes that there are still many obstacles preventing people with disabilities from exercising their fundamental rights. Amongst the goals of the Commission under the Strategy are:

> improving the accessibility of leisure, cultural and recreational organisations, activities, events, venues, goods and services including audiovisual ones; fostering the cross-border transfer of copyright works in accessible format; and promoting use of the scope for exceptions provided by the Directive on copyright.

The Strategy indicates that EU action will support Member States to achieve these goals.

In 2017, the Commission published a Progress Report on the Strategy.[36] In terms of cultural activities, the Progress Report identified a number of activities, most of which relate to copyright law. The activities which were identified as having been taken include the adoption by the Commission of legislative proposals

34 European Disability Forum 2018, *Disappointing Compromise on EU Accessibility Act*, http://www.edf-feph.org/newsroom/news/disappointing-compromise-eu-accessibility-act. Last accessed 6 April 2020.

35 European Commission 2010a, Communication to the European Parliament, the Council, the European Economic and Social Committee and the Committee of the Regions, European Disability Strategy 2010–2020: A Renewed Commitment to a Barrier-Free Europe COM(2010) 0636.

36 Commission Staff Working Document 2017, *Progress Report on the Implementation of the European Disability Strategy (2010–2020)*, Brussels, 2.2.2017 SWD(2017) 29 final.

to implement the Marrakesh Treaty in EU law, a proposal to amend the Information Society Directive with regard to rights for the benefit of persons who are blind, visually impaired, or otherwise print disabled, and a proposal for a new regulation on the cross-border exchange, between the Union and third countries, of accessible format copies of certain works for the benefit of persons who are blind, visually impaired, or otherwise print disabled. As identified earlier, all three legislative initiatives have now been adopted. No initiatives regarding accessible art works and 3D printing are explicitly mentioned in either the Strategy or the Progress Report.

The Progress Report also indicated that disability accessibility requirements had been mainstreamed in EU cultural policies, such as Europeana.eu, 'European Capitals of Culture',[37] and relevant policy collaboration among Member States in the field of culture.

European standards

The European Standardisation Organisations, CEN, CENELEC, and ETSI, have the task of developing European-wide standards. The European Commission can initiate work on such a standard by issuing a standardisation mandate to one or more of the organisations. In 2010, the Commission issued Mandate 473 to CEN, CENELEC, and ETSI, [38] requesting them to develop a standard which would allow for the inclusion of accessibility following a 'Design for All' approach in mainstream standards. The intention was to develop a standard to facilitate the incorporation of accessibility in mainstream standards from an early stage. The approach adopted involved developing a standard which would enable organisations 'to extend the range of users by identifying diverse needs, characteristics, capabilities, and preferences, by directly or indirectly involving users, and by using knowledge about accessibility in its procedures and processes'.[39]

In early 2019, the standardisation bodies adopted the standard 'Design for All – Accessibility following a Design for All approach in products, goods and services – Extending the range of users'.[40] The standard had been approved in late 2017, and was finally published in March 2019.[41] This is a process-oriented standard in that it sets out requirements and recommendations to enable an organisation to design, develop, and offer goods and services so that they can

37 For information on the European Capitals of Culture see: https://ec.europa.eu/programmes/creative-europe/actions/capitals-culture_en. Last accessed 6 April 2020.

38 European Commission 2010b, Standardisation Mandate to CEN, CENELEC, and ETSI to include 'Design for All' in Relevant Standardisation Initiatives, M/473.

39 O'Ferrall E 2018, 'Accessibility of Products and Services Following a Design for All Approach in Standards, Conference Paper', *Congress of the International Ergonomic Association*, abstract available at: https://link.springer.com/chapter/10.1007%2F978-3-319-96071-5_158. Last accessed 6 April 2020.

40 European Committee for Standardization 2019, Design for All – Accessibility following a Design for All approach in products, goods and services – Extending the range of users, EN:17161:2019.

41 *Ibid.*

be understood and used by the widest range of users, including persons with disabilities.[42] It is intended to apply across all goods and services. While it does not refer to access to art works through 3D printing, it is potentially relevant for those organisations that wish to expand access to art works in which they own the copyright.

Council Resolution on accessibility of cultural infrastructure and cultural activities for people with disabilities

In 2003, the Council adopted a Resolution on accessibility of the cultural infrastructure and cultural activities for people with disabilities.[43] This is a very short document which invites Member States to

> Provide information via modern technology and enhance access to cultural activities through e.g. subtitled performances; use of easy-to-read and sign language; guides and catalogues in Braille; use of contrasts of light in exhibitions.

Given that this is a relatively old document, it is not surprising that it does not explicitly mention 3D printing as a means of enhancing access to cultural activities. More generally, copyright issues are not mentioned in the Resolution either.

European Year of Cultural Heritage

The year 2018 was declared the European Year of Cultural Heritage. This was based on a Decision of the European Parliament and of the Council, which refers to the CRPD.[44] Recital 9 notes:

> In accordance with Article 30 of the United Nations Convention on the Rights of Persons with Disabilities, to which the Union and most of the Member States are party, the Parties to the Convention recognise the right of persons with disabilities to take part on an equal basis with others in cultural life and they are to take all appropriate measures to ensure that persons with disabilities, inter alia, enjoy access to places for cultural performances or services, such as theatres, museums, cinemas, libraries and tourism services, and, as far as possible, enjoy access to monuments and sites of national cultural importance.

42 O'Ferrall, 'Accessibility of Products and Services Following a Design for All Approach in Standards, Conference Paper'.

43 Council of the European Union 2003, Resolution of 6 May 2003 on accessibility of cultural infrastructure and cultural activities for people with disabilities, OJ C 134, 7.6.2003, pp. 7–8.

44 European Parliament and Council 2017, Decision (EU) 2017/864 of 17 May 2017 on a European Year of Cultural Heritage (2018), OJ 2017 L 131 pp. 1–9.

Furthermore, Recital 13 refers to the need to foster wider access to cultural heritage and states that '[s]uch wider access can be achieved by reaching out to different audiences and by increasing accessibility to places, buildings, products and services, taking into account special needs and the implications of demographic change'.

A specific objective of the year was to 'promote solutions which make cultural heritage accessible to all, including via digital means, by removing social, cultural and physical barriers, taking into account people with special needs'. Once again, no mention of 3D printing is made, but it can be argued that the Decision created a framework in which such initiatives would be welcomed, and the references to improving access via digital means are potentially relevant.

The EU Disability Card

Lastly, in 2016, the EU launched an EU Disability Card.[45] This has been piloted in eight countries and is a system of mutual recognition ensuring equal access to certain benefits. This means that individuals who have a disability card issued by one Member State should be able to enjoy benefits offered to holders of a nationally issued disability card in other Member States, when visiting those states. Those benefits often include free or reduced price access to museums and cultural activities and / or free admission for a personal assistant. Other benefits include the possibility to borrow a wheelchair when visiting a cultural institution and to receive information in accessible formats. If making 3D prints available to people with visual impairments becomes a benefit available in the future in one or more Member States, the Card could facilitate access to that benefit for disabled visitors from across the EU.

Conclusion

The EU is taking action to support access to culture for people with disabilities, including people with visual impairments. There is some scope for bringing access to culture and 3D printing of art works within the scope of EU primary legislation, but this issue is not specifically mentioned in either the Treaties or the Charter. In terms of copyright exemptions, the main driver of action is the Marrakesh Treaty. Given the lack of progress in adopting the 2008 Equality Directive and the fact that it does not explicitly cover art and culture, it seems unlikely that EU equality law, through the establishment of a wide-ranging reasonable accommodation duty, will lead to the provision of 3D art as a form of individualised accommodation. Moreover, such a duty is generic, meaning that it applies across the range of fields covered by the underlying legislation, rather than specifically requiring the provision of 3D art. However, one possible

45 For information on the EU Disability Card, see http://ec.europa.eu/social/main.jsp?catId=1139&langId=en. Last accessed 6 April 2020.

way in which the EU could promote the availability of art in 3D formats is through providing financial support for such initiatives via the Creative Europe Programme.[46] This could provide funding for pilot projects and sharing of best practices. More generally, while no explicit reference was found to using 3D printing to improve access to art for people with visual disabilities in EU legislation, promoting such access would be in line with current EU policy.

46 See https://ec.europa.eu/info/live-work-travel-eu/culture-heritage-sport-eu/funding-culture_en. Last accessed 6 April 2020.

Part 4

Mapping and critiquing the legal landscape

10 Disability exceptions under Australian copyright and moral rights law

Jani McCutcheon

Introduction

This chapter explores the Australian copyright and moral rights landscape governing 3D reproductions of 2D art. The investigation is timely, because the *Copyright Amendment (Disability Access and Other Measures) Act 2017* (Cth) recently introduced new disability access exceptions to the Copyright Act 1968 (Cth) ('the Act').[1] The changes were prompted in part by Australia's ratification on 10 December 2015 of the World Intellectual Property Organization (WIPO) *Marrakesh Treaty to Facilitate Access to Published Works for Persons Who Are Blind, Visually Impaired, or Otherwise Print Disabled* ('Marrakesh Treaty').[2] The reforms extend beyond disability exceptions, but those pertinent to this chapter:

a replaced the previous exception for persons with a disability, and others acting on their behalf, with a new fair dealing exception in s 113E; and
b replaced the previous statutory licences for institutions assisting persons with a print or intellectual disability with a single exception that applies to organisations assisting persons with a disability, in s 113F.

This chapter will scrutinise the new provisions, with a particular focus on their application to 3D-printed reproductions of artistic works. Such reproductions ostensibly infringe the copyright owner's exclusive right to reproduce the artistic work in material form,[3] particularly because 2D to 3D transformations are deemed reproductions under s 21(3)(a) of the Act. They may also infringe the

1 References to sections of legislation hereafter are references to the Act, unless otherwise indicated. These changes chiefly govern disability exceptions under Australian copyright law, although certain provisions facilitating format shifting may permit 2D to 3D translations of books, newspapers and periodicals, and photographs in limited circumstances. See ss 43C and 47J.

2 *Marrakesh Treaty to Facilitate Access to Published Works for Persons Who Are Blind, Visually Impaired or Otherwise Print Disabled*, opened for signature 27 June, 2014 (entered into force 30 September, 2016).

3 See s31(1)(b)(i).

artist's moral rights of attribution[4] and integrity.[5] No specific disability exemption applies to moral rights infringement, but there is a defence of reasonableness which may cover some ground.[6]

The application of these new disability exceptions to 3D reproductions of artistic works may be unclear, particularly due to the multiplicity of actors involved in the 3D reproduction process, and the heavy focus on access to literary works that underscored the Marrakesh Treaty. As stated in the introduction, 3D printing of artistic works has generated opportunities and issues in relation to inclusive access to art that are only now beginning to be appreciated. The advantages of sensory art projects are clear. However, it is important to investigate the scope of the disability exceptions under Australian law to determine whether they are fit for purpose in facilitating such sensory access and identify any gaps or ambiguities in the law which may hamper it.

The new fair dealing provision

Section 113E provides:

1 A fair dealing with copyright material does not infringe copyright in the material if the dealing is for the purpose of one or more persons with a disability having access to copyright material (whether the dealing is by any of those persons or by another person).
2 The matters to which regard must be had, in determining whether the dealing is a fair dealing for the purposes of this section, include the following matters:
    a the purpose and character of the dealing;
    b the nature of the copyright material;
    c the effect of the dealing upon the potential market for, or value of, the material;
    d if only part of the material is dealt with, the amount and substantiality of the part dealt with, taken in relation to the whole material.

While the provision refers to a 'dealing' (which is undefined), its application will only be triggered if one of the exclusive rights of the copyright owner are exercised,[7] including the right to prevent importations of infringing material.[8]

4 See ss193(1) and 194(2).
5 See ss195AI(1) and 195AK.
6 See ss195AS.
7 See s 31 (works) and ss 85–88 (subject matter other than works).
8 See s 37 (works) and 102 (subject matter other than works).

'Copyright material'

Subsection 10(1) of the Act defines 'copyright material' as anything in which copyright subsists. This would include artistic works. This is a new approach to the Act, which has conventionally duplicated the fair dealing defences across Part III (works) and Part IV (subject matter other than works). This definition was criticised for potentially causing confusion about a new category of subject matter[9]; however, it is also commendable for avoiding repetition of the fair dealing exception across Part III and Part IV. In capturing all 'copyright material', it certainly extends beyond the Marrakesh Treaty, which defines 'works' to mean

> literary and artistic works within the meaning of Article 2(1) of the Berne Convention for the Protection of Literary and Artistic Works, in the form of text, notation and/or related illustrations, whether published or otherwise made publicly available in any media.[10]

Importantly, the breadth of the Australian definition captures all artistic works, which, under Marrakesh, are confined to artistic works in the form of illustrations 'related' to literary text.

'Person with a disability'

Subsection 10(1) defines 'person with a disability' as 'a person with a disability that causes the person difficulty in reading, viewing, hearing or comprehending copyright material in a particular form'.[11] Again, this definition is broader than the Marrakesh Treaty's more limited concept of 'beneficiary person' and its preoccupation with literary works.[12]

The current definition is an improvement on the draft bill, which omitted the word 'comprehending' from the definition.[13] Difficulty in 'viewing' is clearly

9 Australian Copyright Council, *Comments on Exposure Draft of Copyright Amendment (Disability and Other Measures) Bill February 2016*, p. 3, at http://www.copyright.org.au/acc_prod/ACC/Submissions/Exposure_Draft_submission_.aspx (accessed 20 March 2020).

10 Marrakesh Treaty, art 2(a).

11 S 10(1).

12 See Marrakesh Treaty, art 3: 'A beneficiary person is a person who:

a) is blind;
b) has a visual impairment or a perceptual or reading disability which cannot be improved to give visual function substantially equivalent to that of a person who has no such impairment or disability and so is unable to read printed works to substantially the same degree as a person without an impairment or disability; or
c) is otherwise unable, through physical disability, to hold or manipulate a book or to focus or move the eyes to the extent that would be normally acceptable for reading;

regardless of any other disabilities'.

13 The exposure draft of the bill can be found at https://www.communications.gov.au/have-your-say/updating-australias-copyright-laws (accessed 20 March 2020).

suffered by persons with a visual impairment (PVI); however, the changed wording indicates that the exception extends also to persons with a cognitive impairment, such as persons diagnosed with Alzheimer's.

Who has the relevant purpose?

The provision clarifies that the exception is available 'whether the dealing is by [the person with a disability] or by another person'. The wording, unique to this fair dealing defence, pre-empts and cures the problems which may have been caused by *De Garis v Neville Jeffress Pidler Pty Ltd* (1990) 95 ALR 625 ('*De Garis*'), which would have potentially limited the scope of the fair dealing exception to the person with a disability, and not to third parties assisting them.[14] It seems the government heeded warnings about the seriously reduced utility of the exception if *De Garis* was not circumvented.[15] This is a sensible approach, particularly given the reality that persons with a disability might depend on third parties simply because of their disability. It is also consonant with the repealed s200AB(4) of the Act, which also applied to institutions and individuals assisting those with disabilities. However, there is still a question about whether the commercial motivations of any third party effecting the fair dealing might impact the application of the defence, discussed later.

"Having access"

The concept of 'having access' to copyright material may raise some issues. Technically, PVI have 'access' to 2D copyright artworks – they just can't see them. Equally, they have 'access' to books – they just can't read them if they are not in a Braille format. Clearly, the intention was to facilitate *access in a suitable form,* and it is unfortunate that those additional words were not inserted into the section to eradicate any doubt. This interpretation is consistent with the Explanatory Memorandum's statement that s113E was designed to permit persons with a disability to have access to copyright material 'in the format they need with the appropriate features they require',[16] and the government media release which clarified that the provision would 'enable people with a disability to enjoy fair access to copyright material *in formats suitable to their individual needs*'.[17]

14 Jani McCutcheon and Simon Holloway, 'Whose Fair Dealing? Third-Party Reliance on the Fair Dealing Exception for Parody or Satire' (2016) 27 *Australian Intellectual Property Law Journal* 54.

15 See Australian Digital Alliance and Australian Libraries Copyright Committee, Joint Submission to the Department of Communication and the Arts, February 2016, 5–6, at https://www.communications.gov.au/sites/default/files/submissions/australian-digital-alliance-and-australian-libraries-copyright-committee.pdf?acsf_files_redirect (accessed 20 March 2020).

16 Explanatory Memorandum, Copyright Amendment (Disability Access and Other Measures) Bill 2017 (Cth) 15.

17 Australian Government, Department of Communication and the Arts, 'First Steps in Modernising the Copyright Framework', 22 March 2017, at https://www.communications.gov.au/departmental-news/first-steps-modernising-copyright-framework (accessed 20 March 2020).

The next question is whether there are any format restrictions built into the defence. If PVI can 'have access' to an artistic work through a verbal or written description of the work in alternative audio or Braille formats, would the defence extend to modification of 2D art into 3D form to permit tactile interaction with the 2D art? It is suggested that these different formats produce such different sensory perceptions and understandings of the work that all modified formats should, prima facie, be acceptable. The true control over the breadth and extent of alternative formats should be exercised by the fairness criteria, discussed later.

The counterargument is that this kind of manipulation may not have been in Parliament's sights, because the conversion of 2D art into 3D form is still such a rare occurrence. In contrast, books have been produced in Braille versions since 1829.[18] Note, for example, that the explanatory memorandum fails to mention 2D to 3D art transformation, or indeed modification of artistic works in any way.[19] However, this appears inconsequential. The second reading speech described the exception as 'a flexible copyright framework that recognises the various ways people with a disability use accessible format content' and clarified that it is 'designed to be format-neutral to ensure that Australians with a print disability will be able to continue to have fair and equal access to material in line with technological advancements'.[20]

The statutory fairness criteria

Subsection 113E(2) of the Act sets out four non-exhaustive factors that must be considered when determining whether the change in format is a fair dealing. This legislative drafting is unconventional, since, despite the Act having a suite of fair dealing exceptions covering a number of different purposes,[21] only the research or study defence currently includes a similar list of statutory fairness factors.[22] Statutory fairness criteria may also, in any event, be considered superfluous, given that every fair dealing defence begins with the words '[a] *fair* dealing…', mandating a fairness inquiry.

There is perhaps some risk in including statutory fairness criteria. Despite being expressed as inclusive factors, their very presence may encourage an exhaustive navigation of only those criteria as privileged and carefully curated factors. The inclusive nature of the statutory list suggests that other factors, such as cultural sensitivity, might be relevant to the fairness analysis, and it is important that all relevant factors be considered. For example, if a 3D reproduction of Aboriginal art would be antithetical to Aboriginal beliefs or law systems, it might

18 Ginny A. Roth and Elizabeth Fee, 'The Invention of Braille' (2011) 101(3) *American Journal of Public Health* 454, 454.

19 Explanatory Memorandum, Copyright Amendment (Disability Access and Other Measures) Bill 2017 (Cth) 15.

20 Commonwealth, Parliamentary Debates, House of Representatives, 22 March 2017 (Paul Fletcher, Minister for Urban Infrastructure), 36.

21 See generally ss 40–42 inclusive, ss 103A–103C inclusive and s 113E.

22 See ss 40(2) and 103C(2).

point against fairness, even if none of the listed statutory criteria apply. Further, a number of the statutory factors are frankly incongruous in a disability access exception, particularly as it pertains to 3D art translations. This applies principally to the fourth factor, because in the vast majority of cases, fairness will not rest on the amount and substantiality of the part dealt with, since the whole material will need to be reproduced.

Australia has a poorly developed jurisprudence on the fairness component within the fair dealing analysis,[23] including the statutory factors. There is an inclination to regard as relevant US judicial commentary on the very similar US fair use factors.[24] Similar to the fair use analysis in US jurisprudence, the explanatory memorandum states that '[e]ach factor should be considered in a fairness assessment, noting that each factor may have a different degree of significance according to each individual use'.[25] The following discussion will interrogate the statutory fairness criteria in the context of sensory art, except the fourth factor, for the reasons outlined earlier.

The first factor: the purpose and character of the dealing

The explanatory memorandum stated in relation to this factor that it:

> prompts consideration of whether the use is for the purpose of providing a person with a disability with access to copyright material... If the use is made to assist a person with a disability to enjoy copyright material, this factor is likely to be satisfied.[26]

If that is the case, then this first statutory criterion is superfluous, since the substantive provision already covers a 'fair dealing … for the purpose of one or more persons with a disability having access to copyright material'. An important issue in the application of this criterion in the US fair use analysis is whether the use has a commercial purpose,[27] where this is a relevant, but not determinative,

23 Michael Handler and David Rolph, 'A Real Pea Souper: The Panel Case and the Development of the Fair Dealing Defences to Copyright Infringement in Australia' (2003) 27 *Melbourne University Law Review* 381; Australian Law Reform Commission, *Copyright and the Digital Economy* Report No. 122 (2014) para 5.15.

24 See generally, Australian Law Reform Commission, *Copyright and the Digital Economy* Report No. 122 (2014) Ch 5.

25 Explanatory Memorandum, Copyright Amendment (Disability Access and Other Measures) Bill 2017 (Cth) 15. See also Australian Law Reform Commission, *Copyright and the Digital Economy* Report No. 122 (2014) para 5.16 Australian Law Reform Commission, *Copyright and the Digital Economy* Report No. 122 (2014) para 5.25.

26 Explanatory Memorandum, Copyright Amendment (Disability Access and Other Measures) Bill 2017 (Cth) 15.

27 See Australian Law Reform Commission, *Copyright and the Digital Economy* Report No. 122 (2014) paras 5.46–5.55.

factor.[28] It remains unclear what effect the commerciality of any dealing might have. For example, while the exception clearly extends to dealings by persons without a disability for the qualifying purpose, would the exception be excluded if those persons are charged for alternative format copies, as it apparently is under US fair use jurisprudence?[29] Should the outcome then be different depending on whether the charge only covers cost recoupment or constitutes a profit? What happens in the case of mixed purposes? For example, would the fair dealing exception extend to a research organisation engaging in 3D printing of art, which has a primary purpose of perfecting the technology for diverse (and potentially commercial) applications but may have an ancillary purpose of assisting a person with a disability to enjoy the art? It is a pity the explanatory memorandum does not address the effect of commercial purpose. A second important issue in the context of this factor is whether the use is sufficiently transformative.[30] It is suggested that this threshold will ordinarily be met in the case of 3D art translations.

The second factor: the nature of the copyright material

In relation to this factor, the explanatory memorandum states that, consistent with US fair use jurisprudence,[31] '[w]hether material is in print and available, as well as if it is published or unpublished, are relevant issues for consideration'. Sensitivity to the publication status of a work is due, at least in part, to 'the author's right to control the first public appearance of his undisseminated expression'.[32] This means that it 'will normally mean that it is not 'fair' to publish what is not yet before the public'.[33] This perhaps belies an assumption that disability exceptions are, and should be, designed to facilitate access to published material. For example, the Parliamentary debates suggest that the Marrakesh Treaty was designed to overcome the reality that 'the great majority of *published* material worldwide is not presently accessible'.[34] This ignores the question of what, if any, access should be granted to 'unpublished' material.

This question is particularly relevant to this chapter's topic. This is because the second fairness factor can be incongruous in the context of artistic works, which are not conventionally 'published' in the same manner as literary, dramatic and even musical works. This clearly depends on the nature of the artistic work.

28 Campbell v Acuff-Rose Music, Inc, 510 US 569, 584, 114 S Ct 1164, 1174 (1994).
29 Cambridge Univ Press v Patton, 769 F 3d 1232, 1264 (11th Cir 2014).
30 See Australian Law Reform Commission, *Copyright and the Digital Economy* Report No. 122 (2014) paras 5.33–5.45.
31 See, for example, Australian Law Reform Commission, *Copyright and the Digital Economy* Report No. 122 (2014) para 5.59.
32 *Harper & Row Publishers, Inc v Nation Enterprises* (1985) 471 US 539, 555.
33 Australian Law Reform Commission, *Copyright and the Digital Economy* Report No. 122 (2014) para 5.59, citing *Harper & Row Publishers, Inc v Nation Enterprises* (1985) 471 US 539, 555.
34 Commonwealth, *Parliamentary Debates*, House of Representatives, 22 March 2017 (Paul Fletcher, Minister for Urban Infrastructure), 36 (emphasis added).

Photographs, commercial art and illustrations, for example, are more amenable to exploitation through publication, whereas fine art is generally reproduced for the more limited purposes of exhibition and sale catalogues, art books and GLAM and other product licensing schemes. However, sensory art reproductions, or even audio art translations, will not ordinarily be *published*.[35] Most fair dealings will be private, for very particular purposes, and will not result in multiple copies or their dissemination. It is therefore unlikely that this factor will be highly contentious.

The third factor: the effect of the dealing upon the potential market for, or value of, the material

This factor 'requires an analysis of whether the proposed use of copyright material is reasonably fair with regard to the interests of the copyright holder'.[36] Substantial market harm is required for the dealing to be considered unfair.[37] There is little evidence of an existing, fully fledged market for sensory reproductions of artistic works exploited by copyright owners. This is, at least partly, because it has not been technologically possible until now, stultifying the demand that triggers and grows markets. However, the statute speaks of the effect on a 'potential' market, so delayed, emerging or future markets are also apparently relevant.

Technological flux and the innovation in 3D printing technology make it challenging to identify and track the copyright owner's legitimate potential market. To what extent should a copyright owner's delay before entering a technologically fluid market be considered? Does technological possibility necessarily convert to market reality, or do other factors like affordability and likely market demand need to coalesce? The 3D printing, while still developing, clearly already facilitates the conversion of copyright material into a suitable format, and markets are beginning to develop around this. There is, for example, an emerging market for services providing 3D versions of photographs of family members or household pets.[38] As early as 2013, services existed to transform children's drawings into 3D prints.[39] There is a demand for converting 2D character concept

35 If they were, this suggests a commerciality which would correspondingly engage the first factor, discussed earlier.

36 Explanatory Memorandum, Copyright Amendment (Disability Access and Other Measures) Bill 2017 (Cth) 15.

37 Ibid.

38 See, for example, www.my3dselfie.com and the services provided by 3DPhotoworks, at https://www.3dphotoworks.com/ (both accessed 22 March 2020).

39 Geraldine Bouvry, 'Make Your Kids' Drawings Come Alive with 3D Printing' 22 May 2013, at https://www.3ders.org/articles/20130522-make-your-kids-drawings-come-alive-with-3d-printing.html (accessed 22 March 2020).

art into 3D printed figures.[40] And, of course, there are the nascent sensory art projects mentioned in the introduction.

In short, 3D prints can be generated relatively easily, provided there is a high-resolution image, access to a person with the requisite technological knowledge and a decent 3D printer. While visual art reproductions may less frequently be licensed than musical, literary or dramatic works, it is homogenous and there is a visual art licensing market for some forms of art and in certain contexts. Photographers and illustrators tend to make their living by licensing reproductions of their works, and there is a healthy market for objects bearing reproductions of fine art housed in cultural institutions, from coffee cups to postcards and posters.[41] This market could potentially extend to haptically perceptible reproductions. Relevantly for this chapter, the US Second Circuit has recognised the copyright owner's right to prepare a 3D version of a 2D work of art, considering the potential market for 'art rendering' rights as 'not implausible'.[42] If changes in technology increasingly mean that copyright material can be provided more or less on demand and at minimal cost, the ease of tapping into these potential new markets could increase the likelihood that the market is real and not illusory. Particularly in the case of photography and commercial art, which have conventionally traded on its inherent reproducibility, it would be relatively easy for photographers and commercial artists to offer 3D prints of their works or offer them in a 3D printable file format. There is also some poignancy here, because artists are in general notoriously impoverished. They are not monolithic and grasping publishers refusing to supply appropriate format material because they are indifferent to persons with a disability. There may therefore be greater sympathy for an artist taking an interest in crafting a new market to service persons with a disability and demanding a small fee in return.

However, the scope of these potential markets must be carefully considered. Much turns on distinguishing a realistically 'potential' market from a phantom market. Patry argues that '[i]f the term "potential market" is to have any meaning, it must be anchored in an evidentiary possibility that plaintiff may market the work in the future, based on facts in existence at the time of defendant's use'.[43] Gervais argues that 'the prospective market must be reasonably predictable'.[44] And as Patry notes, the market must be one the copyright owner would

40 'Winners of Vancouver Startup Launching Conceptkicker - 2D Art To 3D Printed Figures' 1 December 2014, at https://www.3ders.org/articles/20141201-winners-of-vancouver-startup-launching-conceptkicker-2d-art-to-3d-printed-figures.html (accessed 22 March 2020).

41 While most examples would likely be reproductions of public domain art works, not all are. See, for example, the products, at https://store.hyperallergic.com/collections/all (accessed 22 March 2020).

42 Rogers v. Koons 960 F.2d 301, 309-12 (2d Cir. 1992) (photograph of people holding puppies transformed into 3D sculpture of people holding puppies). See also United Feature Syndicate, Inc. v. Koons 817 F. Supp. 370, 379-82 (S.D.N.Y.1993).

43 William F. Patry, *Patry on Copyright* (2019) § 10:139.

44 Daniel Gervais, submission to Copyright Office Notice of Inquiry and Request for Comments on the Topic of Facilitating Access to Copyrighted Works for the Blind or Other Persons With Disabilities, para 39, p. 14 (2009).

have licensed, not just could have licensed.[45] Otherwise, because the limits of 'potential' markets are theoretically boundless, this factor would always weigh against a fair dealing. This is particularly problematic because enabling the PVI to have 'access' to art *necessitates converting it into* an ostensibly infringing *haptically perceptible form*. Thus, having *access* always necessitates making a *reproduction*. In contrast, sighted people usually gain 'access' to art without the necessity of making a permanent reproduction.[46] If we convert every copyright owner into a possible licensor exploiting a potential haptic market, then the cost burden on the PVI will be untenable, and indeed the primary objective of the exception will be thwarted. All of the other fair dealing exceptions launch from the presumption of access, and then moderate what can be done with works that have been accessed. This fair dealing exception facilitates access in the first place. If we employ the deceptively simple formula 'fact of desired reproduction = exploitable potential market = unfair without a license', it will effectively impose a disability tax. The folly is to assume that a market must or could always follow simply based on the technical potential for reproduction.

In summary, due to the growing ease of effecting 3D translations of art, it is foreseeable that a market could develop whereby, in response to a demand for a 3D version of the work, the copyright owner cooperates with service providers to provide it, or provides a 3D printable file of the work, for a reasonable fee. Certainly, if copyright owners are realistically likely to offer to supply works in suitable formats within a reasonable time for a reasonable fee, this third factor may work against disability access. Conversely, if the copyright owner is not likely to make the work accessible in a haptically perceptible form, then the 3D reproduction is prima facie permissible.

Institutional safeguards

Supplementing the new fair dealing exception is s 113F, which provides:

> An organisation assisting persons with a disability, or a person acting on behalf of such an organisation, does not infringe copyright in copyright material by using the material if:
>
> a the use is for the sole purpose of assisting one or more persons with a disability to access the material in a format that the person or persons require because of the disability (whether the access is provided by or on behalf of the organisation or by another body or person); and
>
> b the organisation, or the person acting on behalf of the organisation, is satisfied that the material (or a relevant part of the material) cannot be obtained in that format within a reasonable time at an ordinary commercial price.

45 William F. Patry, *Patry on Copyright* (2019) § 10:151.

46 Most technical and usually ephemeral reproductions made during the process of, for example, browsing are exempt from infringement. See ss 43A and 43B.

'Organisation assisting persons with a disability' is defined to mean:

a an educational institution; or
b a not-for-profit organisation with a principal function of providing assistance to persons with a disability (whether or not the organisation has other principal functions).[47]

There are points of overlap between this provision and the fair dealing exception. This is because the latter applies, 'whether the dealing is by [one or more persons with a disability] or by another person', where the other person could include a person acting on behalf of an organisation assisting persons with a disability as defined. Both provisions also, of course, excuse uses of copyright material for the qualifying disability access purpose. However, the scope of s 113F is narrower, limited to educational institutions and non-profit disability support entities. Section 113F also clarifies that the purpose must be '*solely*' for disability access, a limitation absent from the fair dealing exception. And, of course, section 113F imposes a unique commercial availability test. This is designed to 'ensure that persons with a disability may have access to copyright material at a similar time and cost as other persons'[48] without unreasonably affecting the commercial interests of the copyright owner, by ensuring 'that Australian publishers and distributors would have the first opportunity to implement market solutions to supply persons with a disability with copyright material in accessible formats'.[49] This test has raised some uncertainties, including whether the test requires the institution to re-check commercial availability each time the material is requested by a user.[50] The test has some overlap with the market protection factor under the fair dealing exception, discussed earlier. However, s 113F clearly contemplates that the organisation need only test for existing availability, which presupposes exploitation by the copyright owner in prevailing, rather than potential, markets.

Presently, there seems little scope for the narrower, independent application of section 113F to sensory art translations, with the fair dealing exception likely to already cover the field. Nevertheless, should educational institutions or qualifying organisations seek to assist PVI to gain access to sensory art reproductions, they are likely to be covered by section 113F. In particular, until the market for sensory art reproductions evolves, it seems likely that the commercial availability test would almost always be discharged.

47 Section 10(1).
48 Explanatory Memorandum, Copyright Amendment (Disability Access and Other Measures) Bill 2017 (Cth) 16.
49 Ibid.
50 See, for example, the Australian Copyright Council's *Print Disability Copyright Guidelines*, p. 15, at https://static-copyright-com-au.s3.amazonaws.com/uploads/2015/05/Print-Disability-Copyright-Guidelines.pdf (accessed 22 March 2020).

Moral rights

The 3D translation of art may infringe the artist's moral right to be attributed as the author of the work[51] or to resist false attribution of authorship[52] when any attributable act, including reproduction, occurs.[53] They may also infringe the author's right of integrity,[54] which protects their art from 'derogatory treatment', defined to mean:

a the doing, in relation to the work, of anything that results in a material distortion of, the destruction or mutilation of or a material alteration to the work that is prejudicial to the author's honour or reputation; or
b an exhibition in public of the work that is prejudicial to the author's honour or reputation because of the manner or place in which the exhibition occurs; or
c the doing of anything else in relation to the work that is prejudicial to the author's honour or reputation.[55]

These provisions to some extent mirror the Marrakesh Treaty, which stipulates that an 'accessible format copy … must respect the integrity of the original work, taking due consideration of the changes needed to make the work accessible in the alternative format and of the accessibility needs of the beneficiary persons'.[56]

It is possible that 3D representations of art works involve material distortions or alterations that compromise the authorial message such that it is prejudicial to the honour or reputation of the author. Special issues arise in relation to artistic works in comparison to non-artistic works, because of the value of the first copy. For fine art, which is seldom reproduced commercially, the most valuable property right is the rare, single-copy chattel recording the artistic vision. This is a major point of distinction between disability access to books and disability access to art. Nowadays, the first copy of the book is usually a digital file on a computer, and it is immaterial to the author or the copyright owner whether the book is presented in Braille or otherwise. However, the artist might legitimately argue that their work was never intended to be modified into 3D form and presented to the world in this way. It is, arguably, a very different work to the original. This is especially the case when substantial modification of the 2D artwork is required to accommodate more efficient haptic perception, which may require simplification of the original composition.[57]

No specific disability exemption applies to moral rights infringement, but there is a defence of reasonableness available for infringements of the right of attribution

51 Section 193(1).
52 Section 195AC.
53 Sections 194(2) and 195AE.
54 Section 195AI(1).
55 Section 195AK.
56 Marrakesh Treaty, art 2(b).
57 See, for example, the simplified and abstracted 3D prints of iconic art images created by artists Adam Lister and Isaac Budmen, at https://design-milk.com/3d-prints-iconic-images-art-culture/ (accessed 22 March 2020).

and the right of integrity.[58] This excuses infringement that is 'reasonable in all the circumstances', which is measured against a number of statutory factors.[59] The reasonableness defence is very likely to function effectively as a moral rights disability exception. In particular, the purpose of the infringement is one of the express factors to take into consideration in the reasonableness analysis[60] (as it is in the fair dealing analysis), and thus the benefits of the disability purpose will be weighed against the prejudice to the author's honour or reputation. However, it is also likely that the Marrakesh Treaty's direction to 'respect the integrity of the original work, taking due consideration of the changes needed to make the work accessible in the alternative format' will factor in this analysis and limit 'reasonable' format modifications to those that are strictly necessary to enable access. Thus, for example, the kind of radical 3D transformative interpretation of a photograph wrought by Jeff Koons' puppies sculpture[61] would likely fall outside the reasonableness defence, even if PVI could touch the sculpture and gain some benefit from it. It is also an open question to what extent the reasonableness defence should accommodate issues of cultural sensitivity, for example, when the modification of Aboriginal art conflicts with Aboriginal belief and law systems. On balance though, moral rights claims are unlikely to successfully defeat disability access to most 3D art translations.

Technical locks

The efficacy of the disability exceptions must also be considered in the context of other factors which may undermine them. Many art objects are photographed (or are photographs), and high-resolution digital photographs or CAD files are frequently the medium through which 3D prints are generated. However, disability access through these photographic or digital surrogates may be hampered by a technological protection measure (TPM). A TPM is defined to include an 'access control technological protection measure' (ACTPM) controlling *access* to copyright material,[62] or a lock that essentially prevents the exercise of an exclusive right, thus preventing the generation of copies.[63] Any given work may utilise one or both of an ACTPM or TPM. Copyright owners may bring an action against a person circumventing an *ACTPM*.[64] However, it is lawful to circumvent an *ACTPM* to enable a person to do an act prescribed by regulations and which is non-infringing under ss113E or 113F.[65] This would allow a lock to be broken to gain *access* to the copyright material for a disability purpose. There is

58 See ss195AS (right of integrity) and 195AR (right of attribution). No defence of reasonableness is available for false attribution of authorship.
59 See ss 195AS(2) and 195AR (2).
60 See s 195AS(2)(b) and 195AR (2)(b).
61 The subject of Rogers v. Koons 960 F.2d 301, 309-12 (2d Cir. 1992).
62 See the definition of 'access control technological protection measure' in s 10(1).
63 See the definition of 'technological protection measure' in s 10(1).
64 See s 116AN(1).
65 See Note 2 to s 113D, s 116AN(9) and *Copyright Regulations 2017* (Cth) reg 40(2)(b).

no similar prohibition on circumventing a *TPM* preventing the making of a copy. Therefore, circumventing both ACTPMs and TPMs is lawful if the disability fair dealing exception applies.

The major difficulty with the TPM regime in the context of disability access (or, indeed, any exception for circumvention liability) concerns access to the devices or services which users ordinarily must rely on in order to carry out acts of circumvention. The Act contains a general prohibition on manufacturing or dealing with circumvention devices in various ways[66] or on providing circumvention services.[67] There are a number of exceptions to liability for limited purposes such as interoperability or encryption research.[68] However, there is no similar exception for disability purposes. This effectively forces the PVI to use unlawfully provided circumvention devices or services to circumvent ACTPMs and TPMs to gain access to works and produce an accessible format copy. Circumvention devices and services which are prima facie unlawful are likely to be far more difficult for PVI to find on the open market and use. This produces an apparent conflict between the Australian TPM regime and the Marrakesh Treaty, which requires contracting parties to ensure that their TPM protection regimes do not 'prevent beneficiary persons from enjoying the limitations and exceptions provided for in this Treaty'.[69] The Act should therefore be amended to exempt from liability dealings in circumvention devices or services to permit disability access under ss113E or 113F.

Contractual constraints

Another potential obstruction to the efficacy of the disability exceptions is contractual constraints or exclusions which conflict with them, or undermine them. Such restraints may seek to contractually prohibit dealings with copyright works, or ACTPM or TPM circumvention, even if those acts are permitted under existing exceptions, including the disability fair dealing exception. Such contractual

66 Section 116AO. S 10(1) defines 'circumvention device' to mean 'a device, component or product (including a computer program) that:

a) is promoted, advertised or marketed as having the purpose or use of circumventing the technological protection measure; or
b) has only a limited commercially significant purpose or use, or no such purpose or use, other than the circumvention of the technological protection measure; or
c) is primarily or solely designed or produced to enable or facilitate the circumvention of the technological protection measure'.

67 Section 116AP. Section 10(1) defines 'circumvention service' to mean 'a service that:

a) is promoted, advertised or marketed as having the purpose or use of circumventing the technological protection measure; or
b) has only a limited commercially significant purpose or use, or no such purpose or use, other than the circumvention of the technological protection measure; or
c) is primarily or solely designed or produced to enable or facilitate the circumvention of the technological protection measure'.

68 See ss 116AO(3)-(6) and 116AP(3)-(6).

69 Marrakesh Treaty, art 7.

overreach has long been contentious,[70] and no Australian government has successfully navigated the conflict between contract and copyright exceptions. The enforceability of such contractual provisions remains uncertain.[71] It is recommended that Australian law be reformed consistent with the 2014 reforms in the United Kingdom, which render contractual overrides unenforceable.[72]

Conclusions

This chapter interrogated the current Australian copyright and moral rights landscape relating to disability access to works of visual art. This framework appears to provide generous accommodation of access, notwithstanding some potentially troubling questions, particularly in relation to the market protection factor in the fair dealing analysis. This will require careful and sensitive interpretation and application by future decision-makers. The combination of novel statutory exceptions and the nascent status of sensory art projects means we have no opportunity to test the efficacy, or even the relevance,[73] of the disability exceptions in the context of visual art. However, the rapid development of 3D printing is likely to change this, and one factor that may influence the shape, speed and use of technological development is the reality or perception of legal risk. Australia's disability exceptions should go some way to clarifying the likely legality of facilitating sensory art projects for the benefit of PVI.

However, a well-worded copyright exception is only one part in enhancing the haptic perception of art. It must be lawful to obtain the devices and services needed to break the technological locks for permitted purposes. There should be legislative clarity that the disability exceptions cannot be avoided or undermined by contract. More practically, stakeholders must be educated about the availability and effect of the disability exceptions, particularly with a view to facilitating 3D translations of modern and contemporary art still under copyright. Therefore, while Australia's recent disability exception reforms are a step in the right direction, there are many more steps to take.

70 Copyright Law Review Committee, *Copyright and Contract* (2002); Martin Kretschmer, Estelle Derclaye, Marcella Favale and Richard Watt, *The Relationship between Copyright and Contract Law* (2010) Report commissioned by the Strategic Advisory Board for Intellectual Property Policy, UK.

71 Australian Law Reform Commission, *Copyright and the Digital Economy* Report No 79 (June 2013), [17.23-17.47].

72 'To the extent that a term of a contract purports to prevent or restrict the doing of any act which, by virtue of this section, would not infringe copyright, that term is unenforceable'. This provision is contained in The Copyright and Rights in Performances (Research, Education, Libraries and Archives) Regulations 2014, The Copyright and Rights in Performances (Disability) Regulations 2014 and The Copyright and Rights in Performances (Quotation and Parody) Regulations 2014.

73 It is probably too early to tell if exclusion from 3D art translations is even a problem needing curing. Note the mixed reactions to one sensory art project at the Seattle Art Museum: 'You are getting the shape of it, but that's really all you are getting'. Sara Toth Stub, 'Museum Use Touch to Engage All Visitors' *Accessible Go* 8 November 2017, at https://accessiblego.com/articles/Museum_Use_Touch_to_Engage_All_Visitors_ (accesed 20 March 2020).

11 United States

Peter J. Karol

Introduction

The United States presents a contradiction with respect to easing access to copyright-protected works for persons with a visual impairment (PVI). On the one hand, in its case and statutory law, it contains robust, progressive, and clear exceptions designed to accommodate access to literary works. On the other hand, it contains next to no such safe harbors specific to the visual arts. Instead, adaptations of those pictorial, graphic, and sculptural works would need to be sheltered under more generalized exceptions such as under the fair use framework.

This raises a central question. Was this lacuna meant as an intentional exclusion of visual artworks from the broad safe harbors given for literary works? Or was it simply an inadvertent by-product of the fact that the crafters of such doctrines may have been unaware of recent technologies that allow the transformation of two-dimensional artworks into three-dimensional objects capable of being perceived haptically by PVI? If the latter, then the Congress might be receptive to passing an amendment designed expressly to incorporate pictorial, graphic and sculptural works into the existing safe harbor framework along lines discussed later in the chapter. If the former, however, then that raises the even more vexing question of why the legislature might have created a two-tiered system that prioritizes accessibility for literary works but not visual ones.

The following chapter seeks to investigate these and related questions from the U.S. perspective. It first explores traditional copyright law. It shows that while fewer mid-century pictorial works might be subject to copyright in the US than is regularly assumed, for those works that are covered by copyright, there is no express statutory exemption to shelter adaptations for PVI. There is, however, a strong case that activities related to the generation of such adaptations would be protected by the fair use doctrine. This section concludes by proposing and arguing in favor of adopting a clear safe harbor for visual art adaptations that parallels the one in place for literary works. It next turns to the limited moral rights doctrines in the U.S., revealing that while federal legislation is unlikely to pose any obstacles to 3D art translations, older state laws could still cause problems to the extent that they are not preempted by federal law. Following this, it briefly raises concerns with possible affirmative claims of copyright in 3D derivative versions of works that might be created.

Copyright law

Copyright protection for visual artworks in the United States

U.S. copyright basics for visual art

Copyright law and analysis in the United States is predominantly governed by the Copyright Act of 1976 (the "Copyright Act").[1] Under the current iteration of that law, broadly defined categories of copyrightable works (such as "literary" and "pictorial, graphic, and sculptural" works) are protected for a baseline term of 70 years after the death of their respective authors.[2] Copyright now attaches at the moment of fixation in a tangible medium of expression (e.g., when paint is applied to canvas) regardless of whether any formalities are followed.[3] Of particular relevance here, copyright owners are exclusively entitled to determine who may "reproduce" and "prepare derivative" versions of the subject work.[4] To this end, the U.S. courts have squarely held it is copyright infringement to create three-dimensional renderings of two-dimensional pictures without the permission of the copyright owner or any applicable defense.[5]

The Difficulty of Determining whether Older Visual Artworks remain under Copyright and Who Owns the Rights

Despite the facial simplicity of these provisions, the determination of whether older paintings (made before the Copyright Act became effective on January 1, 1978) remain under copyright, and for how long, remains a difficult question in many cases. Yet the question is highly relevant to those wishing to adapt artworks of that period for PVI. This is because the copyright status of older works in the U.S. is heavily impacted by the version of the Copyright Act in effect at the time of creation or dissemination.

The good news for those looking to reproduce U.S. mid-century masterworks is that a substantial number of such works have likely fallen into the public domain. For works governed by the Copyright Act of 1909 (which includes much twentieth-century American Art), copyright in artworks was permanently lost if the work was "published" without the use of proper formalities.[6] While merely exposing a painting at a private exhibition was not considered a divesting

1 17 USC §§101 et seq (Copyright Act).
2 Copyright Act, §§ 102(1), 102(5), 201, 302(a).
3 Copyright Act, §102(a).
4 Copyright Act, §§106(1)-(2).
5 Rogers v Koons, 751 F Supp 474, 478 (SDNY 1990), amended on reargument, 777 F Supp 1 (SDNY 1991), and affd, 960 F 2d 301 (2d Cir 1992) (three-dimensional sculpture infringes a two-dimensional photograph) (citing additional cases); Peker v Masters Collection, 96 F Supp 2d 216, 219 (EDNY 2000) (finding infringement of reproduction right where company added oil paint to poster to create the textured look of an oil painting).
6 Craig Joyce et al., *Copyright Law* (9th edn, LexisNexis 2013) 400.

"publication," [7] rights could be lost where a model of an artwork (such as the so-called Chicago Picasso) was publicly exhibited at a museum without copyright notice and reproduced in newspaper images.[8] Moreover, even properly copyrighted works needed to be renewed by the copyright owner (and often were not).[9]

A related question—who owns older copyrights—is also critical for those seeking express permission to reproduce artworks in the U.S. As a general rule, for works created after January 1, 1978, unassigned copyrights in artworks will remain with the artist or the artist's heirs.[10] The just-mentioned axiom, however, does not hold for the countless older visual artworks that were not "published" in the sense described earlier. Indeed, for some time, the contrary rule prevailed in many U.S. jurisdictions. Namely, certain courts held that an unconditional transfer of a painting by an artist was presumed to have included transfer of the common law copyright with it.[11] Thus, where an artist transferred a painting to a university gallery, he was held to have transferred his copyright in that painting to the university as well because he made no express reservation of rights in the bill of sale.[12] In such a case, neither the artist nor the artist's heirs would be able to grant permission to reproduce the work.

In all, for pre-1978 works of visual art in the U.S., it can be complicated even for an expert in copyright law to determine whether that work (a) remains under copyright and (b) if so, whom to ask for permission to reproduce it.

Statutory exceptions for PVI

The Chafee Amendment

Given the perils of determining whether visual artworks remain under copyright and who owns those rights, creators of 3D models for PVI would benefit substantially from a clear statutory exemption sheltering such uses. Unfortunately, no directly applicable exemption currently exists under the U.S. law.

The closest the Copyright Act comes to such a safe harbor is Section 121, created in 1996 through the so-called "Chafee Amendment." This provision provides clear (though narrow) exemptions for authorized entities that reproduce "literary" and "musical" works in formats accessible to PVI.[13] However, as this summary suggests, nowhere does the text of Section 121 reference the

7 Acad of Motion Picture Arts & Scis v Creative House Promotions, Inc, 944 F 2d 1446, 1452 (9th Cir 1991).

8 Letter Edged in Black Press, Inc v Pub Bldg Comm'n of Chicago, 320 F Supp 1303, 1306 (ND Ill 1970).

9 Joyce et al., (n 6) 345–346.

10 Copyright Act, §201(a), (d), §202.

11 Pushman v NY Graphic Soc'y, 39 NE 2d 249, 251 (NY 1942).

12 Ibid.

13 Copyright Act, §121(a).

separate category of "pictorial, graphic, and sculptural works." In fact, the only reference to pictures at all is a passing reference to "descriptions of pictorial works" in computer programs.[14]

A court is thus unlikely to interpret the statute to apply to reproductions of visual art. While Section 110(8) provides another safe harbor for performances of non-dramatic literary works for PVI, it too has no facial application to works of visual art.[15]

The Marrakesh Treaty Implementation Act

While the U.S. did recently further amend the Copyright Act in connection with its ratification and implementation of the Marrakesh Treaty, none of those amendments can fairly be read to cover 3D renderings of freestanding visual artworks.[16] The U.S. added Section 121A of the Act, which specifically exempts acts of importation and exportation of the same literary and musical works exempted domestically in Section 121. In other words, it allowed for international exchange of already-exempted materials.

The failure of this Marrakesh Treaty Implementation Act to even consider visual artworks, while not surprising, appears to have been a missed opportunity in the United States. The treaty itself, although generally understood to cover only literary works and related illustrations, broadly requires contracting parties to provide "a limitation or exception to the right of reproduction ... to facilitate the availability of works in accessible format copies...."[17] And "works" is facially defined in Article 2 to include both "literary" <u>and</u> "artistic" works. [18] Thus, under a literal reading, the treaty text could have justified inclusion of the pictorial and graphic works at issue here. Unfortunately for these purposes, however, that same definition is subsequently limited only to works "in the form of text, notation and/or related illustrations."[19]

Tracking this final clause of the definition of "works," the legislative history to the Marrakesh Treaty Implementation Act confirms it was only meant to cover "illustrations" in the very limited sense of those in literary works. Namely, the legislative history makes clear that Sections 121 and 121A are intended to cover "illustrations ... or photographs" but only insofar as they are "integrated with the text" of a work being adapted.[20] It gives the example of a textbook that might have an illustration in it.[21]

14 Ibid. (b)(2).
15 Copyright Act, §110(8).
16 Copyright Act, §121A.
17 Marrakesh Treaty Article 4(1)(a).
18 Ibid. Article 2(a).
19 Ibid.
20 S Rep No 115-261, at 3 (2018).
21 Ibid.

Fair use

In the absence of a specific statutory exemption for the adaptation of visual artworks, 3D renderers will still be able to turn to the broadly applicable U.S. doctrine of fair use, Section 107 of the Copyright Act.[22] That provision, and recent case law interpreting it, provide a strong defense against infringement in this context, although there remains the risk that a court sympathetic to the copyright holder will deny its applicability in any given case.

Fair use provides an affirmative defense to a claim of copyright infringement and is determined according to four statutory factors: (1) the purpose and character of the use, including whether such use is of a commercial nature or is for non-profit educational purposes; (2) the nature of the copyrighted work; (3) the amount and substantiality of the portion used in relation to the copyrighted work as a whole; and (4) the effect of the use upon the potential market for or value of the copyrighted work.[23]

Fair use analysis generally proceeds factor-by-factor. Although it is a notoriously fact-specific and thus case-specific inquiry,[24] it is still possible to draw some generalizations about how a court might approach a particular use (such as the visual art adaptations at issue here).

As a starting place, strong language in the legislative history of the Copyright Act shows that the Congress intended fair use to protect against reproductions meant to give access to PVI. The House Committee Report that accompanied codification of the fair use doctrine in the Copyright Act of 1976 expressly stated that making copies accessible "for the use of blind persons" posed a "special instance illustrating the application of the fair use doctrine…."[25] Although this reference was made in the context of adapting books, Justice Stevens noted the same principle in the venerable Sony Betamax case concerning audiovisual works:

> Making a copy of a copyrighted work for the convenience of a blind person is expressly identified by the House Committee Report as an example of fair use, with no suggestion that anything more than a purpose to entertain or to inform need motivate the copying.[26]

Given this strong evidence of intent, the U.S. courts are highly likely to approach four-factor analysis of visual adaptive technologies with a presumption in favor of fair use.[27]

22 Copyright Act, §107.

23 Ibid.

24 See, e.g., Cambridge Univ Press v Patton, 769 F 3d 1232, 1258-59 (11th Cir 2014).

25 HR REP NO 94–1476, at 73 (1976), reprinted in 1976 USCCAN 5659, 5686.

26 Sony Corp of Am v Universal City Studios, Inc, 464 US 417, 455, n 40 (1984).

27 This national goal of promoting the use of accessible technologies is also consistent with the stated goal of the 1990 Americans with Disabilities Act "to assure equality of opportunity [and] full participation" for persons with disabilities. 42 USC § 12101 (ADA). This same policy

Not surprisingly, given this powerful endorsement, recent courts considering adaptations for PVI have started their fair use analyses by finding that factor one, the "purpose and character of the use," weighs in favor of reproductions that allow access to copyrighted works to PVI. In particular, a federal appellate court held in favor of fair use on factor one in a major case brought by the Author's Guild against HathiTrust, a digital library engaged in large-scale digitization of literary works for the purpose of providing accessible copies of texts to the print-disabled.[28]

Concededly, the HathiTrust court reached this favorable conclusion despite holding that such digital adaptations were not "transformative" because they were akin to translations that merely amounted to derivative works in new media.[29] If anything, however, visual adaptations are a stronger case for fair use than literary ones, as the technology in the former process requires some alteration of the content of the artwork in order to make it haptically perceptible (thus making it more transformative), whereas audio renderings of literary works correspond more directly to the original.

Under factor one, it is important whether the party claiming fair use is a non-commercial or non-profit entity such as a public museum.[30] In such a case, that will make a finding of fair use more likely. Although it is not strictly required that a proposed fair use be of a non-commercial nature,[31] the fact that a user makes no profit from the accused activity certainly enhances the fair use defense.[32] For this reason, maquettes created through use of the 3D printing technologies, which, while benefiting PVI, might also be consumed and appreciated by the visually able, should not be sold at the museum gift shop, in order to strengthen fair use claims.

Even if a non-profit museum or other similar institution commissions the 3D copy, that does not insulate an outside 3D-printer/vendor doing the rendering. This is especially true if that vendor is itself a commercial entity making a profit from its activities (as may be the case here). The U.S. courts, for instance, have consistently held against commercial copy shops in the so-called "coursepack" cases even though they were generally making copies of academic works for the indirect benefit of non-profit educational institutions and professors.[33] It is thus advisable that any outside vendors used in a 3D-rendering project agree to do so on a not-for-profit basis.

---

motivates the recent spate of ADA lawsuits against U.S. art galleries for failing to make their websites accessible to PVI. Elizabeth A. Harris, 'Galleries from A to Z Sued Over Websites the Blind Can't Use' *New York Times* (New York, 18 February 2019) C1.

28 Authors Guild, Inc v HathiTrust, 755 F 3d 87, 102 (2d Cir 2014).

29 Ibid. 101.

30 Copyright Act, §107(1).

31 See Campbell v Acuff-Rose Music, Inc, 510 US 569, 584, 114 S Ct 1164, 1174 (1994) (commerciality is only one element of the first factor enquiry into its purpose and character).

32 *Cambridge Univ Press* (n 24) 1263.

33 Ibid. 1264 (summarizing same).

Factor two, which focuses on the copyrighted work itself, is likely to cut against a finding of fair use in this case. That is because visual artworks, like the literary works at issue in the Author's Guild case, merit strong protection under the Copyright Act.[34] In any event, factor two is rarely determinative in copyright cases.[35]

Factor three, described by the HathiTrust court as asking "whether the copying used more of the copyrighted work than necessary and whether the copying was excessive[,]" could cut either way in this instance.[36] On the one hand, 3D printers are likely to use almost the entirety of a copyrighted photograph, painting, or drawing in order to maintain maximum fidelity to the original (in an enhanced capacity designed to facilitate access by PVI). This facially works against a finding of fair use.[37]

On the other hand, as the court recognized in HathiTrust, such holistic use may very well not be "excessive" in this context, where the very purpose of the use makes it "necessary to copy the entire copyrighted work, in which case Factor Three does not weigh against a finding of fair use."[38] In HathiTrust itself, for instance, the court held that digitization of the images as well as the entire text was not excessive in the case of literary works under this prong because:

> These image files contain information, such as pictures, charts, diagrams, and the layout of the text on the printed page that cannot be converted to text or speech.... Many legally blind patrons are capable of viewing these images if they are sufficiently magnified or if the color contrasts are increased.[39]

This is very strong language in support of the proposed use in this case, particularly as the technology here is serving the same type of enhancing or quasi-magnification function for PVI described in the HathiTrust case.

Finally, turning to the fourth factor, the effect on the market for or value of the copyrighted work, this too is likely to favor a finding of fair use. There is little to no evidence that artists themselves create or market three-dimensional, haptically perceptible versions of their own works. There would be no need for the undertaking at issue here if artists were making such versions. That is the very problem museums are now trying to solve. Thus, just as in HathiTrust, a court is likely to find in this case that "the present-day market for [artworks] accessible to [PVI] is so insignificant" that there will be no impact on the market for or value of the copyrighted work.[40]

34 See Rogers v Koons, 960 F 2d 301, 310 (2d Cir 1992) (factor two favors copyright owner/photographer over artist that adapted the work into a sculpture).

35 Authors Guild, Inc v HathiTrust, 755 F 3d 87, 102 (2d Cir 2014).

36 Ibid. 98.

37 *Koons* (n 34) 311 (fact that copyrighted photograph was "copied nearly *in toto*" works against finding of fair use under factor three).

38 Ibid.

39 *Authors Guild* (n 35) 103.

40 Ibid. 103 (citing legislative history asserting same with respect to the market for books).

In all, following especially the precedent laid down in the Author's Guild v. HathiTrust case, three-dimensional adaptations of visual artworks are more likely than not to be held protected by fair use if created for the limited purpose of providing access to PVI. As, however, similar uses have been ruled non-transformative, there is still risk that a later court could rule against fair use particularly if the 3D models are sold for commercial gain, fabricated by commercial 3D-printers, or made accessible to non-PVI.

Summarizing the Contradictions in U.S. Copyright Exceptions for PVI and Proposed Amendments

Stepping back and summarizing the U.S. copyright landscape, it is likely that the creation of three-dimensional renderings of two-dimensional artworks without authorization from the copyright holder constitutes a prima facie copyright violation in the U.S. Although the U.S. has fairly strong and clear safe harbors specific to reproductions made for PVI, those safe harbors are facially limited to literary works and likely of little help to the works at issue here. Thus, the museum or other person wishing to create such three-dimensional models will need to resort to the general defense of fair use. Although, in this regard, precedents exist and strong arguments can be made in support of a claim of fair use, there is always some risk associated with fair use assertions, particularly if those creating the models are commercial entities profiting off their creation.

Regrettably, these uncertainties in the U.S. copyright law appear likely to deter the widespread use and dissemination of state-of-the-art technologies for adapting works of fine art for PVI. Due to the complexity of the aforementioned statutory scheme, and the haziness of the U.S. fair use analysis, risk-averse fabricators and museums may balk at proceeding with such projects even if the current law would, in the end, support such endeavors.

Indeed the ambivalent condition of the U.S. copyright law with regards to visual art exceptions appears to be a variant of what the scholar Eric Johnson has recently lamented as the need for a more open "disability perspective" in the U.S. intellectual property law.[41] Johnson has noted how, with respect to copyright, "the statutory law displays an ableist perspective, both in how it has been drafted and in how its language has been interpreted," and gives as an example the aforementioned Jeff Koons case in which the artist was found to be an infringer when he refabricated a photograph in three dimensions, but not when he reproduced portions of a different photograph in two dimensions.[42] This leads to a form of discrimination, wherein sighted persons get the benefit of imagery and information not accessible to PVI.

Although the Chafee and related amendments certainly do inject one perspective of PVI into the corpus of copyright law relating to literary works, insofar as

41 See Eric E. Johnson, 'Intellectual Property's Need for a Disability Perspective' (2010) 20 Geo Mason U Civ Rts LJ 181.

42 Ibid. 202, n 106.

the legislation appears to simply ignore the problem of pictorial works, it reveals its own subtle form of discrimination. Namely, a wide gap has arisen over ease of access to information conveyed in pictorial, graphic, and sculptural works as compared to literary ones.

This raises the natural question of whether the U.S. could and would amend the safe harbor in Section 121 to expressly cover pictorial, graphic, and sculptural works. Although Section 121 has its limitations and critics, it does at least provide an existing, narrowly tailored framework, allowing for the modification of copyrighted works by authorized entities into "accessible formats".[43] The latter term is currently defined without reference to subject matter to mean

> an alternative manner or form that gives an eligible person access to the work when the copy … is used exclusively by the eligible person to permit him or her to have access as feasibly and comfortably as a person without such disability.[44]

As such, the provision would readily map onto visual artworks if amended as follows (showing proposed change in underline):

> [I]t is not an infringement of copyright for an authorized entity to reproduce or to distribute in the United States copies … of a previously published literary work <u>or of a pictorial, graphic and sculptural work</u> … if such copies … are reproduced or distributed in accessible formats exclusively for use by eligible persons.

Such an amendment would be consistent with the intent of the original Chafee Amendment, the legislative history behind the fair use provision, and the lion's share of case law on the subject.

It is difficult, finally, to imagine principled opposition to such an amendment. The exception is limited by its own terms to works made by specialized non-profit entities ("authorized entit[ies]") for the exclusive use of PVI ("eligible"), and leaves untouched the politically challenging category of motion pictures and audiovisual works.

Moral rights legislation

The Visual Artists Rights Act

The United States remains a jurisdiction with relatively weak moral rights protections, having long conceived of and justified copyright law as an economic right.[45] It only recently and begrudgingly adopted a limited federal right of

43 Copyright Act, §121(a).
44 Ibid. (d)(1).
45 See, e.g., Mazer v. Stein, 347 U.S. 201, 219 (1954).

attribution and integrity in 1990 in connection with its accession to the Berne Convention. This legislation, known as the Visual Artists Rights Act (or VARA, for short), is notoriously narrow and likely poses little barrier to the creation of 3D artworks from 2D originals.

Although two-dimensional paintings, drawings, and prints do qualify as protected "work[s] of visual art" under the statute,[46] VARA's protections extend only to the original work itself, and, critically for these purposes, they do not apply to any "reproduction, depiction, portrayal, or other use of a work in, upon, or in any connection with" a "model" of the original.[47]

Although "model" is not itself defined in the statute, it would seem that a 3D rendering for PVI comfortably fits within the ordinary meaning of the term. Indeed, the Oxford English Dictionary defines a "model" as "A three-dimensional representation of a person or thing…."[48]

Moreover, the work (i.e., the original painting or other artwork) has either been used "upon" the model (where the 2D work forms the surface of the 3D model), or "in connection with" the model (where the model is based on the work). Insofar as the work depicted will necessarily be transformed somewhat from the original (to increase its haptic perceptibility), one might argue that the 3D model is no longer a mere "reproduction" of the work. However, the operative language of the exception is broad enough to include the looser concepts of "depiction[s] and portrayal[s]" which imply some degree of creative transformation from the original. Finally, as a last resort, the catch-all phrase "or other use of a work" surely would encompass a non-identical transformative use of the type envisioned here.

The just-described liability exception applies both to rights of attribution and integrity. In other words, so long as the model-maker does not go so far as to harm the original work, for example, by significantly altering it in the 3D translation process, the creation of a model of that original will not violate the moral rights of the artist under the United States law even if the artist believes it to be a "distortion" of her work.

For the sake of completeness, it should also be noted that VARA only applies to a handful of works created before June 1, 1991, namely, works that the artist had created but not "transferred" prior to that date.[49] This would exclude from VARA most works accessioned into museum collections prior to June 1, 1991, so long as the artist had transferred legal title to the work by that time.

46 19 USC §101 (definition of "work of visual art" includes a "painting, drawing, print or sculpture, existing in a single copy" or certain limited edition works).

47 Copyright Act, §106A(c)(3). See Melville B Nimmer and David Nimmer, *Nimmer on Copyright*, vol 3 (Matthew Bender & Company, Inc 2019) § 8D.06[B][2] and [C][2] (reaching same conclusion about "expansive" scope of exception for models, posters, etc).

48 "Definition of Model in English by Oxford Dictionaries" (*Oxford Dictionaries | English*) <https://en.oxforddictionaries.com/definition/model> accessed May 29, 2019.

49 Copyright Act, §106A(d)(2).

Moreover, for newer works created after June 1, 1991, VARA rights end with the author's death.[50]

Finally, the VARA rights just discussed are subject to the fair use defense, making the preceding analysis of fair use applicable here as well.[51]

State moral rights laws

Application of state moral rights law to 3D-printed artworks

A discussion of moral rights in the United States, however, cannot stop at national legislation. Many states have enacted their own version of such laws, with those of California and New York being generally considered the two most venerable and broad in scope. The remainder of this section will focus on those two states with the understanding that the moral rights laws of other states would each require their own attention.

An analysis of overlapping federal and state moral rights claims must proceed in two distinct steps. First, one needs to ask whether the California or New York laws apply to the activities in question here. Second, because federal law remains supreme in the United States, [52] if the answer to the first question is yes, then one needs to ask whether VARA preempts such an attempt by the state to grant a right that VARA exempts.

Looking first to the substantive reach of the California and New York legislation, both arguably do reach more broadly than VARA in a way material to the issues here. Namely, the New York Artists' Authorship Rights Act bars anyone from displaying a "modified form" of a "reproduction" of a painting if attributed to the original artist.[53] This appears to reach the creation of the "modified form" of 3D models of artworks otherwise excluded from VARA, as discussed earlier.

Although California's Art Preservation Act does not expressly extend to a "reproduction" of a painting, it does cover any "alteration" of an "original painting" of "recognized quality." [54] The term "alteration" might be ambiguous enough to reach 3D translations.

Moreover, neither state law (again, contrary to VARA) contains exceptions for older works already in museum collections prior to its passage. California's law, for instance, lasts for 50 years from the death of the artist and applies to works created prior to its passage.[55]

50 Copyright Act, §106A(d)(1). For the small number of pre-1991 museum works to which VARA applies, the term is coextensive with that of copyright (generally, 70 years after death). Ibid (d)(2).

51 Copyright Act, §106A(a) (noting that all VARA rights are "Subject to section 107 [i.e., the fair use provision]".

52 US Const Art VI, Clause 2.

53 See NY Arts & Cult Aff Law § 14.03.

54 Cal Civ Code § 987(c)(1). The "recognized quality" limitation comes from the definition of "Fine art" in section (b)(2).

55 Ibid. (g)(1).

The New York statute covers only modifications that might reasonably result in "damage to the artist's reputation."[56] Thus, a modeler accused of infringement in New York may argue that there can be no harm to an artist's reputation given that all viewers would be informed that the model was created for the purpose of providing access to PVI. No one would think the artist herself created the work in that form. For this reason, anyone proceeding in this fashion would be well-advised to place a disclaimer, noting that this is a modified version of the work created solely for the purpose of exhibiting the work to PVI and is not the original work by the artist. This strategy, though, would have little impact with respect to the integrity provision of the California statute, which is neither limited to alterations impacting the artists' reputations nor to works identifiable with the artist.[57]

In sum, on their face, both California's and New York's state moral rights laws (especially the latter, with its explicit coverage of modified reproductions) are cause for concern to those making 3D models of paintings without the artist's consent.

State moral rights preemption

VARA includes what at first blush appears to be a very strong and far-reaching preemption provision (i.e., a clause blocking equivalent state rights from being asserted after VARA's passage). Namely, VARA purports to invalidate any "right [conferred by VARA] or equivalent right in any work of visual art under the common law or statutes of any State."[58] This makes it appear as though an artist gets to assert VARA or nothing for works covered by the statute, particularly as most of the subject works that one might wish to reproduce in 3D form for PVI are "work[s] of visual art" under VARA's definition (i.e., original paintings, drawings, etc.). This suggests that the state laws just discussed may not be enforceable against 3D printers of 2D art in this context.

Nothing with the U.S. preemption analysis, however, is ever simple. The VARA preemption provision contains at least three exceptions which muddy the waters here. Namely, VARA preemption does not extend to rights which extend posthumously,[59] to older works that are not covered by VARA,[60] or to state laws that "are not equivalent to" VARA rights.[61]

The first problem is that many of the works one might wish to reproduce were created by artists who died within the last 50 years. In such a case, the works are likely within the scope of California's posthumous right of integrity provision and not expressly preempted by VARA.

56 Ibid. (1).
57 Cal Civ Code §987(c)(1).
58 Copyright Act, §301(f)(1).
59 Ibid. (f)(2)(C).
60 Ibid. (f)(1).
61 Ibid. (f)(2)(B).

Take, for instance, Andy Warhol's 1960s-era Campbell's Soup paintings. California's posthumous moral rights law will remain in force for his works until 2037 (he died in 1987). VARA would likely not apply to most of these works in museum collections because of their age, but California's law could still apply because it is not preempted under that posthumous-work exception.

The second problem is that VARA preemption only applies to those "works of visual art to which the rights conferred by Section 106A apply." The authoritative Patry Copyright treatise understands that to mean that "[p]rotection for copies of works covered by VARA, the title to which was transferred before June 1, 1991 ... are not preempted."[62] Arguably, then, where living artists transferred title to older works before 1991, such artists could still rely on state moral rights provisions, even though (or, really, precisely because) VARA does not cover those works.

Finally, with respect to something like the New York legislation, there is the open question of whether the New York right to prevent "reproduction[s]" in "modified forms" is "equivalent" to any right given by VARA, even for works covered by VARA. Recall that VARA appeared to expressly exempt such models from its coverage. On the one hand, this New York legislation is a form of right of attribution and integrity, which is precisely the same as VARA, suggesting that VARA preemption would apply. This is indeed exactly how one court ruled in New York on the question of whether VARA preempts New York's integrity and attribution provisions.[63] On the other hand, an artist in this narrow context could still argue that nothing in VARA applies to attribution rights in the context of reproductions (as opposed to original works), and therefore that there should be no preemption of the New York law in that limited case.[64]

The most, then, that one can say with certainty about preemption is that while a good number of state moral rights actions are certainly barred by VARA, many preemption questions remain unanswered and some state moral rights laws (especially in posthumous cases and those involving pre-1991 works) remain viable and of concern in the current context.

Conclusion on moral rights in the U.S.

The good news for those seeking to render paintings in three dimensions for PVI is that the primary U.S. moral rights provision, VARA, likely poses no bar to doing so. Moreover, in many cases, VARA further prevents state laws from enforcement in this context.

62 William F Patry, *Patry on Copyright*, vol 5 (West Publishing 2017) § 16:47.

63 Bd of Managers of Soho Intl Arts Condo v City of NY, No 01 CIV 1226 DAB, 2003 WL 21403333, at *15, n 19 (SDNY June 17, 2003) (finding both the integrity and attribution rights granted by both statutes "equivalent").

64 As Prof. Nimmer points out in a different context, the Copyright Act contains its own complicated preemption provision, Section 301(a), which could apply in this last case. Nimmer (n 48) § 8D.08. Such an argument, however, failed in a pre-VARA case involving the artist David Wojnarowicz. Wojnarowicz v Am Family Ass'n, 745 F Supp 130, 136 (SDNY 1990).

Unfortunately, however, due to the breadth of certain state moral rights laws and the limitations of VARA preemption, there remains the possibility that an artist (or artist's estate) wishing to prevent three-dimensional renderings of the artist's work could attempt to do so.

Protectability of 3D renderings as derivative works

Looking beyond the question of whether one is initially permitted to adapt two-dimensional artworks for PVI, some fabricators may themselves attempt to assert intellectual property rights in the model that has been created. While, of course, such entities may own patent or other rights in the technology behind the rendering process, I mean to refer here to copyright claims over the finished product (i.e., as a derivative work). The recognition of such IP rights might provide an incentive for companies to undertake this work. On the other hand, it might lead to attempts by 3D printers to foreclose others from using or creating additional models.

First, it is important to note that the U.S. law does not recognize copyright protection in unauthorized derivative works. The provision itself makes clear that derivative copyright protection "does not extend to any part of the work in which such material has been used unlawfully."[65] This, however, still leaves room for derivative work copyright claims where the copyright owner gave permission to create the derivative work or where the material was used lawfully (such as under the fair use exception).

Assuming such authorization, then, the key inquiry under the current U.S. law becomes whether the adapted (three-dimensional) artwork contains "sufficient nontrivial expressive variation in the derivative work to make it distinguishable from the underlying work in some meaningful way."[66] Older cases have thus recognized sufficient originality in mezzotint engravings of public domain old master works, such that the engraver was credited with copyright in the derivative work.[67] In the specific case of three-dimensional renderings made from two-dimensional originals, courts have also historically recognized change in medium and dimensionality as sufficiently original to warrant derivative protection.[68]

That said, the trend appears to be moving in the other direction for derivative replications of visual art. In 1999, a court specifically rejected a claim for copyright in photographic transparencies of public domain artworks, noting that although photography required skill and effort, there was "no spark of originality"

65 Copyright Act § 103. See, e.g.,, Palladium Music, Inc v EatSleepMusic, Inc, 398 F 3d 1193, 1197 (10th Cir 2005) (derivative work copyright in karaoke songs invalid and unenforceable where claimant did not secure underlying permissions).

66 Schrock v Learning Curve Intl, Inc, 586 F 3d 513, 521 (7th Cir 2009).

67 Alfred Bell & Co v Catalda Fine Arts, 191 F 2d 99, 105 (2d Cir 1951).

68 Doran v Sunset House Distrib Corp, 197 F Supp. 940, 944 (SD Cal 1961), affd, 304 F 2d 251 (9th Cir 1962; "the originality here lies in the form— three-dimensional— and the medium— plastic— which plaintiffs have used to express the idea").

in such "slavish copies."[69] In a recent case rejecting copyright in 3D car models made for use in advertising, the court expressly rejected the notion that mere change in medium or dimensions is enough to establish originality for copyright purposes.[70] Even more to the point here, one court expressed skepticism (in the infringement context) that there was originality sufficient to reach derivate work status where a company applied oil paint brush strokes to a flat poster to give it "bumps" and the feel of an oil-paint replica.[71]

In all, whether a U.S. court would find enough originality in the three-dimensional renderings for PVI envisioned here would likely depend on the individual judge and specific facts of the case. Derivative copyrights are more likely to be found where the renderer can point to particular expressive choices made in the adaptation process. Perhaps, for instance, the modeler chose to enhance certain colors but not others, or to add depth and texture in certain areas, that avoid "slavish" mimicry of the original artwork.

It is possible, indeed likely, that adaptations of two-dimensional artworks for PVI would reach this copyrightability threshold. Accordingly, any museum or other party commissioning such works should be sure to clarify in advance, by express agreement, what rights (if any) the 3D renderer and other potential "authors" of any derivatives will have in the completed model.

Conclusion and recommendations

With its flexible fair use standard and strong supporting case law, the U.S. copyright law would be unlikely ultimately to pose an obstacle to rendering two-dimensional artworks in three dimensions for the express purpose of encouraging access to such works by PVI. That said, there is no clear safe harbor insulating such activity in the U.S. as the Marrakesh Treaty Implementation Act, and its predecessor exemptions focus only on literary works. Even a strong fair use case, moreover, is never risk-free, particularly where contractors involved in the rendering process might be commercial entities tempted to sell versions of the models widely to offset some of the costs involved in the process. Moral rights, although likely inapplicable at a federal level, could themselves pose a problem at the state level given the lack of clarity in the case law of preemption.

If, as appears to be the case, this lacuna in U.S. disability law is more the product of accident or ignorance than intentionality, the good news is that there is at least one clear quick fix available in the short-term. Most immediately, in order to encourage widespread use of adaptive technologies, the U.S. Congress could and should immediately amend Sections 121 and 121A of the Copyright Act to

69 Bridgeman Art Library, Ltd v.Corel Corp, 36 F Supp 2d 191, 197 (SDNY 1999).

70 Meshwerks, Inc v Toyota Motor Sales USA, Inc, 528 F 3d 1258, 1267 (10th Cir 2008).

71 Peker v Masters Collection, 96 F Supp 2d 216, 221 (EDNY 2000) ("though their creation may require special skills, they do not possess any originality that would warrant an independent copyright").

bring pictorial, graphic, and sculptural works into the Chafee Amendment's safe harbor, as detailed earlier.

A second, admittedly more difficult, task would be to clarify the state of moral rights preemption with respect to allowing the uninhibited creation of three-dimensional artworks for PVI. Not only, however, would that force the Congress to enter the fraught realm of federal-state relations, but such subject-specific drafting could prove highly challenging in the preemption context.

But even if legislators could only be convinced to make the former change, which appears politically and technically feasible, such a safe harbor would go a long way toward comforting skittish fabricators or museum boards worried about copyright infringement liability.

12 Copyright in the public interest

Canada's perceptual disability framework

Lucie Guibault and Anthony Rosborough

Introduction

With the enactment of the *Accessible Canada Act*,[1] the Canadian Parliament has taken yet another tangible step towards enhancing the full and equal participation of all persons, especially persons with disabilities, in society. This Act, together with an array of regulations adopted by the three levels of government (federal, provincial and municipal), allows persons with disabilities to increasingly occupy their legitimate place in Canadian society. One of the sectors where persons with disabilities are rapidly gaining ground is the world of the arts. For several years already, the Canada Council for the Arts has developed and implemented a strategy to promote equality in the arts for deaf Canadians and Canadians with disabilities. The aim is to ensure that all Canadians can foster their artistic aspirations through the study, enjoyment and production of works in the arts.[2]

Participation of all Canadians in the cultural and artistic life is not a given, however, especially not for persons with disabilities. Among the forms of systemic discrimination against persons with disabilities which the Canada Council for the Arts identified in a 2012 report is a "lack of alternate format, adapted services and sign languages throughout arts ecology [that] create barriers to participating and engaging in the arts (e.g., lack of audio description, tactile tours, adapted equipment, interpretation, captioning, etc.)".[3] While this same report suggests promoting "greater physical, sensory and programming access to the arts ecology", it does not specify how this can be achieved.

3D printing may raise a range of copyright concerns, when 3D reproductions are carried out without the prior authorisation of the holder of rights in the artistic work at the source of the reproduction. The question addressed in this chapter is whether making and displaying 3D reproductions of works of visual

1 *Accessible Canada Act*, SC 2019, c C-10.

2 Canada Council for the Arts, 'Expanding the Arts: Deaf and Disability Arts, Access and Equality Strategy – Full Report', (Equity Office, Council Secretariat and Strategic Initiatives Canada Council for the Arts. Ottawa, May 2012).

3 Ibid. 4.

art for the benefit of persons with disabilities is lawful under Canadian copyright law. Our analysis rests on the interpretation of the provisions in the Copyright Act, in the light of the relevant case law and scholarly literature. No court has yet considered this issue. However, arguments can be made in support of making such reproductions, in view of the Supreme Court of Canada's broad and flexible approach to the exceptions in the Copyright Act and of Canada's ratification of both the *Marrakesh Treaty on Copyright for the Benefit of Blind and Visually Impaired Persons*[4] (the "Marrakesh Treaty") and the United Nations (UN) *Convention on the Rights of Persons with Disabilities*[5] (UNRPD).

This chapter is further divided in four parts. Part II provides a short description of the technique involved in making 3D reproductions of two-dimensional artistic works; Part III describes how the rights granted under the Canadian Copyright Act are put in question through the realisation of a 3D reproduction of a work. More specifically, this part looks at how 3D printing may affect the rights owner's economic and moral rights, as well as at how the application of technological protection measures may create obstacles to the creation of 3D reproductions. Part IV discusses the exceptions contained in the Copyright Act that seem to support the making of such uses for the benefit of persons with visual impairment (PVI). Our analysis focuses on the fair dealing defence and on the specific exception enacted in favour of PVI. Part V draws conclusions on the lawful character of 3D reproductions of works made for the purpose of enabling PVI to gain sensory experience of visual artworks.

For the purposes of this chapter, we assume that the work of visual art from which a 3D reproduction is made, is (still) protected by copyright law. Rights owners may wish to enforce their rights on original works that are either tangible or digital-born. However, since our focus lies on the tangible product that PVI can touch, the copyright status of the intermediary copies realised in the course of getting to the 3D reproduction, like 3D CAD files, will not be the object of attention.

Technical process of 3D reconstruction

The process of creating a three-dimensional object from a single two-dimensional image of artwork can be regarded as involving three distinct phases or steps within the context of copyright law's economic rights. First, photogrammetric software requires a digital photograph or image of the work in order to place it in a three-dimensional environment. This stage of the process will be referred to as the "digitisation" stage. In essence, the digitisation stage involves some degree of initial reproduction in that a digital manifestation of the work is required by

4 World Intellectual Property Organization, Marrakesh Treaty to Facilitate Access to Published Works by Persons Who Are Blind, Visually Impaired, or Otherwise Print Disables (adopted 28 June 2013, entered into force 30 September 2016).

5 Convention on the Rights of Persons with Disabilities (adopted 13 December 2006, entered into force 3 May 2008) 2515 UNTS 3 (UNRPD).

3D printing computer software. Secondly, the photogrammetric software (and in conjunction with its user) will manipulate the digital image to create a file readable by the 3D printer. This will almost always involve some degree of shape parameter creation and selection of the depth, contour or overall shape of the object. In order to make these decisions, the user must interpret the original work and determine how it would be best represented in three dimensions. This second phase of the process of 3D creation will be referred to as the "manipulation" stage. Thirdly and finally, the 3D printer will produce a three-dimensional object as its final output to be used for perceptibility purposes. The 3D printers can use myriad printing mediums for the creation of an object which vary in texture and density. These attributes (also chosen by the user) may impact the experience or perception of the 3D artistic work. This final stage will be referred to as the "production" stage. As will be further outlined in the next part, the scope of economic and moral rights under Canada's copyright regime that are impacted by this process vary in accordance with each of the aforementioned three phases.

Scope of rights

To contextualise our analysis, imagine that a museum or an art gallery plans to make some of the two-dimensional works in their collections accessible to persons with a disability through 3D printing. These works include paintings, drawings and photographs; the works can be tangible and hanging on the walls of the museum or gallery, or they can be "digital-born" and made available with the help of digital devices. This operation demands that each original work be transformed, through at least two of the three phases enumerated earlier, into its tactile rendition and be displayed in public. In this section, we examine how such a project is likely to impact the author's economic and moral rights, according to the Canadian *Copyright Act.*

Economic rights

Canada's *Copyright Act* sets out a broad array of exclusive economic rights held by copyright owners at s.3(1). The legislative drafting of the Act suggests three "main" economic rights (namely, reproduction, performance and publication) along with a longer list of "included" rights (e.g., translation, adaptation and communication to the public). Recent jurisprudence from the Supreme Court of Canada has called into question the appropriate interpretation of this framework by finding that the latter "included" rights are mere branches of the main three.[6] Nevertheless, scholarly commentary and subsequent amendments to the Act suggest strongly that the enumerated economic rights in the Act should

6 *Entertainment Software Association v Society of Composers, Authors and Music Publishers of Canada*, 2012 SCC 34, [2012] 2 SCR 231.

be treated as distinct rights which are actionable and licensable by owners.[7] With this in mind, this section will highlight key economic rights that would be impacted during the process of creating a three-dimensional object from a two-dimensional artwork, including the rights of reproduction, translation and exhibition in public.

Reproduction

The right of reproduction is the core of virtually all copyright regimes, and Canada's framework is no exception. The Canadian approach to the right of reproduction was canvassed thoroughly by the Supreme Court in the landmark case, *Théberge v Gallerie d'Art du Petit Champlain.*[8] At issue in *Théberge* was whether the creation of canvas-backed artwork from lawfully licenced prints constituted "reproduction" under the Act. The process at issue involved transferring the ink layer of the printed image to a new medium, which was often canvas. Importantly, the process did not multiply the number of copies of the work, but merely transformed the physical materials in which it is embodied. Justice Binnie, writing for the majority, found that in such circumstances there can be no reproduction in the absence of multiplication.

In addition to the requirement of multiplication, the Canadian conceptualisation of reproduction contains an additional nuance. Namely, the Act protects against acts which reproduce either entire works or "substantial parts thereof". Therefore, in certain cases, it is necessary to determine the threshold for substantiality. Determining whether a substantial part has been taken was precisely the issue in *Cinar Corporation v Robinson*,[9] in which the Supreme Court must decide over the similarity between two children's television series. In assessing what constitutes a "substantial part", the Supreme Court held that "substantial part" is a flexible notion that is a matter of "fact and degree".[10] The Court found that substantiality is more a question of quality rather than quantity and is nevertheless relative to the originality of the work subject to protection. More broadly, Canadian courts have held that the analytical factors for an assessment of substantiality include the extent to which the use adversely affects the rightsholder by diminishing the value of the copyright, whether the material taken is the proper subject of copyright, and whether the material taken is used in the same or in a similar fashion as the rightsholder's use.

7 Elizabeth Judge, 'Righting a Right: Entertainment Software Association v. SOCAN and the Exclusive Rights of Copyright for Works' in Michael Geist (ed), *The Copyright Pentalogy: How the Supreme Court of Canada Shook the Foundations of Canadian Copyright Law* (University of Ottawa Press 2013).

8 *Théberge v Gallerie d'Art du Petit Champlain*, 2002 SCC 34.

9 *Cinar Corporation v. Robinson*, 2013 SCC 73.

10 Ibid. [26].

Producing a 3D printed object from a single two-dimensional image can engage the right of reproduction at various phases of the process.[11] Where the source two-dimensional artwork is not already in the form of a digital image, it will need to be captured as such at the initial digitisation phase. The recording and storage of a digital reproduction of the two-dimensional source work would likely constitute an act of *prima facie* reproduction. Given the fact that the digital file is an exact image of the source work, it would leave little room to argue that the parts of the work being reproduced are anything less than substantial.

Secondly, the right of reproduction can be engaged during the manipulation phase when the user creates a file readable by the 3D printer. While the creation of a 3D printable file will involve user input and will undoubtedly transform the underlying source artwork, it is likely that this would nevertheless fall within the range of reproducing a "substantial part". This is because the exercise of creating a 3D print file of the source artwork is intended to precisely reproduce the originality of the work, albeit in an electronic format. Therefore, in assessing the quality of the parts taken from the source artwork, the 3D print file would likely fall within the Canadian Act's "substantial part" conceptualisation of reproduction.

Finally, the creation of the 3D printed object at the production phase may also infringe the right of reproduction. While the object produced cannot be an exact copy of the source artwork, it is conceivable that, in most instances, it would rise to the level of a substantial part. Though it is possible that user decisions made at the manipulation stage could introduce enough originality to overshadow the parts taken from the source artwork, such a finding is unlikely. This is because the process of creating such objects for PVI is precisely to reproduce (to the greatest extent possible) the expression and originality elucidated by the source artwork. Therefore, the most successful 3D object productions for such purposes would be those most likely to engage the right of reproduction.

Translation

Common to most copyright frameworks internationally, the translation right stands as one of the oldest economic rights, stemming largely from the era where novels and written works were the primary focus of copyright. Nevertheless, since that time, the translation right has been interpreted in an evolutionary fashion by Canadian courts, in the context of both computer programmes and changing formats of works. Importantly, the word "translation" is not defined by the Canadian Copyright Act. Authoritative commentary on the subject has defined translation in this context as "turning of something from one human language to another."[12] Importantly, in order to satisfy the criteria for a translation, the

11 See: *Bayliner Marine Corp. v Doral Boats Ltd.* (1985), 5 CPR (3d) 289 (Federal Court); *Spiro-Flex Indust. Ltd. v Progressive Sealing Inc.*, 1986 CanLII 771 (BC SC), 13 CPR (3d) 311.

12 John S. McKeown, *Fox on Canadian Law of Copyright and Industrial Designs* (4th edn, Carswell) 21:9.

resulting work must also be original.[13] In more recent times, Canadian courts have been asked on several occasions to determine whether the creation of digital formats of previously analog works amounts to translations. In the trial decision of *Keatley Surveying Ltd v Teranet,* the Ontario Superior Court was unequivocal in finding that such digitisations do not amount to a translation.[14]

In creating 3D printed objects of two-dimensional artwork, however, the Canadian framework leaves some ambiguity as to whether this could be interpreted as a translation. This stems in large part from the idea/expression dichotomy and the ambiguity surrounding what constitutes a "human language". For example, in *Apple Computer Inc v Mackintosh Computers,* the Canadian Federal Court of Appeal had to decide whether the conversion of computer code from one language to another was a translation. In reversing the trial judge's findings on this issue, the Court of Appeal looked primarily to whether the character of the original work had been retained. It found that translation should not be given such a broad interpretation as to include transformation of an expression into a new medium or form of representation.[15]

Based on the aforementioned, it is not altogether clear whether the creation of 3D printed objects from two-dimensional source artwork could be considered translations within the meaning of the Act. Though the image created at the digitisation stage would not likely be considered a translation under the Act, the actual production of the 3D object poses more complex variables for analysis. More specifically, the creation of the object involves a greater interpretive exercise than merely transposing computer code from one language to another. However, the notion of a "human language" casts doubt on whether the 3D printed object would fall within this conceptualisation. This requires further judicial comment on the limits of what constitutes a "human language" and whether this could include the use of physical objects for the purposes of aiding in perceptual disabilities. It is conceivable that there are strong policy arguments for including such objects under the umbrella of human language, but it is not altogether clear whether this would be sufficient to guide courts. In any event, finding that 3D printed objects are "translations" would also demand consideration of the extent to which the object retains the original expression of the source artwork, given that a mere transformation of the source work's expression would likely not rise to the level of a translation.

Exhibition in public

The Canadian *Copyright Act* provides rights owners with the exclusive right to "present at a public exhibition, for a purpose other than sale or hire", artistic and sculptural works.[16] There is a paucity of case law in Canada interpreting this

13 *Keatley Surveying Ltd v Teranet Inc.*, 2012 ONSC 7120, [119].

14 Ibid. [122].

15 *Apple Computer Inc v Mackintosh Computers Ltd*, [1988] 1 FC 673, [37].

16 *Copyright Act*, RSC 1985, c C-42, s 3(1)(g).

provision, but it is analogous in many ways to the right of public performance. Key to determining the scope of this right is an analysis of what constitutes the "public". Canadian courts have generally looked to the potential audience rather than the degree to which the actual audience at an exhibition or performance constituted "the public".[17]

The extent to which a 3D printed object may impact the right of public exhibition would ultimately depend on the uses for which it is put. In order to ensure that PVI have access to and can benefit from these objects, it is likely that these objects would be made broadly available to the public, including displays at art galleries and museums. In such cases, if the original expression of the source work is preserved in the creation of the 3D object and rises to the level of a "substantial part", the public exhibition of these objects would likely infringe upon the rights owner's public exhibition right.

Moral rights

In contrast to the robust authors' rights systems of continental European countries, Canada's moral rights framework is more aligned with the Anglo-American copyright tradition by including only the minimums required by the *Berne Convention for the Protection of Artistic and Literary Works* (the "Berne Convention"). This includes the right of attribution and the right of integrity. The Supreme Court of Canada has observed that Canadian copyright laws have been generally more concerned with economic rights than moral rights, and generally treat artistic and literary works as articles of commerce rather than extensions of artists' personalities.[18] Irrespective of the degree to which moral rights are emphasised by the Canadian Act, however, the legislative drafting makes certain that moral rights are to be clearly distinguished from economic rights.

According to the Act, the right of attribution provides authors with the right to be associated with the work where it is "reasonable in the circumstances". Canadian courts have not directly interpreted the scope of what is reasonable in the circumstances in this context, but have generally looked to whether attribution is feasible without impacting other aspects of the work. In the case of a 3D printed object, there are myriad ways in which the author could be associated with the work, including a physically perceptible mark or Braille that can convey the name of the author or communication of the author's name through audio. By placing these objects in art galleries, museums and environments accessible to the public, there are therefore numerous options available to ensure that the right of attribution is satisfied, and it is therefore likely that it would be reasonable in the circumstances to do so.

The right of integrity is ordinarily the branch of moral rights to receive the most attention and scrutiny under Canadian law, despite the paucity of case law focusing exclusively on the subject. According to the Act, the author's right to

17 *Canadian Admiral Corporation Ltd v Rediffusion Inc.*, [1954] Ex CR 382; 20 CPR 75.
18 *Théberge*, (n 10), [12]–[15].

the integrity of the work is infringed only if the work is "distorted, mutilated or otherwise modified" in a way that is prejudicial to the honour and reputation of the author.[19] The Act does not provide any further clarification of how prejudice to the honour or reputation to authors should be determined. Jurisprudence has since established the need for both the author's subjective view of his or her honour and reputation[20] and objective evidence in the form of expert opinion.[21] The approach taken by Canadian courts has also often left behind a somewhat circular structure of reasoning, wherein the concepts of "distortion and mutilation" and "prejudice to honour and reputation" appear to be one and the same.[22] The overarching result is that the Canadian approach to integrity rights requires a high evidentiary standard and sits upon unclear conceptual foundations.

It is nevertheless conceivable that a 3D printed object could implicate the author's integrity rights if, as the result of its transformation from two dimensions to three, the alterations have the effect of distorting or mutilating the work in a prejudicial way. Of course, the requirement of expert evidence on this subject makes it much more difficult for the author to allege prejudicial distortion or mutilation on arbitrary grounds. Authors making such a claim would also have to address the awkward position they would find themselves in by alleging that changes to their works that broaden accessibility to them would be subjectively prejudicial.

If the 3D printed object departs substantially from the source artwork, a claim for the infringement of integrity rights is theoretically possible. The prospect of such a claim should be balanced by a caveat in the Act, however. The Act clarifies that a change in the "physical means by which a work is exposed or the physical structure containing a work" does not in and of itself constitute distortion or mutilation of the work.[23] This caveat calls into question the extent to which the creation of a 3D printed object could be considered merely a change in the physical means by which a work is exposed or its physical structure. Given that some additional input from the user would be required at the manipulation stage, the quasi-creative interpretation of the source artwork and creation of new physical parameters may lead to the conclusion that this goes beyond merely changing the physical manifestation of the work.

With the foregoing in mind, the Canadian moral rights framework (though limited in comparison to other jurisdictions) could act as an impediment to the transformation of artwork into three dimensions. While the right of attribution is one that is relatively easily addressed by art galleries and museums who showcase these works, the impact on the author's right of integrity depends on the nuances of each 3D printed object and the extent to which they may be deemed prejudicial to the author's honour or reputation. The paucity of Canadian case

19 *Copyright Act*, (n 16), s 14.1(1).
20 *Snow v The Eaton Centre Ltd.*, (1982) 70 CPR (2d) 105.
21 *Thomson v Afterlife Network*, 2019 FC 545.
22 *Copyright Act*, (n 16), s 28.2(2).
23 *Copyright Act*, (n 16), s 28.2(3).

law interpreting cases in this area presents difficulties in predetermining the types of alterations or modifications to the artwork that would fall subject to integrity rights. However, the requirement of objective evidence of prejudice lends support for the notion that only 3D printed works which depart radically from other aesthetic aspects of the work would be at issue.

Technological Protection Measures (TPMs)

In addition to the economic and moral rights protected under the Act, the Canadian *Copyright Act* also protects TPMs. Namely, in accordance with Article 11 of the WIPO Copyright Treaty, Canada's Act prohibits acts of TPM circumvention, and the manufacture, import and sale of devices that enable circumvention. These measures were implemented in Canada in 2012, under the *Copyright Modernization Act*[10]. The *Copyright Act* defines "technological protection measure" as a device or component that "controls access to a work" or restricts the exercise of the economic rights under the Act.[11] The protection for TPMs under Canada's legislation is quite strong – restricting circumvention attached to even legally acquired works or for which an exception would otherwise apply.[12] The Act defines "circumvention" broadly, including anything that "avoids, bypasses, removes, deactivates, or impairs the technological protection measure."[13] As is the case in other jurisdictions, Canada's implementation of strong TPM protections has been controversial.

The 2D artistic works sought to be transposed into 3D printed objects must generally first be rendered in some digital form, or may even be "digital-born". For example, it may be that an art gallery or museum wishes to create a 3D object out of a digital photograph or recording. In these cases, TPMs or rights management tools may make the conversion of these works into 3D printed objects impossible or exceptionally difficult. For example, copyright owners could use encryption to prevent the use of the data within the digital file, or embed into the file a unique identification marker which can track and monitor its subsequent use. In such cases, museums and art galleries would face significant legally entrenched impediments to converting these words into 3D printed objects. In this respect, TPMs can provide rights owners with an additional and powerful layer of control and protection over their works in a way that could inhibit the production of 3D printed objects to assist persons with disabilities. Thankfully, the Canadian Act contains exceptions allowing circumvention of TPMs for purposes that would likely fall within the transformation of artwork into 3D printed objects. This exception will be more thoroughly canvassed in the proceeding section.

Copyright exceptions and limitations

In many instances, Canadian users of copyright protected material rely in their dealings with these works on either, or both, the fair dealing defence and an enumerated list of statutory exceptions. Fair dealing is a defence to a copyright infringement claim that covers uses of protected works for specific purposes or under specific circumstances, including for research purposes, criticism and education. In interpreting the fair dealing provision, Canada's courts have taken a broad and purposive approach to the framework, with the goal of avoiding outcomes antithetical to the broader purposes of Canadian copyright law.[24] The fair dealing defence offers an additional instrument in the hands of museums and galleries to justify acts of reproduction and performance in public that might not be covered by the list of statutory exceptions. This section evaluates the fair dealing framework and exceptions contained in the Act as they would apply to 3D printing for the purposes of assisting persons with disabilities. It demonstrates that the jurisprudence of the Supreme Court and Canada's broad implementation of the Marrakesh Treaty provides ample room for the realisation and display of 3D reproductions of artistic works, even without the prior consent of the rightsholder.

Fair dealing

Fair dealing under Canadian copyright law has been recognised as an integral part of the Act. In *CCH Canadian Ltd v Law Society of Upper Canada*,[25] the Supreme Court provided a fulsome analysis of the role of fair dealing in achieving a balance between the rights of authors and the rights of users. In this regard, fair dealing is regarded as not merely a defence to otherwise infringing conduct, but a user's right.

In order to show that a dealing is fair under s. 29 of the *Copyright Act*, a defendant must prove: (1) that the dealing was for one of the purposes enumerated in s. 29 and (2) that it is fair. The current version of the *Copyright Act* lists research, private study, education, parody or satire as acceptable purposes for a fair dealing defence. Addressing the research or study purpose, the Supreme Court stressed in *CCH* that '"Research" must be given a large and liberal interpretation in order to ensure that users' rights are not unduly constrained'.[26] The Court further asserted that fair dealing is a "user's right", and the relevant perspective when considering whether the dealing is for an allowable purpose under the first stage of *CCH* is that of the user.

No specific purpose listed in s. 29 of the Act covers the 3D printing and displaying of artistic works for the benefit of PVI. Seen from the perspective of PVI, however, it could be argued that the purpose of making a 3D reproduction would qualify as a form of research and private study of the artistic works.

24 *Keatley Surveying Ltd. v Teranet Inc.*, 2019 SCC 43, [44]–[47].

25 *CCH Canadian Ltd. v Law Society of Upper Canada*, 2004 SCC 13, [23]–[25].

26 Ibid. [51].

In *Alberta (Education Minister) v. Access Copyright*,[16] which involved the making of reproduction of works for use in elementary and secondary schools, the Supreme Court stressed that

> "... [T]here is no such separate purpose on the part of the teacher. Teachers have no ulterior motive when providing copies to students. Nor can teachers be characterized as having the completely separate purpose of "instruction"; they are there to facilitate the students' research and private study. It seems to me to be axiomatic that most students lack the expertise to find or request the materials required for their own research and private study, and rely on the guidance of their teachers'.

The role of a museum or a gallery in realising the 3D reproduction for the benefit of PVI is tantamount to that of the teachers in *Alberta v Access Copyright*: without the guidance of the museum or gallery, the patrons would not be able to find and request the materials that they wish to experience.

Similarly, in *Alberta v Access Copyright*, the Supreme Court added that "the word 'private' in 'private study' should not be understood as requiring users to view copyrighted works in splendid isolation. Studying and learning are essentially personal endeavours, whether they are engaged in with others or in solitude". This statement could be applied to the situation where a 3D reproduction of an artistic work is displayed in a museum or gallery: the public exhibition of such a work does not affect the "private study" character of the experience lived by PVI.

Finally, the Supreme Court stressed in *SOCAN v Bell*[17] that fair dealing for research purposes should not be restricted to research that entails creative purposes:

> limiting research to creative purposes would also run counter to the ordinary meaning of "research", which can include many activities that do not demand the establishment of new facts or conclusions. It can be piecemeal, informal, exploratory, or confirmatory. It can in fact be undertaken for no purpose except personal interest.

These words find special resonance in the context of 3D printing and displaying of artistic works for PVI: the beneficiaries of the 3D prints will presumably experience the works for their personal interest, which may or may not lead to creative activity.

In short, the Supreme Court's broad and flexible interpretation of the purposes for which a defence of fair dealing is acceptable would most likely support the case where a museum or gallery engaged in 3D printing and displaying of artistic works for the benefit of PVI as a legitimate purpose.

The next step consists in determining whether the actual 3D printing and displaying of an artistic work by a museum or gallery meets the fairness criteria set out by the Supreme Court in *CCH*. These criteria are the following: the character of the dealing, the amount of the dealing, the alternatives to the dealing, the nature of the dealing and the effect of the dealing. Whether a use is fair is a matter of fact to be analysed on a case-by-case basis. Based on the current case law of the Supreme Court, it could be reasonably argued that museums and galleries would enjoy sufficient leeway to engage in the 3D reproduction and display of artistic works for the benefit of PVI, as such use would certainly meet the requirement of the character and the nature of the dealing. Moreover, since there are no known comparable alternatives to the dealing and since the effect of the dealing on the original work would presumably be minimal, these criteria would tend to favour a finding of fairness. The main word of caution pertains to the amount of the dealing, which again would be assessed in each individual case. The 3D reproduction of an artistic work in a manner which reveals the essential character of the work to PVI necessarily entails its entire reproduction. In this sense, the amount of the use might militate against a finding of fairness. But the fairness enquiry is holistic, and the amount could be mitigated by both its necessity to achieve disability access and the merit of the disability access purpose.

Perceptual disability exception

S. 32(1) of the Canadian *Copyright Act* has contained an exception for the benefit of users with a perceptual disability since 1997. Nevertheless, the provisions of the Marrakesh Treaty were implemented by Act of Parliament in 2016,[27] which amended the Copyright Act to introduce a mechanism for the cross-border exchange of adapted formats for PVIs.[28] The definition of "perceptual disability" adopted in 1997 covers

> a disability that prevents or inhibits a person from reading or hearing a literary, musical, dramatic or artistic work in its original format, and includes such a disability resulting from (a) severe or total impairment of sight or hearing or the inability to focus or move one's eyes, (b) the inability to hold or manipulate a book, or (c) an impairment relating to comprehension.[29]

It is worth emphasising that in contrast with the provisions of the Marrakesh Treaty, which apply strictly to books and printed matter,[30] the Canadian implementation is much broader in scope, as it also expressly applies to artistic works.

27 Bill C-11, *An Act to Amend the Copyright Act (access to copyrighted works or other subject-matter for persons with perceptual disabilities)*, 1st Sess, 42nd Parl, 2015–2016 (as assented to 22 June 2016).

28 *Copyright Act*, (n 16), s 32.01.

29 *Copyright Act*, (n 16), s 2.

30 Marrakesh Treaty (n 4), art 2.

S. 32(1) of the Copyright Act reads as follows:

> **32(1)** It is not an infringement of copyright for a person with a perceptual disability, for a person acting at the request of such a person or for a non-profit organisation acting for the benefit of such a person to

a reproduce a literary, musical, artistic or dramatic work, other than a cinematographic work, in a format specially designed for persons with a perceptual disability.

This section, which remained unmodified following the implementation of the Marrakesh Treaty, clearly authorises either the person with a perceptual disability herself or another person or non-profit organisation acting on this person's behalf to reproduce an artistic work in a format specially designed for persons with a perceptual disability. The Act does not specify the kind of formats that might be acceptable. Arguably, any format that is "specially designed for persons with a perceptual disability" would be acceptable, which would include the 3D print of an artistic work. On the other hand, subsection 32(2) specifies that the exception does not apply where the work or sound recording is commercially available in a format specially designed to meet the needs of the person with the perceptual disability who requested it. This restriction would not likely apply to the realisation of a 3D print from a two-dimensional artistic work, like a painting, a drawing, a photograph or a map, as it is highly improbable that a 3D version of an artistic work would be commercially available. As a result, and in accordance with the Canadian principles of statutory interpretation, if the Parliament had wanted to restrict the making of adapted formats and prevent 3D printing of artistic works, it would have expressly provided so in the Act.

The authorisation to make an adapted format is granted not only to persons with a perceptual disability but also to any other person or non-profit organisation at the request or for the benefit of such persons. S. 32.02 of the Act specifies that a non-profit organisation mentioned in sections 32 and 32.01 includes a department, agency or other portion of any order of government, including a municipal or local government, when it is acting on a non-profit basis. In our opinion, this section should be read in conjunction with s. 2 of the Act which defines "library, archive or museum" as:

a an institution, whether or not incorporated, that is not established or conducted for profit or that does not form a part of, or is not administered or directly or indirectly controlled by, a body that is established or conducted for profit, in which is held and maintained a collection of documents and other materials that is open to the public or to researchers, or

b any other non-profit institution prescribed by regulation.

The non-profit organisation targeted by s. 32.02 arguably extends to a museum as defined in s. 2, so long as the latter acts on a non-profit basis. This interpretation also corresponds to the interpretation given to the provisions of the Marrakesh

Treaty.[31] Whether a gallery would likely fall within the scope of the provision and be permitted to adapt the format of an artistic work through 3D printing depends on whether it would qualify as a non-profit institution or not.

Once an adapted version of the work is realised, the next question is whether displaying the 3D reproduction of the original work in public would be allowed. The provision that most closely addresses display in art galleries and museums is s. 32(1)(b.1), which allows a person with a perceptual disability, a person acting at the request of such a person or for a non-profit organisation acting for the benefit of such a person to

> provide a person with a perceptual disability with, or provide such a person with access to, a work or other subject-matter to which any of paragraphs (a) to (b) applies, in a format specially designed for persons with a perceptual disability, and do any other act that is necessary for that purpose.

Clearly, if either the person with a disability or a non-profit organisation acting for the benefit of such a person, like a museum or a gallery, is allowed to make a copy in an adapted format, they should also be able to grant the beneficiary access to that format without any further restriction. Interpreting subsection 32(1)(b.1) of the *Copyright Act* differently would leave the entire provision devoid of any practical effect.

TPM circumvention

As addressed earlier, TPMs may impose significant limitations on the creation of 3D printed objects for people with perceptual disabilities. In addressing the consequences of this, the Act permits circumvention of TPMs for the purposes of making a work perceptible to a person with a perceptual disability. The legislative framework enabling circumvention of TPMs for perceptual disabilities is quite robust, and it allows numerous parties to circumvent TPMs, including the person with the perceptual disability, a "person acting at their request" and non-profit organisations.[32] Therefore, it is likely that an art gallery or museum's circumvention of TPMs for the purposes of making two-dimensional artworks perceptible as 3D reproductions would fall under this exception.

The Canadian Act also permits the Canadian federal government to enact further regulations which can permit additional grounds for circumventing TPMs, provided several factors are considered. Those factors include whether the inability to circumvent the TPM could "adversely affect the use a person may make of a work" and whether the work is "commercially available in a medium

31 Laurence Hefler, Molly K. Land, Ruth L. Okediji, and Jerome H. Reichman, *The World Blind Union Guide to the Marrakesh Treaty: Facilitating Access to Books for Print-Disabled Individuals*, (OUP 2017) 25.

32 *Copyright Act*, (n 16), s 41.16(1).

and in a quality that is appropriate for educational uses".[33] Taken together, it is likely that Canada's federal government could enact regulations permitting TPM circumvention for the specific case of transforming two-dimensional artwork into three dimensional objects. If the blanket exception in the Act is not currently broad enough to cover such activities (which seems unlikely), the ease of enacting additional regulations suggests that it would not be terribly difficult to include them.

Conclusion

This chapter explores whether, under the current Canadian copyright regime, the making and displaying of 3D reproductions of works of visual art for the benefit of persons with a disability would be considered lawful. For the purposes of this chapter, we posit that such reproductions would typically be performed either by a person with a disability or, more likely, by a museum or art gallery on behalf of such a person. Since this issue has yet to be examined by the courts, our assessment remains speculative. The creation and public exhibition of a three-dimensional reproduction of an artistic work would no doubt impact the rights granted under the *Copyright Act*. However, we believe that a non-profit organisation, such as a museum, would probably be able to successfully invoke the defence of fair dealing for the purpose of research and private study, or the application of the statutory exception for the benefit of persons with a perceptual disability. This interpretation gives the greatest meaning to Canada's ambition to make society as inclusive as possible for persons with a disability, including in the cultural and artistic life.[34]

33 *Copyright Act*, (n 16), s 41.21(2).

34 Economic and Social Development Canada, 'Building an Inclusive Canada: National Disability Summit: What We Learned Report' (Building an Inclusive Canada: National Disability Summit, Ottawa, 2019) 8.

13 Copyright limitations in Brazil[1]

Sérgio Branco[2] *and Beatriz Nunes*[3]

Introduction

Brazilian Copyright Law (hereafter referred to as BCL) grants authors both moral rights and economic rights. Moral rights, akin to personality rights, are inalienable and irrevocable.[4] Economic rights, on the other hand, concern the economic exploitation of a protected work. Article 29 of the BCL determines that *"the express prior authorization of the author of a literary, artistic or scientific work shall be required for any kind of use, such as (…)"*. This text is, evidently, exemplificative and is followed by a list of ten subsections that illustrate modalities of use, including partial or full reproduction, editing, adaptation, translation and computer storage.

Additionally, BCL creates mechanisms that provide balance between the interests of the copyright holder and the interests of society. This article critically analyzes the exceptions in BCL that protect people with a disability or people with a visual impairment (PVI), as well as the challenges imposed by the technological advancements that have taken place over the last decades. The chapter will focus on the application of the exceptions to the use of 3D printing technology so as to provide PVI access to artworks.

Limitations concerning disabilities in BCL

Article 29 of the BCL determines that any use should be preceded by the prior and explicit consent of the author. Limitations allow for the use of copyright-protected works without the prior express consent required by that provision in certain circumstances and to serve the interest of others.

Article 46, subsection I, lists several limitations to the rights accorded under Article 29. The provision protects different interests by exempting, for example,

1 The present article was originally written in Portuguese by both authors and was then translated by Beatriz Nunes.
2 Co-founder and Director of the Institute for Technology & Society of Rio de Janeiro (ITS Rio).
3 Specialist in Intellectual Property (PUC Rio). Currently works as Freelance Translator.
4 Article 27 BCL. Moral rights are inalienable and irrevocable.

the reproduction of news or informative articles or reports of public speeches (subparagraphs *a* and *b*).

Article 46, subsection 1, paragraph (d), is the only limitation which directly concerns PVI. It provides that it is not a violation of copyright to reproduce:

> literary, artistic or scientific works for the exclusive use of the visually handicapped, provided that the reproduction is done without gainful intent, either in Braille or by means of another process using a medium designed for such users.

Notably, the legislator opted for the expression "*visually handicapped*" instead of "blind". The former has a broader scope: many people who have sight problems are not necessarily blind, so the law will protect anyone who experiences a visual disability.

The exception requires that the reproduction be done "without gainful intent". It is uncertain if this means that only non-profit entities can reproduce and distribute works created for PVI. There is clearly no express condition to this effect imposed by the legislator. It therefore seems defendable that even an ordinary commercial publishing house would be allowed to offer this kind of work provided there is no gainful intent. We interpret this to mean that the reproduction should not result in, or be motivated by, profit.

Finally, the provision requires that the reproduction be in the form of the Braille system or of "another process using a medium designed for" PVI. For the purposes of this chapter, this raises the obvious question of whether 3D printing is such a process. Clearly, 3D printing is not a medium specifically "designed for" PVI, although, as this book makes clear, it can clearly benefit PVI.

This limitation has the potential to provide considerable social benefits for the 500,000 people in Brazil that are blind and 6,000,000 people with any degree of visual disability.[5] Despite this, there are no high court decisions concerning it. This perhaps reflects Brazil's (and the world's) failure to adequately provide PVI with access to artistic and cultural works. According to the World Blind Union, in 2013, "only some 7% of published books are ever made accessible (in formats such as Braille, audio and/or large print) in the richest countries, and less than 1% in poorer ones". According to the World Blind Union, "*this is a 'book famine'*".[6] Sadly, the same can be said regarding artistic works and their accessibility.

There is much discussion on whether the limitations in BCL should be interpreted restrictively or whether they can be given a broad interpretation. Despite the views of renowned copyright scholars such as Eliane Y. Abrão[7] and Carlos

5 Statistics on visual impairment in Brazil. Available at: <https://www.fundacaodorina.org.br/a-fundacao/deficiencia-visual/estatisticas-da-deficiencia-visual/>. Accessed on 10 March 2020.

6 World Blind Union. Press release – WIPO Negotiations Treaty for Blind People. Available at: <http://www.worldblindunion.org/English/news/Pages/JUne-17-Press-Release-for-WIPO-Book-Treaty.aspx>. Accessed on 10 March 2020.

7 "The list of works that are not dependent on the author's prior authorization for public use is exhaustive, categorical, because a limitation is an exception to the general rule, and when the

Alberto Bittar,[8] the Supreme Court of Justice (STJ), one of the highest courts in Brazil, has recently ruled that the limitations, considering the necessary balance between copyright protection and other constitutional principles, should be interpreted broadly.[9]

This interpretation is fundamental to the fulfillment of the rights and freedoms that are constitutionally granted (such as a right to education and freedom of speech). Moreover, it is consistent with the Disability Statute (Law no. 13.146),[10] enacted in 2015, which granted a series of rights to Brazilians with disabilities. Among them, article 42[11] states that a person with a disability has the right to culture, sport, tourism and leisure in equal opportunity with other persons. In addition, paragraph 1 determines that the refusal to offer intellectual works in a format accessible to persons with disabilities, on any grounds, including the claim of intellectual property rights protection, is prohibited. Superficially, this appears to provide stronger protection to PVI than the limitation in the BCL.

---

legislator fails to consider it as such, it will automatically demand an authorization prior to use". (Freely translated from the original by the authors). Abrão, Eliane Y. *Direitos de Autor e Direitos Conexos*. São Paulo: Migalhas, 2014, p. 342.

8 "On the other hand, it exhaustively lists the possibilities of free use (…)". Bittar, Carlos Alberto. *Direito de Autor*. Rio de Janeiro: Forense Universitária, 2004.

9 Appeal to the Federal Court no. 964.404 - ES (2007/0144450-5), Rep. Judge: Min. Paulo de Tarso Sanseverino: "If the limitations dealt with in articles 46, 47 and 48 of Law no. 9.610/98 represent the appreciation by the legislator of fundamental rights and guarantees as opposed to a right to copyright, which is also a fundamental right (article 5, subsection XXVII, of the CRFB), the mentioned limitations (articles 46, 47 and 48) derive from the pondering of certain values and situations, and thus cannot be considered as the totality of existing limitations." In this very sense, also considering the limitations of Law no. 9.610/98 non-exhaustive, see: Leonardo Macedo Poli, cited earlier, and Allan Rocha de Souza (The Social Function of Copyright: a civil-constitutional interpretation of the limits of legal protection: Brazil: 1988):

> I emphasize that an opposite interpretation would lead to the violation of rights or fundamental guarantees that, in certain concrete cases, should take precedence over copyright. It would also lead to the disrespect of the duty to optimize fundamental rights and guarantees (article 5, §1, of the CRFB), which bind not only the Legislative Power, but also the Judiciary Power.
>
> (Freely translated from the original)

Although the beginning of the text has a twisted and cryptic wording, what the decision emphasizes is that copyright cannot be viewed as absolute and must be weighed against other constitutional rights, such as freedom of expression. Thus, if copyright must reflect the result of weighting between multiple rights, the list of limitations cannot be considered as a closed list.

10 Disability Statute, Law no. 13. 146/2015. Available at: <http://www.planalto.gov.br/ccivil_03/_ato2015-2018/2015/lei/l13146.htm>. Accessed on 10 March 2020.

11 Article 42:

> Persons with disabilities have the right to culture, sport, tourism and leisure on equal terms with other persons, and are guaranteed access to: I – cultural assets in accessible format; II – television, cinema, theater and other cultural and sporting activities in accessible format; and III – monuments and places of cultural importance and spaces offering cultural and sporting services or events. §1° The refusal to offer intellectual works in an accessible format to persons with disabilities is prohibited, on any grounds, including the claim of intellectual property rights protection.

However, there are likely to be practical difficulties applying the PVI limitation in the BCL, particularly to 3D printing. Brazilian judges have little or no background in copyright litigation, and issue diverse and, at times, contradictory decisions, which lead to uncertainty. The STJ's decision to interpret limitations broadly is fundamental for the adaptation of both the wording and application of the limitations to the development and adoption of new technologies. However, undoubtedly, the best solution would be to revise the legal text so as to explicitly mention which uses are allowed under the limitation system of the BCL, or at least express those uses in technology-neutral language which do not need to be updated with each technological development. Technologies constantly surpass existing legislation, and 3D printing technology is an example not contemplated by the current law (although it has been applied and used in Brazil for educational, artistic, scientific and, most significantly, for accessibility purposes).[12]

3D printing, accessibility and copyright

The term 3D printing includes various additive manufacturing techniques. It is a form of rapid prototyping in which three-dimensional digital models from a digital file are created by adding materials that accumulate layer by layer.[13] There are a variety of 3D printing methods, each of which works differently and uses specific materials, which can range from plastic filaments to even human tissue and food/edible matter.[14]

The 3D printing is currently used for a variety of purposes, from printing actual, functioning human organs to custom-made prostheses, or even applying the technology to the high-fashion industry. In short, the technology in question reproduces a physical object, giving it tangible life by transforming data from a digital file into something physical, "touchable".

The combination of 3D scanners and 3D printing technologies is already applied, for example, as an enabler for consuming artworks at various accessible art

12 In 2017, UNIFEBE (located in Santa Catarina/Brazil), inaugurated a Center for Innovation, the *Laboratório In 3D*, the first MakerBot Innovation Center in Brazil. The lab started with 8 3D MakerBot printers. See: <https://www.wishbox.net.br/blog/centro-de-inovacao-com-impressoras-3d-unifebe/#btn-continuar-lendo>. Accessed on 10 March 2020. Teachers can use 3D printers to encourage students to think about projects, parts, problem solving, etc. In an increasingly digital world, understanding new needs is critical to training and learning process. Many schools are investing in new technologies, such as 3D printers. São Paulo has invested in new computer equipment and 3D printers for the municipal school system, aiming to creatively stimulate children and young adults (See: <https://3dlab.com.br/impressao-3d-na-educacao/>. Accessed on 10 March 2020.

13 Nunes, Beatriz Laus Marinho. "*Printing Fashion: The Impact of 3D Printing in the Intellectual Property Regime and in the Fashion Industry*", pp. 39–40. Available at: <https://www.maxwell.vrac.puc-rio.br/37300/37300.PDF>. Accessed on 10 March 2020.

14 Fávero, Luciana. "*Blindness and the Visual Arts: How Assistive Technologies Can Be an Inclusion Tool*", p. 57. Available at: <http://repositorio.unicamp.br/jspui/bitstream/REPOSIP/333152/1/Favero_Luciana_M.pdf>. Accessed on 10 March 2020. See also in this book the chapter by Noel Daemen.

exhibitions, just as 3D scanners are used for the purpose of preserving an object. However, the issue is complicated when it comes to applying the 3D printing technology, given that the technology provides a re-materialization of a certain object or artwork. In theory, this re-materialization would depend on consent/authorization by the copyright holder of the artwork in question since BCL determines, as per article 29, that every copy of a given artwork should be preceded by prior and explicit authorization, if it is not yet in the public domain.

The existing legislation is silent when it comes to new technologies that are becoming increasingly accessible and essential for the fulfillment of constitutional rights (such as access to education and culture for everyone regardless of any social, physical or any other difference).

The current copyright system lists all copyright limitations. Those limitations are silent on the possibility of reproducing copyrighted objects through 3D printers and/or scanners. As mentioned, this form of reproduction has been developed and applied for educational purposes, accessibility, as well as in the recovery of artworks. In all cases, the final objective is to provide access to education and culture, especially for those with a disability, thus promoting greater accessibility. The technology is also applied for restoration and conservation purposes, as occurred, for instance, in the case of the National Museum (in Rio de Janeiro).[15]

Although existing legislation makes no reference to 3D printing, there are already several projects around the world that use 3D printing and 3D scanners for educational and accessibility purposes for the benefit of PVI. By way of example, the "Touching the Prado"[16] project, from the Prado Museum in Spain, launched its first initiative focused on visually impaired visitors, based on innovation and technology. As a result of this project, six works that represented different pictorial genres found in the Museum's collections can now be touched. The project, which was developed in collaboration with professionals in the visual impairment sector, allows for the reality of the painting to be perceived so that those who are visually impaired can "mentally" recreate the work of art, thus providing an emotional perception of the work in those who cannot see it. In other words, PVI will also experience a heightened degree of artistic-aesthetic-creative enjoyment of those works of art. Not only are they presented with 3D images but also with didactic material about the artworks in Braille.

15 The National Museum was destroyed by a fire in September 2018. Researchers had been developing a project for the creation of three-dimensional replicas on 3D printers for over 20 years, and had the idea of reconstructing some of the works of art as well as the lost parts with the material resulting from the fire itself. Hundreds of items, including Luzia's skull (the face of South America's oldest human fossil), Egyptian amulets, fossils, millennial vessels and even a mummy's coffin have undergone a process of recreation and full-size assembly, with printing being the final step – see <https://g1.globo.com/rj/rio-de-janeiro/noticia/2018/09/21/pesquisadores-recriam-parte-do-acervo-do-museu-nacional-incluindo-o-cranio-de-luzia-com-impressoras-3d.ghtml>. Accessed on 14 March 2020.

16 *Museo del Prado*. Available at: <https://www.museodelprado.es/en/whats-on/exhibition/touching-the-prado/29c8c453-ac66-4102-88bd-e6e1d5036ffa>. Accessed on 10 March 2020.

Similarly, in Rio Grande do Sul (Brazil), a digital repository gathers 3D models of paintings and other works of art from museums, as well as buildings and monuments,[17] in order to foster the conservation of historical and cultural heritage. Just like the Spanish project, they use 3D printing to provide access to culture for PVI. The 3D models, as explained by one of the project's creators, besides being available to anyone with Internet access, allow the works to be analyzed from different angles and enable access to people with disabilities, since the replicas are both tangible and palpable.[18]

Another project, the "Tactile Books Project", conceived by a team from the University of Colorado Boulder (USA) led by Tom Yeh, used the 3D printing technology for the development of children's literature classics, in Braille, and added 3D printed tactile graphics (illustrations, images, objects, etc.). Tactile pictures make the content of a book relatable and legible, and help in the development of a child's tactile acuity and mobility, their sense of seeing or feeling of their environment, as well as their confidence in exploring and building relationships and associations through touch.[19] The goal of the project is thus to develop a software that transforms images in children's books into 3D forms, through the use of computation algorithms, providing an interface that allows parents and teachers to print their own customized picture books using the 3D technology. As Yeh explains: "Ideally a parent could choose a book, take a picture of a page, and send the picture to a 3D printer, which would result in a 3D tactile book".[20]

How would current legislation apply in the cases described? Would they be included in copyright limitations? These are 3D reproductions that convey the intent of the artist or author (especially in the case of children's books) to PVI. Under Article 46, I, subparagraph "d" BCL, it is important to note that the law refers to "literary, *artistic* or scientific works" and not only to literary works. By

17 *LDSM - Repositório 3D do Laboratório de Design e Seleção de Materiais.* Available at: <https://www.ufrgs.br/ldsm/3d/>. Accessed on 10 March 2020.

18 Raposo, Camila. *Repositório digital reúne modelos 3D de peças de museus, prédios e monumentos.* Available at: <http://www.ufrgs.br/secom/ciencia/repositorio-digital-reune-modelos-3d-de-pecas-de-museus-predios-e-monumentos/>. Accessed on 10 March 2020.

19 Stangl, Abigale, Kim, Jeeeun and Yeh, Tom. (2014). *3D Printed Tactile Picture Books for Children with Visual Impairments.* Available at: <https://www.researchgate.net/publication/300388617_3D_printed_tactile_picture_books_for_children_with_visual_impairments> Accessed on 10 March 2020.

20 In Brazil, 3D printing technology has also been applied for the purposes of providing PVI with the possibility of better or fully experiencing an important moment. The Brazilian company *Cammada*, in partnership with TV Globo, which is a famous Brazilian open television network, granted such a moment for a young visually impaired girl. *Cammada's* founding partner, João Faro, selected a sequence of images of the goals scored by her father, a Brazilian football player, and printed them in tactile graphics using a 3D printer. These images, now in Braille and in 3D, were presented to the player's visually impaired daughter so she could "see" and thus fully experience her father's passes, which, at the time, were significant in Brazilian football history. See: Cammada. Available at: <http://blog.cammada.com/>. Accessed on 10 March 2020.

mentioning artistic works, the interpretation can be broader to include the reproduction of paintings, sculptures and other examples of visual arts.

The 3D printing already allows the complete reproduction of a particular object, including works of art, as well as the integration of Braille on any surface. Therefore, the use of 3D printing technology would, based on a broad interpretation, be considered lawful according to the aforementioned limitation. The 3D printing technology can fulfill an educational objective, as it offers new opportunities for PVI and is also a way of facilitating the exercise of the right of access to culture. This must be considered when assessing the technology at hand vis-à-vis the laws in force.

Conclusion

Copyright limitations, which play a key role in the copyright protection system, are constantly challenged by the advent of new technologies. The faithful, physical, 3D reproduction of artworks protected by copyright was, until recently, considered unthinkable. Taking into consideration this constant technological evolution in our society, the current copyright system must be rethought or, at the very least, interpreted more broadly to contemplate new technologies, including the use of 3D printers and scanners.

Moreover, it is important to consider and acknowledge the benefit of new experiences provided as a result of the use of 3D printing, whether intended for PVI or for a broader audience. 3D printing is promising in this context. Its use in combination with research, such as that developed by researchers from Rio Grande do Sul, has allowed for the faithful reproduction of artworks with tactile qualities, enabling access by everyone.

This makes it essential to interpret the existing limitations in the BCL broadly in order to facilitate 3D printing for the purpose of providing access to culture, knowledge and leisure by PVI. To achieve greater certainty, this may require changes to existing legislation or even the creation of specific legislation. Only then will we be fulfilling the command to promote, as the Brazilian Federal Constitution imposes, the construction of a free, just and solidary society.

14 UK pathways towards an equal access to creative works

Sabine Jacques

Introduction

Some readers of this book may not have had previous cause to contemplate how persons with a visual impairment (PVI) access visual creative works. To do so, they must rely upon other senses, such as hearing or touch. In the case of a literary work, for example, PVI may require a Braille version or a copy of the work in a format compatible with screen reading software. Unfortunately, converting a work into a software-compatible file may be problematic, and a Braille version may fail to convey the same user experience as the 'original'. We can also think of analogous issues with other two-dimensional ('2-D') art works (such as drawings, paintings or photographs) or three-dimensional ('3-D') works (such as large statues or works of architecture) which are just too large to be fully appreciated via the sense of touch. Different kinds of works (such as improvisational theatre) may simply be inaccessible or ill-suited for tactual exploration.

Yet international human rights law protects against discrimination and advocates for equal access to culture. This is demonstrated by principles of non-discrimination, equality and ability to take part in cultural life proclaimed by the Universal Declaration of Human Rights,[1] the European Convention on Human Rights,[2] the International Covenant on Economic, Social and Cultural Rights,[3] the Convention on the Rights of Persons with Disabilities[4] and the EU Charter of Fundamental Rights.[5]

This chapter first traces the development of UK copyright law with respect to the disability exceptions enshrined in sections 31A to 31F of the Copyright,

1 Articles 19 and 27 Universal Declaration of Human Rights ('UDHR') 1948.

2 Article 10(1) of the European Convention on Human Rights ('ECHR') 1950.

3 Article 15 of the International Covenant on Economic, Social and Cultural Rights 1966.

4 Article 30 of the Convention on the Rights of Persons with Disabilities 2006. Notably, this instrument requires taking into account the needs of PVI beyond literary works, to include 'literature, artefacts, radio, screen and television productions, performance and visual arts'. See P. Harpur, *Discrimination, Copyright and Equality: Opening the E-book for the Print-Disabled* (CUP, 2017) 60.

5 Articles 11 and 21 of the Charter of Fundamental Rights of the European Union *OJ* C 326, 26.10.2012, 391–407.

Designs and Patents Act 1988 (CDPA)[6] and demonstrates how the exception permits a broader range of uses than the minimum required by international standards. The chapter then concentrates on visual disability to assess whether the UK provisions are capable of adapting with technological developments which offer new ways to create accessible copies. It looks specifically at the potential wealth of opportunities offered by 3-D scanning and printing techniques.

A translation or a reproduction?

Before turning to the scope of disability exceptions under UK copyright law, it is necessary to identify which of the right-holder's exclusive rights may be engaged in the case of the transformation of a 2-D artwork, such as a painting, into a 3-D object, such as a sculpture. One might wonder whether this action triggers the reproduction right, the adaptation right or perhaps both. This is not a mere theoretical question, as the right-holder may be different in each case, meaning different authorisations are required. Additionally, as we shall see later, the UK disability exceptions do not apply to the adaptation right. Consequently, if producing an accessible copy and any intermediate copies is deemed to be an act of adaptation, then these would always require the right-holder's permission.

Pursuant to the CDPA, the exclusive right of adaptation[7] includes a change of format of the work (e.g. turning a literary work into a play or cinematographic work, or vice versa;[8] or turning a literary or dramatic work into a comic strip).[9] It also includes the right to translate a protected work. Although 'translation' generally involves a change of language whilst the original content and form is maintained, the term also encompasses a change of format or medium.[10] However, as aptly argued by Vaver,[11] under copyright law, producing a Braille version of a literary work which simply involves replacing each word with the Braille dot pattern is a conversion into an accessible form, and not a *translation*.[12] Rather, the end result is an exact reproduction of the original words in a symbolic representation.

Similarly, as UK copyright law defines 'reproduction' as a reproduction into 'any material form', the conversion of a 2-D work into a 3-D form dimensional work should also be understood as triggering the reproduction right rather than being a translation or adaptation. This is reinforced by the fact that CDPA[13] explicitly excludes artistic works (including visual arts) from the scope of the

6 1988 c. 48 amended by The Copyright and Rights in Performances (Disability) Regulations 2014 No. 1384.

7 Section 21(3)(a)(i) CDPA.

8 Section 21(3)(a)(ii) CDPA.

9 Section 21(3)(a)(iii) CDPA.

10 Oxford English Dictionary, third edition, March 2019.

11 D. Vaver, 'Translation and Copyright: A Canadian Focus' (1994) 16(4) *EIPR*, 159–166, 159.

12 *Express Newspapers plc v News (UK) Ltd* [1990] 1 WLR 1320; *Walter v Lane* [1899] 2 Ch. 749, 758, aff'd [1900] AC 539. Also confirmed in *Ladbroke v William Hill* [1964] 1 All ER.

13 Section 21(1) CDPA.

adaptation right. Thus, accessible 'conversions' of paintings, prints, photos, crafts and sculptures and so forth are dealt with exclusively under the reproduction right. However, the position could be different in a scenario in which a character which is only described, rather than illustrated, in a book is 'translated' into a 3-D printed form. This act might trigger the adaptation right in respect of that literary work.[14]

Overall, whilst some overlap of exclusive rights (perhaps in the case of a film or a literary work) is possible,[15] this should be avoided where possible. Vaver suggests (relying upon Goldstein's work)[16] that to differentiate between a reproduction and a translation is to compare its destination market with that for the original. Where the two markets are different, then it is more likely that we are dealing with a *translation or adaptation* than a reproduction.[17] Again, this rule of thumb suggests that an accessible 3-D form is a reproduction because the aim is not to create a new market for a work, but to enable people with disabilities to access the original market.

Background to the UK copyright disability exceptions

In terms of international copyright law, the Marrakesh Treaty,[18] eventually adopted in 2013, seeks to provide an effective, equitable framework which respects the rights of copyright holders but still permits those who are blind, visually impaired or otherwise print-disabled to access copyright-protected materials. It does this by providing an exception which permits the making of accessible copies, subject to certain requirements.[19]

Prior to the Marrakesh Treaty, the EU had taken steps to harmonise the copyright disability exception through the Information Society Directive 2001/29/EC ('InfoSoc Directive').[20] Article 5(3)(b) of this Directive permits EU Member States to introduce a disability exception into national copyright law with respect to the reproduction, communication to the public and making available to the public rights – provided that the use is for non-commercial purposes and

14 Going beyond what is authorised under section 21(3)(iii) CDPA, which envisaged turning literary works into images only for the purpose of a 'book, newspaper, magazine or similar periodical'. See also J. McCutcheon, 'Making Art from Words: The Picturisation Adaptation Right' in J. McCutcheon & F. McGaughey (eds) *The Research Handbook on Art and Law* (forthcoming 2020, Edward Elgar Publishing Ltd), available at SSRN: https://ssrn.com/abstract=3389634.

15 Section 21(5) CDPA. For more see L. Bently, B. Sherman, D. Gangjee & P. Johnson, *Intellectual Property Law* (Oxford, 5th ed., 2018) 177.

16 P. Goldstein, 'Derivative Rights and Derivative Works in Copyright' (1982) 30 *Jo. Cop. Soc. USA* 209.

17 *Supra* n. 15, 159.

18 The Marrakesh Treaty to Facilitate Access to Published Works for Persons Who Are Blind, Visually Impaired, or Otherwise Print Disabled 2013 ('Marrakesh Treaty').

19 For more on the international legal frameworks, see further, Schneider, this volume.

20 Directive 2001/29/EC of the European Parliament and of the Council of 22 May 2001 on the harmonisation of certain aspects of copyright and related rights in the information society *OJ* L 167, 22.6.2001, 10–19. On the EU dimension, see further, Ramalho, this volume.

required for equal access by the person with the disability. However, as this exception is not mandatory, the option to do so has not been taken up in all EU Member States.

In the case of the UK, the UK legislator took the InfoSoc Directive as an opportunity to establish the practice developed under the disabilities legislation within the copyright framework. The scope of the permitted use goes much further than the Marrakesh minimum, as the disability exceptions are not limited by the nature of the disability or impairment but are based upon broad notions of inclusion and non-discrimination. This can be traced back to the Disability Discrimination Act 1995,[21] replaced by the Equality Act 2010.[22] This anti-discrimination legislation imposes a duty upon those who provide goods, services and facilities to make 'reasonable adjustments' to ensure that persons with disabilities are not placed at a 'substantial disadvantage' compared to those without disability. In other words, making reasonable adjustment is not an altruistic act, but a legal responsibility, and failure to do so is unlawful discrimination under the Act.[23]

For publishers, the need to make reasonable adjustments requires them to provide a 'reasonable alternative method'[24] for making their products accessible to PVI. In practice, a publisher either offered an accessible format of the work – generally in the form of large print, audio or Braille – or established a licensing scheme so that others may produce accessible formats. One advantage of the latter is that it becomes possible to tailor the form of the accessible version to an individual's particular disability.

The following section explains the further evolution of these provisions and identifies who may rely upon them as a possible defence to any claim of copyright infringement.

In the EU, the European Commission responded to the Marrakesh Treaty with Directive 2017/1564[25] and Regulation 2017/1563,[26] which were adopted in September 2017. The Regulation came into force directly on 12 October 2018, and EU Member States were required to transpose the Directive into

21 1995 c. 50. Note, the Disability Discrimination Act 1995 is still in force in Northern Ireland.

22 2010 c. 15.

23 Section 21 of the Equality Act 2010.

24 Section 21(2)(d) of the Disability Discrimination Act 1995 and similarly in section 20 of the Equality Act 2010.

25 Directive (EU) 2017/1564 of the European Parliament and of the Council of 13/9/2017 on certain permitted uses of certain works and other subject matter protected by copyright and related rights for the benefit of persons who are blind, visually impaired or otherwise print-disabled and amending Directive 2001/29/EC on the harmonisation of certain aspects of copyright and related rights in the information society OJ L 242, 20.9.2017, 6–13.

26 Regulation (EU) 2017/1563 of the European Parliament and of the Council of 13/9/2017 on the cross-border exchange, between the Union and third countries, of accessible format copies of certain works and other subject matter protected by copyright and related rights for the benefit of persons who are blind, visually impaired or otherwise print-disabled OJ L 242, 20.9.2017, 1–5.

national legislation before that date. In the UK,[27] consultations were undertaken to determine whether current national legislation was compliant with the obligations under the Marrakesh Treaty[28][29] and the EU Directive. This resulted in a revision of the disability exceptions.[30]

Previously, the exception included the requirement of a prior check to determine whether a suitable accessible copy was already commercially available. This created uncertainty as to whether the exception applied in a situation where a publisher had made an 'accessible copy' of the work available, but which might not be suitable for a user's particular disability. The 2018 revision removed this precondition, which is a particularly welcome reduction of the burden on users and bodies acting on their behalf.

Although right-holders had called for a compensation scheme to be introduced with respect to the potential increased unauthorised use of their works, this was rejected based upon a lack of sound economic evidence that they suffered any real harm.[31] Additionally, the UK government elected to open up the disability exceptions beyond the 'making and supply' of accessible copies required by the Directive to also permit communication to the public or public performance of accessible format copies.[32]

Finally, the exception was broadened to encompass more kinds of works. Whereas the Marrakesh Treaty limits itself to literary and artistic works 'in the form of text, notations and/or related illustrations',[33] the CDPA disability exceptions now apply to all categories of copyright-protected works,[34] including entrepreneurial works such as broadcasts and sound recordings. As the exceptions are mandatory,[35] these cannot be circumvented by contractual provisions.

Who benefits from the UK copyright disability exceptions?

The original UK copyright exceptions, introduced in 2002, only applied to literary, dramatic, musical and artistic works and only benefitted users who were

27 Whilst the UK's EU membership remains uncertain following the 'Brexit' referendum result in 2016, as the UK is itself a member of the Berne Convention and has indicated it intends to ratify the Marrakesh Treaty (if and when) it leaves the EU, UK law must still conform with the provisions of this treaty. The initial leaving date of 29/3/2019 has since been extended until 31/10/2019. Presently, the UK is still a member of the EU.

28 UK Intellectual Property Office ('IPO'), Consultation On UK's Implementation of the Marrakesh Treaty (8 May 2018), available at https://assets.publishing.service.gov.uk/government/uploads/system/uploads/attachment_data/file/705158/marrakesh-treaty.pdf

29 UK IPO, Government Response to Marrakesh Consultation (10/9/2018), available at https://assets.publishing.service.gov.uk/government/uploads/system/uploads/attachment_data/file/738669/Marrakesh-Government-Response.pdf

30 The Copyright and Related Rights (Marrakesh Treaty etc.) (Amendment) Regulations 2018, No. 995.

31 *Supra* n. 31.

32 Sections 31B & 31BA CDPA.

33 Article 2 of the Marrakesh Treaty.

34 Section 1(1) CDPA.

35 Section 31F(8) CDPA.

blind, visually impaired or could not physically hold a book.[36] It permitted persons with a disability to make accessible copies themselves or for these to be made by educational institutions and not-for-profit organisations.[37]

Since the revisions in 2014[38] and 2018,[39]discussed earlier, the scope of the exception now extends to all disability types, including any physical disability that prevents users from holding or manipulating a book as well as perceptual or cognitive disabilities, such as dyslexia or a hearing impairment.[40] The only limitation in terms of visual disability is that a user will not be considered disabled if the impairment can be improved to an acceptable level, such as by use of corrective lenses.[41] The intent is that the exceptions apply to anyone whose disability prevents them from enjoying the work in the same manner as a person who does not have that disability. The UK approach contrasts with the Marrakesh Treaty, which is only limited to blindness, visual impairment and related disabilities, and fails to provide any standards for establishing when a person *is* blind or which visual impairments qualify. The Marrakesh terminology is, therefore, open to different national interpretations based on different national standards for blindness, meaning that an individual may qualify in one country but not in another.

Individuals are not the only ones to benefit from a disability exceptions. To facilitate access to creative works, certain organisations may benefit too. A second provision extends the beneficiaries beyond educational institutions to not-for-profit organisations without the need for a specific licence. The CDPA collectively calls these qualifying organisations 'authorised bodies'.

Despite some differences between the Marrakesh and the UK provisions, both similarly require accessible copies to be made from lawful copies or those obtained lawfully.[42] Both prohibit any changes made to the work beyond what is necessary for the purpose of making an accessible format for an individual with a disability.[43] Finally, the copying (including the conversion) and the exclusive supply to a beneficiary party can only be done on a not-for-profit basis (by an individual, educational institutions or a not-for-profit organisation).[44]

Relying upon the CDPA disability exceptions

The net result of the recent legislative activity, discussed earlier, is that a user in the UK now has two ways to obtain a lawful accessible copy of a copyright-protected

36 Copyright (Visually Impaired Persons) Act 2002, 2002 c. 33. For more, see D. Bradshaw, 'Making Books and Other Copyright Works Accessible, without Infringement, to the Visually Impaired: A Review of the Practical Operation of the Applicable, and Recently-Enacted, UK Legislation' (2005) 4 *Intellectual Property Quarterly* 335, 335–360.

37 Section 31B(12) CDPA as introduced in 2003.

38 Ensuring compliance with the Equality Act 2010, see sections 31A-31F CDPA. *Supra* n. 10.

39 *Supra* n. 32.

40 In accordance with article 3 of the Marrakesh Treaty.

41 Section 31F(3) CDPA.

42 Sections 31A(1)(a) & 31B(1)(a) CDPA.

43 Section 31F(5)(b) CDPA.

44 Section 31F(6) CDPA.

work: they may make their own copy, or they may obtain a suitable copy from an authorised body. In each case, the CDPA imposes certain requirements for lawful use.[45] First, the making of an accessible format under the exception is for the user's *own* personal use,[46] that is, the beneficiary may not make multiple accessible copies for wider distribution, for example, online for a fee. Second,[47] as Lord Morris explained during the second reading of the bill, introducing this requirement in 2002:

> A visually impaired person can only have an accessible copy [...] where they have lawfully in their possession or are lawfully able to use, such as in a reference library, what is called a "master copy" of the copyright material. Of course, the master copy will generally have involved payment of copyright royalties to the owners.[48]

Arguably, this second 'lawful possession' requirement constitutes a hurdle for disabled persons in pursuit of equal access to cultural works. For example, the Internet abounds with images which sighted people take for granted while conducting a search or scrolling through their social media feeds. However, as such media are likely to include unauthorised reproductions of copyright-protected works, PVI wishing to make an accessible copy will not be able to rely upon the disability exceptions. They will have to enter into lawful possession of the work prior to the making of this accessible copy that may involve added burden if the right-holder is difficult to identify. Whilst such a position is justifiable under copyright law, it does create inequalities in terms of accessible content between individuals.

The provisions impose additional obligations where an accessible copy is made by an authorised body acting on behalf of beneficiaries. Not only must they make and supply accessible copies based upon lawful access of a protected work, but the body must also take appropriate steps to prevent unauthorised reproduction or distribution of the resulting copies, or its communication or making them available to the public.[49] Since UK copyright law is required to grant copyright-holders a high level of protection,[50] authorised bodies must maintain *and* make available records which demonstrate compliance with these statutory requirements,[51] either through online (e.g. a website) or offline (e.g. a catalogue) channels.[52]

45 Section 31A CDPA.
46 Section 31A(2)(b) CDPA.
47 Section 31A(2) CDPA.
48 Hansard, H.L. Vol.637, col.905 (July 12, 2002).
49 Section 31B(1A)(b) CDPA.
50 Also a way to ensure compliance with the three-step test as enshrined in article 9(2) Berne Convention for the Protection of Literary and Artistic Works of 9 September 1886 as amended at Paris on 28 September 1979, and repeated in the Agreement on Trade-related Aspects of Intellectual Property Rights of 1994.
51 Section 31B(1A)(c) CDPA.
52 Section 31B(1A)(d) CDPA.

Importantly, an authorised body is permitted to make intermediate copies of a work which assists in the making of an accessible copy,[53] and these intermediate copies may be stored and/or lent to other authorised bodies, which may then also supply accessible copies. A specific example may help to appreciate the significance of this provision. We shall look at making an accessible copy of a painting which involves 3-D printing to translate it into a tactile 3-D form.

The 3-D printing process typically involves two phases, digitalisation and printing, which might result in various intermediate copies.[54] During the first phase of digitalisation, a digital copy of the work is made. This is akin to an electronic scanned version of a book being turned into an accessible copy by processing the scan using Optical Character Recognition software. This phase can itself be subdivided into four steps.[55]

First, there is the identification of the correct display on the scan bed of a 3-D scanner. In our painting example, the person scanning must take account of the position of the painting on the scan bed, the lighting, distances, glossing, background and so forth. The choices made at this stage determine the quality of the 3-D printed copy. The second step involves the actual scanning to produce a digital file (often called a CAD file). The scanning process may be manual (i.e. a person physically moves around the painting on the scan bed), partially automated (e.g. placing the painting on a rotary table while the person overseeing the scan remains static) or completely automated. In the third step, the digital file is reworked to remove any anomalies. In the final step, the file is converted into a form (known as a CAM file) suitable for manufacturing a 3-D replica using a 3-D printer.[56]

However, scanning is not the only way to make a 3-D printed object. Potentially, a suitable digital file may already exist and be available for a user simply to download from a platform. Yet, using an existing file is only permitted for the making of an accessible copy according to the UK disability exceptions if it is a lawful copy. Additionally, there is the possibility that this file of instructions might itself constitute a protected copyright work. In *Abraham Moon & Sons Ltd v Thornber & Ors*,[57] the court considered allegations of infringement of a 'ticket stamp' – the set of written instructions for setting up a loom for the manufacture of a particular fabric design. It recognised the ticket stamp as an artistic work (as well as a literary work), even though it lacked any visual representations, because it served as the record of a visual image, which would have visual significance to fabric designers.[58] Extrapolating this logic to our area of interest, it seems arguable that a file containing instructions for the 3-D manufacture of a 3-D

53 Section 31BA(1) CDPA.

54 See further, Daemen, this volume.

55 M. Laar & J. W. Gunnick, *The Shape of Things to Come: An Introduction to the Design, Rapid Manufacturing and Business Opportunities of Customized Products* (Berenschot, 2009) 15–22.

56 Ibid.

57 [2012] EWPCC 37 (05 October 2012).

58 Ibid., at [90].

form could similarly qualify as an artistic and/or literary work (if the originality requirement is met).

Overall, it is evident that lawfully making a 3-D version of a protected visual work is far from straightforward. Even if the CAM file itself constitutes a lawful copy of a protected painting, or if the painting is a work already in the public domain, the file itself may enjoy separate copyright protection. It is also easy to imagine scenarios in which the right-holders of the 'original' work and the CAM file may be different. Furthermore, the act of scanning may have the effect of 'reviving' copyright in public domain works.

This may render the making of other digital files enabling 3-D versions of works more difficult, as it is likely that these will amount to a substantial reproduction of the original. Claimants able to demonstrate that the 3-D copy has been made in accordance to their instructions would presumably be successful in court despite the absence of direct reproduction of the claimant's work.[59]

Even though the description of the various stages has been simplified, our example illustrates how intermediate copies may arise between the original work (the painting) and the accessible version (a 3-D version of the painting). Although the UK disability exceptions are relatively broad, it has been conceived with permitting access to literary and cinematographic works. Application to visual art remains unchartered territory, and making of 3-D accessible versions of works may fall outside its scope. In particular, if any intermediate copies fall outside the scope of permitted acts, the effectiveness of the UK copyright disability exceptions is undermined. Would-be beneficiaries may be forced to seek permission both from the right-holder of the visual artwork *and* the right-holder of the digital CAM file which they need to access. Also, based upon *Abraham Moon*,[60] the digital file might qualify as a literary work which would qualify for the adaptation right under s.21 CDPA, meaning our previous concern regarding the overlap between reproduction and adaptation right is revived.[61]

Supplying accessible copies against remuneration

It is evident from the language and the scope of the UK disability exceptions, that the legislator attached importance to principles of equality and non-discrimination. Nevertheless, the provisions also strike a balance to ensure that equal access does not jeopardise copyright holders' existing business models, including the 'official' licensing schemes already in place.

The Marrakesh Treaty permits authorised bodies that are not-for-profit organisations to receive remuneration for the accessible copies which they make and supply.[62] Although a UK regulation[63] in 2014 permitted the then eligible

59 Ibid., at [91].
60 *Supra* n. 59.
61 *Supra* section 2 of this chapter.
62 Article 4.5 Marrakesh Treaty.
63 *Supra*, n. 6.

organisations to levy a charge which did not 'exceed the cost of the making and supplying' copies[64] (attempting to head off litigation concerning the appropriate level of remuneration),[65] this was rescinded in the 2018 revisions. Although the reason surrounding the change is somewhat unclear, it seems that the provision was removed to more faithfully replicate the exception in EU Directive 2017/1564.[66]

Removal of a provision which permits a body to recoup costs strongly suggests that the current UK disability exceptions only apply to those which provide accessible copies to users free of charge.[67] This might have a detrimental effect on organisations which might otherwise invest in innovative ways to render works accessible. Nevertheless, requiring an authorised body to provide free accessible copies may be justified.[68] Firstly, it simplifies the process of obtaining accessible copies, which should encourage beneficiaries and authorised bodies to exercise their rights. Secondly, removing all financial barriers to access ensures that no discrimination between individuals occurs based upon personal financial circumstances. Finally, the disability exceptions are aligned with most other UK copyright exceptions which are not contingent upon remuneration.

In practice, the lack of international harmonisation on this issue is undesirable. Wider dissemination of creative works between signatory parties to the Marrakesh Treaty may be hindered if some countries operate a compensation scheme while others do not, and it is unclear what happens, for example, if free accessible copies made in the UK are exported to a country where compensation is payable.[69]

Supporting greater dissemination of accessible copies

While UK copyright law may regulate activities occurring within this jurisdiction, in practice, cross-border supply of accessible works occurs. For example, the UK-based Copyright Licensing Agency (CLA) grants a 'print disability licence'

64 Former section 31A(3) CDPA.

65 Notably, there is no guidance in the Marrakesh Treaty on what constitutes an appropriate remuneration. J. Li & N. Selvadurai, Reconciling the Enforcement of Copyright with the Upholding of Human Rights: A Consideration of the Marrakesh Treaty to Facilitate Access to Published Works for the Blind, Visually Impaired and Print Disabled (2014) 36(10) *European Intellectual Property Review* 653, 653–664.

66 Section 31A(3) and 31B(10) were both removed from the CDPA by 2018 Regulations (SI 2018/995).

67 In accordance to article 3(6) of Directive 2017/1564 (*supra* n. 26) which goes further than the Marrakesh Treaty. For more, see J. Kouletakis, 'No Man Is an Island: A Critical Analysis of the UK's Implementation of the Marrakesh Treaty' forthcoming in *SCRIPTed*, available at https://rke.abertay.ac.uk/ws/portalfiles/portal/16201896/Kouletakis_NoManIsAnIsland_Accepted_2019.pdf.

68 L. R. Helfer, M. K. Land, R. L. Okediji & J. H. Reichman, *The World blind Union Guide to the Marrakesh Treaty* (2017) 123–124, available at https://www.wipo.int/edocs/mdocs/copyright/en/wipo_cr_mow_17/wipo_cr_mow_17_topic_2_c.pdf.

69 Ibid., at [124–127].

which allows non-UK, EU authorised bodies located outside the UK to distribute accessible copies within the EU. Undoubtedly, introducing a specific copyright exception for the making of accessible copies facilitates access by persons with a disability. Yet, a significant barrier remains unless there is a mechanism to enable cross-border access of works.

The Marrakesh Treaty requires signatories to permit cross-border supply of accessible formats to beneficiaries or authorised entities in all other contracting states. Any barriers to the importation of such copies from other contracting states must be removed.[70] On implementing the Treaty, the UK concluded that the existing CDPA provisions were already compliant, since there were no existing restrictions on the export of accessible copies.[71] Additionally, the CDPA[72] already specifies that importation of accessible formats into the UK does not violate UK copyright law.

While this may suggest that cross-border supply and importation are unproblematic, it is naïve to assume that transnational activities are straightforward in practice. For example, national legislation may comply with the Marrakesh framework, yet still establish different standards for qualification as a beneficiary. Current low levels of harmonisation on this, and other issues, must surely create difficulties when nationally authorised bodies from different jurisdictions try to cooperate.

Contractual override

In 2011, a wide-ranging review of UK copyright law recommended a blanket ban to prevent contractual overriding of any of the CDPA's exceptions and limitations.[73] Although the UK government adopted a more tailored approach instead, the disability exceptions are ones which cannot be circumvented by a contractual clause.[74] Consequently, any contract clause, whether in a copyright licence, a subscription agreement or elsewhere, which purports to bypass the disability exceptions, is now unenforceable. This is a welcome departure from the UK's usual golden rule of freedom of contract and goes further than the prohibition on unreasonably restrictive licence terms, which it replaced.[75]

In a digital environment, this provision is even more crucial, since purchase of any electronic material is contingent upon acceptance of standard, lengthy 'Terms and Conditions'. These typically include broad, generic and unavoidable clauses which may be at odds with some uses permitted by copyright exceptions.

70 Articles 5 and 6 Marrakesh Treaty.

71 *Supra* n. 31, 9–10.

72 Section 27 CDPA.

73 I. Hargreaves, *Digital Opportunity: A Review of Intellectual Property and Growth* (May 2011), available at https://assets.publishing.service.gov.uk/government/uploads/system/uploads/attachment_data/file/32563/ipreview-finalreport.pdf

74 Section 31F(8) CDPA.

75 Under the Consumer Rights Act 2015, Part 2. 2015, c. 15.

Simply put, beneficiaries of the UK disability exceptions are permitted to make accessible copies for people with disabilities, irrespective of what a provider's contract might say.

Digital Rights Management Systems (DRMs)

Digital rights management systems (DRMs) associated with digital media inevitably make it more difficult to make accessible copies,[76] since their 'raison d'être' is to protect a right-holder's interests by preventing unauthorised reproduction. A long- recognised short-coming of DRMs is their inability to distinguish between an unlawful copy and one which is made for a lawful purpose (such as the reliance on a disability exception by a beneficiary). The difficulty is amplified since the very act of circumventing DRMs, without the right-holder's permission, itself constitutes a violation of the circumvention prohibition.[77] As a result, DRMs may, in some cases, act as a practical override of the disability exceptions.

DRMs are also used to control what a user may do with a work which they have acquired lawfully. For example, encryption may enable a reader to increase font size but prevent standard screen-reading software from narrating the text. Clearly, this is problematic. Larger font may assist some PVI to enjoy a literary work, but it discriminates against others. Equally, encryption tools may similarly hinder making 3-D reproductions of 2-D artistic works, discussed earlier. Although 3-D printing can be tailored to a user's specific circumstances, DRMs could vitiate this key advantage. It is paramount to preserve flexibility and adaptability in order to provide equal access to cultural works.

The UK copyright law does attempt to address such concerns. If a specific DRM prevents legitimate access to a protected work, an individual beneficiary, or the representative of a particular affected group which has been unable to secure redress from the right-holder, may complain to the Secretary of State.[78] If the complaint is upheld and the intended use falls under the CDPA disability exceptions, the right-holder may either be required to permit the act or to identify an existing licensing scheme which would provide the complainant access to the work. Should the right-holder fail to comply with the Secretary of State's request, the complainant then has standing to commence legal proceedings. While the mere existence of these provisions might compel some right-holders to comply, their efficiency must be doubted, since a formal complaint has yet to be lodged. Additionally, these provisions do not extend beyond the minimum scope required by the Marrakesh Treaty. Under the broader UK disability exceptions,[79] which could extend to the making of a 3-D version of a painting based on a digital file, it is therefore lawful to use DRMs to limit the scope of the disability exceptions.

76 Sections 296 to 296ZG CDPA.
77 Section 296ZA CDPA. See also article 6(4) InfoSoc Directive.
78 Section 296ZE(2)-(3) CDPA.
79 Section 296ZE(1) CDPA.

Disability exceptions and moral rights

An account of the UK disability exceptions would be incomplete without some mention of moral rights. According to UK copyright law, exceptions (including the one under discussion) are confined to economic rights. The work's creator(s) – who is not necessarily the right-holder – also enjoy more-limited 'moral rights' protection in recognition that a creative work carries the imprint of the author's personality.[80] Moral rights also benefit society. By enabling an author to be identified with the work they have created (paternity right)[81] and ensuring that the creative expression remains as the author intended (integrity right),[82] the public interest is furthered by the ability to access works in their original work.[83] Equally, the public is able to discern the author's identity through the obligation to attribute the author of the work.

The disability exceptions do not appear to conflict with the attribution (or paternity) right,[84] or its obverse, the right of a person to object to any misattribution as author of any authorial work, or film, which they have not in fact authored.[85] An accessible copy will not infringe the author's attribution right, provided authorship is properly acknowledged. Similarly, as beneficiaries of the UK disability exceptions will typically strive to provide wholly accurate information about the work in question, it seems rare that the right against false attribution will be a concern.

The integrity right, which protects against the distortion, mutilation and other modification of a work,[86] is more relevant to the topic of this chapter. Making an accessible copy of a 2-D work by creating a 3-D form clearly alters the original work,[87] including sequentially altering the work through intermediate copies. However, this right is only infringed if a reasonable person would regard the altered version to be prejudicial to the author's honour and reputation.[88] Thus, it also seems straightforward to reconcile the making of a bona fide accessible copy of a work with the integrity right.[89] Indeed, since the very aim of the accessible

80 R.C. Bird & L.M. Ponte, 'Protecting Moral Rights in the United States and the United Kingdom: Challenges and Opportunities under the U.K.'s New Performances Regulations' (2006) 24 *Boston University International Law Journal* 213, 217; G. Davies & K.Q.C. Garnett, *Moral Rights* (Sweet & Maxwell, 2010) 3.

81 Sections 77–79 CDPA.

82 Sections 80–83 CDPA.

83 G. Dworkin, 'Moral Rights in English Law – The Shape of Rights to Come Basic Features of the Droit Moral' (1986) 8(11) *EIPR* 329, 330.

84 Section 78 CDPA requires an author who wishes to rely upon this right to assert it.

85 Section 84 CDPA. ff.

86 Section 80 CDPA.

87 This right derives from article 6bis(1) of the Berne Convention.

88 Such as in defamation law tests. *Confetti Records v. Warner Music UK Ltd* [2003] EMLR 790, [149–150]; *Pasterfield v. Denham* [1999] FSR 168, [182]; *Delves-Broughton v. House of Harlot* [2012] PCC 29, [24]; *Tidy v. Trustees of the National History Museum* [1995] 39 IPR 501 per Rattee J (*Tidy v. Trustees*).

89 For example, a reduction of a work's size was not held to infringe the integrity right of its author. Ibid., *Tidy v. Trustees.*

copy is to remain as true as possible to the spirit of the original, it seems unlikely that an authorised body would subject a protected work to a treatment which would be prejudicial to the author's honour or reputation.

On balance, while the CDPA lacks any provisions governing the interplay between moral rights and the disability exceptions, a use permitted by the disability exceptions is unlikely to constitute moral rights infringement.

What might the future hold?

The UK's current disability exceptions framework is heavily influenced by the Marrakesh Treaty and EU instruments, but is also under-pinned by a strong and pre-existing commitment to uphold principles of equality and non-discrimination and thereby ensure access to cultural works.

The current political uncertainty linked to the UK's vote to leave the European Union may have an impact on the future interpretations of the provisions discussed in this chapter. A recent EU Directive has been adopted which aims to modernise EU copyright rules.[90] Relevant to our purpose, Recital 21 of the Directive states that the existing copyright exception relating to use by an educational institution for the purposes of illustration and teaching should be understood as covering 'the specific accessibility needs of persons with a disability in the context of illustration for teaching'. Over time, more educational establishments are likely to invest in 3-D printers, as this and related technology becomes mainstream. A broadening of this 'teaching' exception has the potential to supplement disability exceptions and benefit students with a disability by improving their learning experience. As EU Member States have, until 7 June 2021, to transpose this Directive into national law, it remains to be seen whether the UK leaves the EU before this implementation period and/or whether the CDPA is amended nevertheless to mirror its provisions. Whatever the future holds, it seems likely that the EU jurisprudence will continue to influence UK copyright for decades to come.

Technological advances have created opportunities, including the 3-D printing of visual works, making it possible for graphic elements in a story book, for example, to be brought to life in tangible form. This challenges the 'traditional' understanding of what an 'accessible copy' is, which, in turn, muddies the water of the activities falling within the scope of permitted use. Simultaneously, as the number and the type of digital works increased, so too has the use of digital locks, as right-holders strive to control unauthorised copies. This highlights the need for the effectiveness of the current DRMs complaints procedure to be reviewed.

Although the Marrakesh Treaty seeks to promote cross-licensing of accessible copies between signatory countries, these aims may be thwarted because the

90 Directive (EU) 2019/790 of the European Parliament and of the Council of 17 April 2019 on copyright and related rights in the Digital Single Market and amending Directives 96/9/EC and 2001/29/EC *OJ* L 130, 17.5.2019, 92–125.

Treaty leaves open whether remuneration is payable. Where different practices exist, cooperation between authorised bodies in those countries becomes more problematic. UK bodies may be unable to access current EU licensing schemes, depending upon the terms of the UK's (possible) exit of the EU.[91]

Concluding thoughts

For PVI, 3-D printing technology opens new possibilities to art through a sensory approach. The tools are now available to create a 3-D version of a 2-D work which a person can touch, allowing them to feel works which they could not otherwise imagine. The technology also affords unprecedented opportunities to customise an output matched to the particular needs of a specific disability, although lawful routes to accessibility still remain untrodden in many situations.

Copyright protects a wide range of cultural works by granting private property rights to authors. But this is only justified to the extent to which society *as a whole* benefits from access to these works. But for the disability exceptions, persons with a disability owning a lawful copy of the work could be prevented from making an accessible copy without specific authorisation from the rightholder(s). Over time, these important disability exceptions have been revised to extend to Braille versions of literary works and subtitles for broadcasts, and beyond individual users with disabilities to educational establishments and not-for-profit organisations. Provided their use meets certain requirements, these bodies no longer require a licence to make accessible copies on behalf of others. Furthermore, the UK scheme goes beyond its international and EU obligations by extending the exceptions to all types of copyright-protected works and to all types of disabilities and impairments.

Issues, nevertheless, remain, especially when making tactile objects of visual artworks. We have seen that curtailments upon DRMs use do not apply across the full scope of the UK disability exceptions, and that the exception does not extend to the adaptation of literary works, which might protect a digital file used in the course of 3-D printing. These potential lacunae call for further investigation to determine whether legal intervention is necessary.

The relaxation of a copyright-holders' control over their works in order to render these more accessible to people with disabilities is to be applauded. Not only is this in line with the international legal framework, but it meets human rights-based objectives of wider dissemination of works and equal access to information. In a recent initiative, staff at the Victoria and Albert Museum made 3-D scans of some of its sculptures collection and then ran workshops at a nearby hospital, offering patients the opportunity to redesign their own 'masterpiece'.[92] Although the aim of this scheme was to alleviate the frustration of undergoing

91 *Supra*, n. 29.

92 A. Flowers, *Taking Sculptures for a Walk: 3D Printing and Museum Outreach* (April 6, 2018), available at https://www.vam.ac.uk/blog/digital/taking-sculptures-for-a-walk-3d-printing-and-museum-outreach

hospital treatment, it is easy to appreciate how readily adaptable and beneficial it would be for PVI or other disabilities. It underscores the importance of adequate and flexible copyright disability exceptions. Beyond equal opportunity and accessibility issues, the adoption of inclusive copyright provisions, which permit a greater proportion of society to engage with creative works, should also empower them to participate actively in forming culture by developing and harnessing their own creativity. This is not only beneficial to them as individuals, it reinforces the overarching aims of the copyright system to incentivise more and more kinds of creative works and benefit society as a whole.

15 China

Tianxiang He

Introduction

Humans are not born equal. In terms of accessing or appreciating copyright works, the blind, visually impaired, and otherwise print disabled people (hereinafter PVI) are at a disadvantage when compared with fully abled users. This is a fact that should not be neglected by our legislators when designing our laws. The PVI should enjoy the same rights as able-bodied people in accessing copyright works. But in practice, the market supply of works in accessible format is quite limited. The economic considerations behind the lack of supply is that the potential market is too small and that the cost for copyright clearance is just too high.[1] Copyright exceptions, when appropriately designed, can help to solve the problem by offering a legitimate channel for the public to utilize copyright works freely.

This chapter discusses whether the Copyright Law of China[2] and related regulation(s) provide adequate exceptions for the PVI to appreciate works of visual art by translating two-dimensional forms such as paintings into three-dimensional objects, and, if not, what should be done to promote that goal further. For that purpose, this chapter first examines China's international obligations in providing copyright exceptions for the PVI and clarifies to what extent China has satisfied these obligations in sections 'China's international obligations' and 'China's current setting'. Section 'Access to visual art under the existing Chinese legal framework' then checks whether China's existing copyright exceptions cover the use of visual art works by the PVI. The last section of this chapter investigates how China can revise its current legal setting and provide more room for PVI to experience two-dimensional visual art works in their three-dimensional forms.

1 Shae Fitzpatrick, 'Setting Its Sights on the Marrakesh Treaty: The U.S. Role in Alleviating the Book Famine for Persons with Print Disabilities' (2014) 37 *Boston College International and Comparative Law Review* 143–144.

2 Copyright Law of the People's Republic of China, 2010 (hereinafter CLC).

China's international obligations

China has ratified the United Nations Convention on the Rights of Persons with Disabilities (hereinafter CRPD)[3] on August 2008, and must therefore take all appropriate measures to ensure that persons with disabilities can have access to cultural materials in accessible formats, per the right of the disabled persons to equally take part in cultural life provided by Article 30(1)(a) of the CRPD. According to Article 30(3) of the CRPD, if the national law of a signatory country implements a certain mechanism that constitutes an unreasonable or discriminatory barrier to said rights of the disabled, the relevant country will have to take necessary steps, including the possibility of providing exceptions for the disabled, to fix the problem.

In addition to the WIPO treaties and the TRIPS Agreement, China has also signed the Marrakesh Treaty[4] in June 2013, but has yet to ratify it. The Copyright Law of China (CLC) and a related regulation already provide two copyright exceptions for PVI. Still, these exceptions were devised prior to the Marrakesh Treaty, and their ability to meet the obligations set by that Treaty is yet to be assessed.[5]

It should be mentioned that Article 2(a) of the Marrakesh Treaty defines the 'works' as 'literary and artistic works … in the form of text, notation and/or related illustrations…'. Accordingly, the covered literary and artistic works are restricted to those 'in the form of text, notation and/or related illustrations', which excludes most visual art works. However, Article 12 of the Marrakesh Treaty added a 'development provision', which allows its signatories to set other copyright limitations and exceptions that are not provided by the Treaty, taking into consideration their economic situation and their social and cultural needs. This 'development provision' is very important for China, as it gives its signatories a degree of legislative flexibility to expand the scope of their copyright exceptions to cover visual art works. In any event, China will have an obligation to provide specific exceptions for the PVI in its national law after it ratifies the Marrakesh Treaty.

To sum up, China currently has a general obligation under the CRPD to make sure that its national laws do not unreasonably or discriminatorily prevent persons with disabilities from accessing cultural materials. Providing new copyright exceptions in its national law will definitely be a solution for China to consider. The Marrakesh Treaty further sets out specific obligations for its Contracting Parties to provide relevant copyright exceptions for the PVI. In order to ascertain the extent to which China should provide copyright exceptions for the PVI

3 Convention on the Rights of Persons with Disabilities, 13 December, 2006 (hereinafter CRPD).

4 Marrakesh Treaty to Facilitate Access to Published Works for Persons Who Are Blind, Visually Impaired, or Otherwise Print Disabled, 27 June, 2013.

5 The detailed examination of the exceptions provided by the CLC is conducted in section "Access to visual art under the existing Chinese legal framework".

to experience visual art, it is thus necessary to first check China's stance vis-à-vis the Marrakesh Treaty, to then assess what could be built from there.

China's current setting

Copyright exceptions for the visually disabled

As per Article 22 of the CLC, a published work may be used under 12 different circumstances listed in Article 22,

> without permission from, and without payment of remuneration to, the copyright owner, provided that the name of the author and the title of the work are mentioned, and the other rights enjoyed by the copyright owner in accordance with this Law are not prejudiced.

Among the listed exceptions, Article 22(12), which provides that 'a transliteration of a published work into Braille for publication' can be exempted, is the only circumstance relevant to PVI within the CLC. In other words, this exception is given to the making of a Braille version of a published work, and the beneficiaries will then be limited to PVI who are capable of reading Braille. Moreover, as Braille consists of patterns of raised dots representing different letters and PVI will read each letter by touching those raised dots, the exception is more relevant to literary works than visual art works.

As the law presently stands, it seems that the listed 12 exceptions in Article 22 of CLC are quite limited and not flexible enough. But the 2013 Regulations for the Implementation of the CLC,[6] which is a set of supplementary rules enacted by the State Council of China (SCC) and the National Copyright Administration, provide some detailed explanations for that article. According to Article 21 of the 2013 RICL:

> The exploitation of a published work which may be exploited without permission from the copyright owner in accordance with the relevant provisions of the Copyright Law shall not impair the normal exploitation of the work concerned, nor unreasonably prejudice the legitimate interests of the copyright owner.

This Article serves as a complement to the listed exceptions. A specific use must first fall under one of the listed exceptions. Article 21 of the 2013 RICL will then serve as a ceiling over the list to restrict the exception further. The wording is inspired by Article 9 of the Berne Convention and subsequent international treaties.[7] In combination with subsection (2) of Article 22 of CLC, it is clear

6 Regulations for the Implementation of the Copyright Law of the People's Republic of China, 2013 (hereinafter RICL).

7 Berne Convention, Article 9; Agreement on Trade-Related Aspects of Intellectual Property Rights (TRIPS Agreement), Article 13; WCT, Article 10; WPPT, Article 16.2; The Beijing Treaty, Article 13.2; Marrakesh Treaty, Article 11.

that the extent of the excepted uses should not 'impair the normal exploitation of the work concerned, nor unreasonably prejudice the legitimate interests of the copyright owner'. This kind of setting can only provide limited help for PVI in accessing visual art works because it further restricts an exception that seems to be geared toward literary works to begin with.

The other exception related to PVI is provided by the 2013 Regulation on the Protection of the Right to Communicate Works to the Public over Information Networks (hereinafter 'Information Network Regulation'). It is an administrative regulation promulgated by the SCC to supplement the implementation of CLC with regard to Internet-related articles. Article 6(6) of this Regulation provides an exception to the right to communicate works to the public over information networks in favor of the blind. It states that a person who provides published written works of others through the information network to the blind 'in a way as particularly perceptible to the blind and not for the purpose of making a profit',[8] can do so without obtaining permission from, or paying remuneration to, the copyright owner. The word 'Braille' is not directly mentioned. However, it describes the accessible format covered as 'specific means that [the blind] can perceive'. According to the lawmaker, the quoted description was designed to cover readings that only the blind can perceive.[9] But such a narrow coverage makes it unclear which 'accessible formats' other than Braille can only be perceived by the blind. For example, the audiobooks referred to in the Marrakesh Treaty[10] can be perceived by both the blind and able-bodied people. Therefore, following such a narrow view means that audiobooks cannot be covered by Article 6(6) of the Information Network Regulation. From a practical perspective, the scope of the 'beneficiary' and the 'accessible format' set by the exception of Article 6(6) of the Information Network Regulation is then similar to that of Article 22(12) of the CLC.

It is clear from the aforementioned that the copyright exceptions related to the disabled provided by the CLC and the Information Network Regulation are quite limited. In terms of accessing visual art works, there is no exception explicitly provided for PVI.

Bridging the gap

As one of the signatories of the Marrakesh Treaty, China will be bound by the treaty after it deposits the instrument of ratification with the Director General of the World Intellectual Property Organization (WIPO).[11] Before ratifying the treaty, China needs to review its relevant national laws to ensure compliance with its obligations under the Marrakesh Treaty. China may also take the opportunity

8 Information Network Regulation, Article 6(6).

9 Jerry Jie Hua, 'Implementation of the Marrakesh Treaty for Visually Impaired Persons into the Chinese Copyright Law' [2017] 3(1) *China and WTO Review* 21, note 57.

10 Footnote 1 of the Marrakesh Treaty states that 'Agreed statement concerning Article 2(a): For the purposes of this Treaty, it is understood that this definition includes such works in audio form, such as audiobooks'.

11 Marrakesh Treaty, Article 19(b).

to go beyond the Marrakesh standard and expressly provide access to visual art works by PVI.

Still, China has yet to meet its obligations under the Marrakesh Treaty in many aspects, which are discussed in the following text.

Scope of 'beneficiary person'

According to Article 3 of the Marrakesh Treaty, the term 'beneficiary person' under the Marrakesh Treaty refers to 3 kinds of PVI: those (a) who are completely blind, (b) who are not completely blind but nevertheless are visually impaired,[12] and (c) who are otherwise unable to read due to physical disabilities. By comparison, the existing copyright exceptions provided in China can only benefit category (a). Furthermore, the scope of applicability of the exceptions provided for 'the blind' is even more limited in China, as it only covers the group of blind people who can read Braille.

Scope of 'accessible format copy'

While the CLC and the Information Network Regulation limit the 'accessible format' to Braille, Article 2(b) of the Marrakesh Treaty provides a broader definition for this term:

> a copy of a work in an alternative manner or form which gives a beneficiary person access to the work, including to permit the person to have access as feasibly and comfortably as a person without visual impairment or other print disability.

Scope of 'works'

As discussed, the copyright exceptions offered by the CLC and the Information Network Regulation are by and large limited to 'literary works', as it is generally not possible for a visual art work to be transliterated into Braille. By contrast, Article 2(a) of the Marrakesh Treaty is applicable to some artistic works (illustrations related to literary works). The coverage of this Article is broader than the CLC, but it is still not an ideal setting as most visual art works will not be covered.

Types of rights restricted

According to Article 4(1)(a) of the Marrakesh Treaty, the types of rights restricted by the copyright limitations or exceptions should include 'the right of reproduction, the right of distribution, and the right of making available to the public as provided by the WCT'.

12 Hua (n 9) 20.

Exceptions provided by Article 22(12) of the CLC and Article 6(6) of the Information Network Regulation do not clarify what types of rights are concerned. However, for an act to be covered by said exception, that is, to transliterate a published work into Braille for publication, the act of reproduction, distribution, and/or communication to the public over information networks will inevitably be involved. Therefore, the exceptions, as mentioned earlier, will be relevant to the right of reproduction, the right of distribution, and the right to communicate works to the public over information networks.

The ambit of the permitted activities under the exceptions of Article 22(12) of the CLC and Article 6(6) of the Information Network Regulation, which are determined by the relevant types of rights being restricted, seems thus to be similar to those required under the Marrakesh Treaty. But as discussed, since the scope of 'beneficiary person', 'accessible format copy', and 'works' covered by these exceptions is quite narrow, it is deemed that 'the actual permitted activities do not parallel the intentions of the Marrakesh Treaty'.[13]

Exceptions for the circumvention of technological measures

According to Article 7 of the Marrakesh Treaty, China, as a Contracting Party, has an obligation to provide exceptions to the prohibition of circumventing technological measures, for the benefit of PVI.[14]

China does offer a relevant exception to that end in Article 12(2) of the Information Network Regulation:

> technical measures can be circumvented for the benefit of blind people where any of the written works as already published is provided without profit purposes to the blind through the information network in a unique way as particularly perceptible by the blind, and the aforesaid works can only be acquired through the information network.

However, this exception fails to meet the requirement of Article 7 of the Marrakesh Treaty, as its scope of applicability is much more limited.[15] Therefore, it is necessary for China to broaden the current exception or to provide more exceptions to the circumvention of technological measures, as nowadays PVI rely heavily on new technologies (such as 3D printing) to experience visual art works, in which technological measures are usually employed.

13 Hua (n 9) 25.

14 Marrakesh Treaty, Article 7:

> Contracting Parties shall take appropriate measures, as necessary, to ensure that when they provide adequate legal protection and effective legal remedies against the circumvention of effective technological measures, this legal protection does not prevent beneficiary persons from enjoying the limitations and exceptions provided for in this Treaty.

15 Hua (n 9) 28.

Exceptions for cross-border exchange of accessible format copies

Article 5(1) of the Marrakesh Treaty provides that

> [C]ontracting Parties shall provide that if an accessible format copy is made under a limitation or exception or pursuant to operation of law, that accessible format copy may be distributed or made available by an authorized entity to a beneficiary person or an authorized entity in another Contracting Party.

Accordingly, the Contracting Parties must provide exceptions for the cross-border exchange of accessible format copies between them.

In addition, Article 9(1) of the Marrakesh Treaty also provides that '[C]ontracting Parties shall endeavor to foster the cross-border exchange of accessible format copies by encouraging the voluntary sharing of information to assist authorized entities in identifying one another...'.

It is clear that Contracting Parties have an obligation to cooperate in order to facilitate the cross-border exchange of accessible format copies. However, there are no equivalent provisions in the current CLC and related regulations that address the aforementioned obligations.

To sum up, China does offer copyright exceptions for the disabled in Article 22(12) of the CLC and Article 6(6) of the Information Network Regulation. But the exceptions are quite narrow. For example, Article 22(12) of the CLC can only apply to reproducing a published literary work in the form of Braille, which is a skill that requires training. As a result, only blind people who can read Braille are able to enjoy this exception.[16] More importantly, most visual art works are not likely to be covered by the exception, as they cannot be transliterated into Braille. The same issue applies to the exception concerning the circumvention of technological measures provided by Article 12(2) of the Information Network Regulation. Due to the restricted applicability of these exceptions, the relevant permitted activities are limited as well. In addition, the CLC and related regulations have no provisions that can address the obligations regarding the cross-border exchange of accessible format copies for disabled persons.

The copyright exceptions for the disabled offered by China seem to fail to meet the requirements of the Marrakesh Treaty. The exceptions do not cover all visual art works either. Hence, amendments to the related parts of the CLC or even new regulations are needed to both meet the requirements of the Marrakesh Treaty and further facilitate PVI's access to visual art works.

16 Jingyi Li, 'Copyright Exemptions to Facilitate Access to Published Works for the Print Disabled – The Gap between National Laws and the Standards Required by the Marrakesh Treaty' (2014) 45(7) *IIC International Review of Intellectual Property and Competition Law* 747.

Access to visual art under the existing Chinese legal framework

Most visual art works are outside the scope of exceptions of the CLC

Copyright exceptions related to PVI in the current CLC and the Information Network Regulation do not specifically cover visual art works. Article 3 of the CLC lists 12 types of protected works, including written works, musical, dramatic, *quyi* (a traditional Chinese performance art form), choreographic works, works of fine art, and photographic works. Article 22(12) of CLC stipulates that the 'translation of a published work into Braille and publication of the work so translated' can be exempted. However, the exception does not make clear which types of works listed in Article 3 of the CLC may amount to a 'published work'. Although it is clear from the wording of Article 22(12) of the CLC that no limitation is set on the type of work covered, only literary works and some pictorial works are caught by it, as only text, notation, and illustrations can be translated into Braille.[17] Consequently, only literary works and certain types of graphic works are covered by this exception.

Article 6(6) of the Information Network Regulation further allows users to provide 'published literary works' in a 'particular way as perceptible to the blind'. It is clear from the wording of this Article that the type of works covered is literary works. However, the expression 'particular way as perceptible to the blind' means a way that is exclusive to the blind and cannot be perceived by able-bodied people.[18] According to its drafter, 'the 'particular way' mentioned in Article 6(6) means ways that can only be perceived by the blind, such as Braille in the form of embossment printed by a printer'.[19] Considering the restrictions over the definitions of the beneficiary persons (blind people) and the accessible format copy (Braille) set by the legislator, the copyright exceptions related to PVI in the CLC and the Information Network Regulation may not even cover audiobooks and books designed for PVI, and, certainly, most visual art works are not included either.

A possible solution provided by the new amendment draft of the CLC?

The ongoing third revision of the CLC aims to echo China's national strategy to promote indigenous innovation and to build an 'innovative country'.[20] The first

17 Qian Wang, 'Discussion on the Influence of the Marrakesh Treaty on the Copyright Legislations of China' (2013) *Law Science* 56 (in Chinese).

18 Wang (n 17) 54.

19 Jianhua Zhang (Ed.), *Interpretation of the Regulation on the Protection of the Right to Network Dissemination of Information of China* (China Legal Publishing House 2006) 28 (in Chinese).

20 *Explanations on the Copyright Law of the People's Republic of China (Draft Revision for Review) for Public Consultation* (NCAC, 6 June, 2014) <http://www.gov.cn/xinwen/site1/20140610/73841402364850364.doc> accessed 13 July, 2019; *See also* Li Luo, 'Chinese Copyright Law: the Third Revision' (2012) 18 *CLJP/JDCP Journals* 50.

draft was officially opened for public consultation by the National Copyright Administration of China (NCAC) on March 31, 2012.[21] NCAC subsequently published the second draft on July 2, 2012,[22] and the third on June 6, 2014.[23] The fourth and the most recent draft was published for public consultation on April 30, 2020.[24]

The proposed Third Draft Amendment (hereinafter the Draft Amendment) has added a thirteenth exception of 'other circumstances' to Article 43 (the equivalent to Article 22 in the current CLC) as a 'catch-all' exception:

> 'Article 43
>
> In the following cases, a work may be exploited without permission from, and without payment of remuneration to, the copyright owner, provided that the name or appellation of the author and the source and title of the work are mentioned, and the other rights enjoyed by the copyright owner by virtue of this Law are not prejudiced:
>
> (1) copy snippets from another person's published work for purposes of the user's own personal study, research.
>
> ...
>
> (13) Other circumstances.

Interpreted broadly, this provision could not only meet the obligations set by the Marrakesh Treaty, but also exempt 3D reproductions of 2D visual art works for the benefit of PVI. In addition, the draft also included a subsection as Article 43.2: 'the use of a published work pursuant to the above provisions, may not prejudice the normal use of the work and may not unreasonably prejudice the lawful rights and interests of the copyright owner'. This subsection replicates the wording of Article 21 of the 2013 RICL.

However, it is noteworthy that the twelfth exception, which establishes that the 'transliteration of a published work into Braille for publication' is exempted, remained unchanged in Article 43 of the Draft Amendment of the CLC. It will be a logical assumption that the legislators of the Amendment have no intention

21 *Notice on Promulgating the Copyright Law of the People's Republic of China (Draft Revision) for Public Consultation* (NCAC, 31 March, 2012) <http://www.gapp.gov.cn/govinteract/1081/84479.html> accessed 13 July, 2019.

22 *NCAC on Promulgating the Copyright Law of the People's Republic of China (Second Draft Revision) for Public Consultation* (NCAC, 2 July, 2012) <http://www.gov.cn/gzdt/2012-07/10/content_2180033.htm> accessed 13 July, 2019.

23 *Notice About Circular of the Legislative Affairs Office of the State Council on Promulgating the Copyright Law of the People's Republic of China (Draft Revision for Review) for Public Consultation*, (Legislative Affairs Office of the State Council of P. R. China, 6 June, 2014) <http://www.gov.cn/xinwen/2014-06/10/content_2697701.htm> accessed 13 July, 2019.

24 Although the fourth revision has changed the original wording of the twelfth exception into "provide published works in a way as particularly perceptible to the print disabled people", it is still quite limited hence is not ideal. This Chapter will use the third revision as the model for discussion. *Revision Proposal for the Copyright Law of China for Public Consultation*], (National People's Congress, 30 April, 2020) <http://www.npc.gov.cn/flcaw/userIndex.html?lid=ff80808171ba0ccc0171be96df3a02b0> accessed 5 June, 2020.

of expanding the scope of 'works' and 'beneficiaries' under said exception. The explanation of the new draft further supports this assumption: nothing was mentioned about expanding the scope of 'works' and 'beneficiaries', and the Marrakesh Treaty was not mentioned either.[25] In August 2017, the National People's Congress published a report on the implementation of Copyright Law. Its first part, 'Main Work and Effectiveness of Implementing Copyright Law', states that

> China has also ratified or acceded to international treaties such as the Berne Convention for the Protection of Literary and Artistic Works and the Beijing Treaty on Audiovisual Performances, and has taken the initiative to conform to international rules for copyright protection.[26]

Even though the Marrakesh Treaty was signed by China early in 2013, the aforementioned report and the Draft Amendment proposal were silent on that fact, and the latter has made no specific change to copyright law intended to comply with the Marrakesh Treaty requirements. Thus, it is presumed that China did not take the Marrakesh Treaty into consideration when drafting the third amendment and did not plan to expand the scope of the twelfth exception of the CLC.

As to the proposed new exception, the change will turn the closed-list model into an open one.[27] Ideally, one can arguably combine Article 43.1(13) and Article 43.2 and claim that subparagraph (13) was inserted to cover all possible situations in the future. The 'two-step' test in Article 43.2 will then always function as the 'ceiling' of all the limitations and exceptions.

However, if we interpret the law in a systematic way, it is clear that if the exception related to the disabled is already granted by the CLC, then probably providing PVI with 3D reproductions of 2D visual art works cannot be assessed again as 'other circumstances' under subparagraph (13). The court has to exclude all the 12 listed circumstances before relying on subparagraph (13). Nevertheless, there might also be an alternative interpretation: as the exception related to the disabled only concerns 'the blind' and the 'translation of a published work into Braille',[28] it is possible to say that it does not cover those people that are visually impaired and are otherwise unable to enjoy visual art works due to physical disabilities. As a result, the unauthorized reproduction of visual art works by PVI other than 'blind' people could theoretically be exempted under the newly added thirteenth exception 'other circumstances', if the proposed draft of the CLC is to be adopted in the future. Still, it has been pointed out that it is 'extremely unlikely that exceptions that do not specifically provide for the needs of the blind or other visually impaired people would provide a comprehensive solution to the

25 NCAC (n 20).

26 Chen Wang, Report of the Law Enforcement Inspection Unit of the Standing Committee of the National People's Congress on the Inspection of the Implementation of the Copyright Law of the People's Republic of China at the 29th meeting of the Standing Committee of the Twelfth National People's Congress (28 August, 2017) <http://www.npc.gov.cn/zgrdw/npc/zfjc/zfjcelys/2017-08/28/content_2027447.htm> accessed 13 July, 2019.

27 Peter K Yu, 'Customizing Fair Use Transplants' (2018) 7 *Laws* 10.

28 CLC, 2010, Article 22(12).

needs of those facing a print disability'.[29] In other words, the proposed revision draft of the CLC is not ideal for enabling PVI to experience artistic works.

To conclude, the CLC and the Information Network Regulation grant exceptions for the blind to enjoy literary works (including text, notation, and/or related illustrations) without the permission of the copyright owner only if they are translated into Braille or any other form that is perceptible by the blind. The proposed Draft Amendment of the CLC aims to add a 'catch-all' exception, which can give more room to Chinese courts for delivering interpretations favorable to PVI. But as discussed earlier, the new 'catch-all' exception of the Draft Amendment to the CLC was not designed to, and probably will not, grant PVI adequate protection in accessing visual art works. Hence, it is not an ideal solution.

Facilitating PVI's access to visual art works in China

As mentioned earlier, the Marrakesh Treaty covers a much wider scope of beneficiaries and permitted activities than the CLC. However, the Marrakesh protection does not enable PVI to enjoy all types of artistic works. Neither does the CLC. China should thus amend its copyright law and related regulations to accommodate the needs of PVI in China. For that purpose, this part discusses proposed changes to Chinese copyright law.

Revise the copyright exception related to PVI to promote enjoyment of visual art works

As discussed, the current exceptions provided by the CLC and related regulations are far from satisfactory with regard to the promotion of greater accessibility to visual art works by PVI. They can be improved on the following aspects.

To begin with, the exceptions should include not just the blind, but also the visually impaired and otherwise print-disabled people as its beneficiaries.

The accessible format should also be expanded from Braille to any format that gives a beneficiary person access to the work. Limiting the accessible format to just Braille ignores those blind people who have not learned Braille, as well as other PVI. For them, there are more effective ways to access copyright works (namely, for literary works, audiobooks, and perhaps large prints are all good alternatives). The 3D printing technology can now be used to help PVI touch and feel the art. The Unseen Art Project, which aims to recreate classical art paintings in 3D,[30] is a good example of how the technology can be utilized to facilitate PVI's access to visual arts. Thus, the 'Braille' requirement in the

29 World Intellectual Property Organization, Study on Copyright Limitations and Exceptions for the Visually Impaired, SCCR/15/7 (20 February, 2007) <https://www.wipo.int/edocs/mdocs/copyright/en/sccr_15/sccr_15_7.pdf> 29.

30 Unseen Art: 3D-Printed Art for the Visually Impaired, ADV/CLB <http://www.adventureclub.fi/unseen/>.

two exceptions mentioned earlier should be amended accordingly. The works covered should be extended to literary and artistic works in general, so that future developments that can assist PVI in experiencing various kinds of works can be covered.

Finally, the types of rights restricted by the exceptions of the CLC and the Information Network Regulation should at least include the right of reproduction, the right of distribution, and the right of communication to the public through information networks (but preferably also other relevant rights, as elaborated later).

China is still a developing country, which has a considerable number of PVI (12.33 million people nationwide in 2006),[31] and has yet to even meet the Marrakesh requirements. China should thus consider legislative changes that can improve PVI's access to copyrighted works.

A critical question: to what extent should China offer a broader VIP exception?

China should update its copyright exceptions to a Marrakesh-plus level so that visual art works can be covered and enjoyed by PVI. The design of new exceptions should take into account the current stage of technological development that can enable PVI to experience copyright works.

What kinds of visual art works?

The CLC does not refer to a specific type of protected works as visual art works, but it does contain types of works that can be deemed visual art, which include works of fine art and architecture (Article 3(4)), photographic works (Article 3(5)), graphic works and model works (Article 3(7)), cinematographic works (Article 3(6)), and stage arts such as dramatic, *quyi*, choreographic, and acrobatic works (Article 3(3)).

New technologies may facilitate the enjoyment of three-dimensional visual art works such as model works, works of fine art (e.g. sculptures), and works of architecture by PVI. For example, 3D printing technology could produce a small version of a work of architecture or sculpture, which PVI could sense through touch. A specific institution, such as a museum, could make use of the exception and provide a space for the PVI to touch and feel the beauty of those works.

As the Unseen Art Project mentioned earlier demonstrates, 3D printing can also help PVI enjoy two-dimensional artistic works such as paintings.

It is therefore suggested that China should consider revising the current exceptions related to PVI to cover 3D printing of visual arts in the future.

31 The Second Nationwide Sampling Survey on the Disabled Key Data Communique (National Bureau of Statistics of China, 1 December, 2006) <http://www.gov.cn/ztzl/gacjr/content_459223.htm> accessed 13 July, 2019.

The permitted acts under the new exception

The rights of reproduction, rental, adaptation, distribution, translation, compilation, performance, communication to the public through information networks, and even the right of showing the aforementioned works should be clearly mentioned in the exception.

In terms of two-dimensional visual art works, making accessible copies and offering them to PVI will involve the rights of reproduction, rental, adaption, distribution, and/or communication to the public through information networks. Specifically, providing PVI with access to two-dimensional visual art works may involve changing the size of the works or simplifying the works. This may concern the rights of reproduction and adaptation. For example, 3D printing technology may be used to reproduce the essential parts of a painting such as the main figure of a portrait, but the remaining parts that are less concrete and important, such as the clouds or the cattle in the background, might have to be discarded. Moreover, the right of communication to the public through information networks will be relevant where PVI want to access design files online and print a copy of the work using a 3D printer at home.

Future outlook

As discussed, although there are PVI-related exceptions in the CLC (Article 22(12)) and in the Information Network Regulation (Article 6(6)), the current setting is unsatisfactory.

The current copyright exception in Article 22(12) of the CLC should be developed further so that more flexibility can be introduced; but the legislator should also aim to maintain as much legal certainty as possible. Experiences from other civil law jurisdictions in East Asia such as Japan can be used as a reference point. In May 2018, Japan amended its copyright law and changed the structure of its closed-list copyright exceptions model to a semi-open model.[32] Some of the listed exceptions were reconstructed into a multilayered (general clause – list – catch-all) style.[33]

China could adopt a similar solution in the following terms:

Article 22(12): It is permissible to exploit a work, in any way and to the extent considered necessary, in any of the following cases or other cases where such exploitation is to enable the blind, visually impaired, or otherwise print-disabled to enjoy the work through means such as reproduction, adaptation, public performance, projection, distribution, and communication to the public over information networks, for non-commercial purposes, provided, however, that this

32 Japanese Copyright Law, Law No. 48 of 1970, amended by Act No. 30 of 2018, Article 30-50 (2018), translated at Japanese Law Translation <http://www.japaneselawtranslation.go.jp/law/detail/?ft=2&re=02&dn=1&yo=%E8%91%97%E4%BD%9C%E6%A8%A9&x=61&y=5&ia=03&ph=&ky=&page=1> accessed 13 July, 2019.

33 See article 30–34 of the Japanese Copyright Law and also on this book the chapter on Japan.

does not apply if the exploitation would unreasonably prejudice the interests of the copyright owner in light of the nature and purposes of such work, as well as the circumstances of such exploitation:

1 Translation of a published work into Braille and publication of the work so translated;
2 Transforming a two-dimensional artistic work into a three-dimensional copy;
3 ...
4 In addition to the cases set forth in the preceding paragraphs, transformation of a published work into any other accessible formats.

The suggested new drafting contains the following changes:

A general rule that encompasses a purpose element (exploitation is to enable the blind, visually impaired, or otherwise print disabled to enjoy a copyright work) and a market element (this does not apply if the exploitation would unreasonably prejudice the interests of the copyright owner in light of the nature and purposes of such work, as well as the circumstances of such exploitation).

The examples of translating a published work into Braille (the original Article 22(12)) and transforming a two-dimensional artistic work into a three-dimensional copy are clearly provided. The jurisprudence related to the original Article shall be kept. Furthermore, the wording of the second example is flexible enough to cover not only 3D printing technology but also any future technologies that can achieve the same result.

Finally, a catch-all clause was inserted as the last subparagraph to cover 'transformation of a published work into any other accessible formats'.

With this drafting, the CLC could achieve not only flexibility via a semi-opened clause that covers any future technological advancements, but also certainty with examples that are deemed acceptable, such as activities using 3D printing technology to help PVI experience two-dimensional artistic works. When legislators find new examples that comply with the general clause, they can then be listed so that courts will enjoy a high level of certainty.

This exception expands the notion of beneficiaries from merely the blind to all the visually impaired or otherwise print-disabled people. Its wording covers all types of works but also all accessible formats.

This Article might cause a conflict between the right of PVI to access visual arts and the exclusive right(s) of the copyright owners, as it is obviously a Marrakesh-plus exception with a very wide coverage, and the copies generated under this exception may constitute market substitution. Therefore, a few restrictions are provided so that the damage will be kept to a minimum. First, it is mandated that the ways of utilization should be of non-commercial nature, which will prevent encroachments from potential competitors in the market. Second, the exception is created only to benefit PVI. As a result, any format that contains superfluous features will not be covered by the exception (for example, colors in a 3D printed copy). Third, the Berne three-step test still applies. This will make sure that any act that will 'impair the normal exploitation of the work concerned' or 'unreasonably prejudice the legitimate interests of the copyright owner' will not be covered by the exception.

However, one exception in the CLC is still not good enough. Considering that the State Council of China has been authorized by the CLC to establish specific rules with regard to collective management organization (Article 8), computer software, and the right of communication of information networks (Article 59), it would be adequate for a separate Article of the CLC to authorize the State Council to generate a separate regulatory document to protect the interests of PVI in accessing copyright works.[34]

34 Similar proposal was raised by Prof. Qian Wang as well. See Wang (n 17) 63.

16 Costa Rican copyright legislation and disability exceptions

The case study of 3D printing

Andres Guadamuz

Introduction

This chapter looks at the specifics of Costa Rican copyright legislation with regard to the disability exceptions and limitations; in keeping with the theme of the book, it will look at the case study of the protection (or lack thereof) given to 3D printed works in general, and most specifically how various exceptions and limitations may impact the use of 3D printing to represent artistic works.

This is a difficult time for the subject of studying disability exceptions in Costa Rica. The number and scope of existing exceptions is limited. As it will be discussed, there are no exceptions in existence for persons with a disability. Moreover, the country only ratified the Marrakesh Treaty last year; it has neither passed any accompanying legislation yet nor changed its legislation to accommodate the provisions contained in the Treaty. Therefore, it will be the contention of this chapter that there is inadequate coverage of exceptions for persons with a disability in general, and until there are changes, the subject is not adequately covered.

Moreover, there is also no adequate cover of 3D printed works in general. This, combined with the lack of disability exceptions so far, means that using 3D printing to reproduce artistic works would consist of an infringement of copyright law with no viable defences.

Things may improve slightly in the future with full implementation of the Marrakesh Treaty,[1] but at the moment it is evident that there is no adequate coverage of this subject in general.

On the bright side, the core copyright law is not entirely clear on the type of protection given to 3D printed works in general, and this is a grey area that could benefit those artists interested in using the technology to allow accessibility to artistic works. Similarly, the lack of general enforcement in Costa Rica would allow practices to develop until there is a clearer picture of where the law stands with regards to both 3D printed works and exceptions and limitations.

1 "Slightly" because, as made clear in other chapters of this book, the Marrakesh Treaty only covers some types of artistic works (illustrations related to literary works).

Costa Rican law and copyright protection

Costa Rican copyright protection and artistic works

Costa Rican copyright legislation is typical of the Civil Law tradition in its coverage for artistic works. The copyright law protects artistic works of various types in a broad and open-ended definition of artistic subject matter, and it offers a non-exhaustive list of works that are protected by the legislation, including several types of artistic works such as "works of drawing, painting, architecture, sculpture, engraving and lithography, photographic works and those expressed by procedure analogous to photography".[2]

In general, there has not been any challenge to this open-ended definition, and whenever there has been a conflict related to copyright works, the courts have been willing to accept a broad interpretation of Article 1. For example, in 2008, the constitutional court ruled on a dispute between the country's collective rights organisation for music, Asociación de Compositores y Autores Musicales (ACAM) and several bars in the capital that were playing music without a licence. While the case rested mostly on licensing issues, the decision goes into a long description of protected subject matter, and it describes that the definition is not exhaustive.[3]

Therefore, it is fair to assume that several categories that are not covered in Article 1 would also have copyright protection, and this would cover "newer" technologies such as computer games, mobile phone applications (apps), and other types of artistic works.

With regard to the relevant exclusive rights of the author, the national legislation confers the right of reproduction and adaptation in Article 16.1. These rights are conferred practically with no explanation as to their reach and interpretation within the text of the law, and the case law has been sparse in any explanation of the scope of the right.

In relation to the right of reproduction, its interpretation seems to be broad: any unauthorised act of reproduction is an infringement, and most of the copying that makes it to court pertains to direct reproduction.[4]

The most relevant case concerning artistic reproduction involves a professional photographer that takes pictures of touristic locations in the northern region of the country; he took a photograph of the famous Arenal Volcano while it was erupting, and turned it into posters and postcards for sale in various hotels in the area. An employee of the national electricity company Instituto Costarricense de Electricidad (ICE) purchased a poster of the photograph at a hotel to keep in his office, and this was taken by another employee, who took a photograph of the poster and used the image to put in phone cards. The lower court bizarrely

2 Art 1.

3 See: Sala Constitucional, Resolución N° 04532–2008, 25 de Marzo del 2008.

4 See for example, Tribunal Segundo, Resolución N° 00376–2002, 30 de Setiembre del 2002; and Tribunal Segundo, Resolución N° 00360–2000, 1 de Setiembre del 2000.

decided that the photographer did not have a legitimate interest to bring an action, but the upper administrative court ruled that the ICE had infringed by reproducing the work without permission.[5]

With regard to adaptation, the text of the law is similarly curt, with no definition of what is considered to be an adaptation. Moreover, a thorough search for case law related to adaptation produced no results with regards to artistic works.

If the 2D artistic work is in the public domain, the law is clear that only the work that is original to the author would be subject to protection. Article 8 reads:

> Whoever adapts, translates, modifies, re-forges, collects, parodies or extracts, in any way, the substance of a public domain work, is the exclusive owner of his own work; but he cannot oppose others to do the same with that work in the public domain. If these acts are carried out with works or productions that are in the private domain, the authorization of the right holder will be necessary. Databases are protected as compilations.[6]

Conversely, this means that any exclusive act requires authorisation, and therefore printing a work without permission would amount to copyright infringement, as explained earlier.

Given the scenario that gives rise to this chapter, if a work of art that is in the public domain is printed by an additive manufacturing process, Costa Rican law is clear that this work is likely not to carry its own protection, and it will also be in the public domain, as it is difficult to see how it would contain elements that are not in the public domain. If the work is protected, then any 3D prints would require authorisation.

Moral rights in Costa Rican law

A subject that requires a brief independent analysis is that of moral rights. Costa Rica follows the continental tradition of strong protection for moral rights. Despite this tradition, the treatment given to moral rights in the Costa Rican copyright act is relatively short. It recognises several types of moral rights, particularly the right of integrity, the right of paternity, and the right to remove the work from circulation. The law establishes that these are independent from economic rights of the author in the sense that they are inalienable, but they last as long as the economic rights. Article 14 covers four types of moral rights:

a Unless otherwise agreed, keep the work unpublished, being able to postpone, by will, its publication and reproduction for a period of up to fifty (50) years after his death.

5 Tribunal Contencioso Administrativo Sección I, Resolución Nº 00095–2006, 3 de Marzo del 2006.

6 All translations by the author.

b Claim the authorship of the work.
c Oppose any deformation, mutilation or other modification of the work or any attack on it that causes damage to his honor or reputation.
d Unless otherwise agreed, withdraw the work from the circulation, after compensation to those affected by their action.

Several court decisions have strengthened the power and inalienable character of moral rights. In a 2002 decision regarding moral rights, the top civil court (Sala Segunda) defined the nature of moral rights in Costa Rican legislation in this manner:

> It is a non-economic, inherent and absolute right. –It is non-economic because it is not likely to be calculated in money, although it produces indirect or mediated economic consequences such as, for example, the possibility of obtaining greater income -in normal contracting or when it comes to fixing the compensation for injuries to your rights- as a result of the increase of the prestige of the author and his work by its distribution united to the name of its creator. -It is inherent in the quality of the author, that is to say that it is linked to the person of the creator, which is why mortis causa is not transmitted, the heirs only receive the exercise of some of the faculties that integrate it - the negative or defensive ones-, but not the moral right itself. -It is absolute because it is opposable to any person -erga omnes-, that is, that allows the owner to face all others, including the third party who has received full rights over the work. The powers that make up the moral right have different content.[7]

Given the strong level of protection, there are no exceptions in the act for moral rights; most of the exceptions refer to economic rights. This is relevant for the possible application of exceptions for persons with a disability, as authors could try to block adaptations or reproductions of an artistic work by claiming that it infringes their moral rights. This is again another circumstance in which the lack of specific exceptions persons with a disability could affect users.

Exceptions and limitations

Costa Rican copyright legislation contains an exhaustive amount of exceptions and limitations, much like all countries that have a close-ended approach to the subject.[8] While many of the existing exceptions are typical of those found in other jurisdictions, it is important to point out that a number of exceptions and limitations were amended as a result of the implementation of a multilateral agreement between Central American countries and the United States, the

7 Tribunal Segundo Civil, Sección II, Resolución N° 00376–2002.

8 For more on the subject, see: Geiger C, 'Implementing an International Instrument for Interpreting Copyright Limitations and Exceptions' (2009) 40:6 *IIC* 627.

Dominican Republic-Central American Free Trade Agreement (DR-CAFTA),[9] which overhauled the copyright system in those countries with heavy influence by copyright maximalists, containing TRIPS plus copyright standards.[10]

In particular, DR-CAFTA introduced limits to provisions regarding temporary copies,[11] strengthened the protection given to digital rights management and rights management information,[12] and reinforced the application of the three-step test to the signatory countries.[13] The text reads:

> [...] each Party shall confine limitations or exceptions to exclusive rights to certain special cases that do not conflict with a normal exploitation of the work, performance, or phonogram, and do not unreasonably prejudice the legitimate interests of the right holder.

While this is in line with the international standards (e.g. the Berne Convention), it is interesting that the agreement felt it necessary to stress the limits of copyright exceptions, to the extent that it needed to incorporate the principle into national law with the passing of the agreement.

In what concerns exceptions for use by persons with a disability, it is unfortunate that at the time of writing, there is not a single exception for this purpose in Costa Rican legislation. For example, out of the limited number of exceptions, there are four articles dealing with journalistic and news reporting,[14] and three for educational use.[15] This reflects the importance given by Costa Rican society to both journalistic freedom and education, and it also says a lot about the relative neglect that the country has given to the rights of persons with a disability, at least in comparison to other rights.

Thankfully, things may be about to improve. Costa Rica is one of the original signatories to the Marrakesh Treaty,[16] and it ratified it in June 28, 2013. The Treaty came into force in Costa Rica in January 9, 2018 with the passing of the Ley N° 9454,[17] which incorporates into national legislation the full text of the Treaty. The Marrakesh Treaty features some exceptions to facilitate access

9 Full text here: https://ustr.gov/trade-agreements/free-trade-agreements/cafta-dr-dominican-republic-central-america-fta.

10 For more on this subject, see: Brown A et al., 'The Impact of Free Trade Agreements on Information Technology Based Business' (2010) 2:1 *Geopolitics, History and International Relations* 62.

11 Article 15.5.1.

12 Article 15.1.

13 On the three-step test, see Senftleben MRF, *Copyright, Limitations, and the Three-Step Test: An Analysis of the Three-Step Test in International and EC Copyright Law* (Kluwer Law International 2004).

14 Arts. 67, 68, 69, and 76.

15 Arts. 73, 73bis, and 74.

16 Marrakesh Treaty to Facilitate Access to Published Works for Persons Who Are Blind, Visually Impaired, or Otherwise Print-Disabled (2013).

17 Ley N° 9454 del 27 de junio del 2018, correspondiente a la aprobación del Tratado de Marrakech para facilitar el acceso a las obras publicadas a las personas ciegas, con discapacidad visual o con otras dificultades para acceder al texto impreso.

to copyright works for persons with visual disabilities. The works covered under the Treaty are literary and artistic works "in the form of text, notation and/or related illustrations, whether published or otherwise made publicly available in any media". This means that, while this development will add much needed disability-related exceptions to national legislation, it will still fall short, as it does not cover all copyright works.

It is important to re-state that the law only incorporated the full text of the Treaty into Costa Rican legislation, which is commonly the first stage of adoption in Costa Rica; hence, the actual changes to copyright law have not taken place yet. While the Treaty is in force and it can be used as a source of law by the courts, the exception does not exist yet in the Act. The exceptions exist in a sort of legislative limbo: they could have effect, but we still need to wait for the law to incorporate the exception explicitly.

Various laws will need to be amended as a result, specifically the existing copyright law will have to add the Treaty's revisions to the list of exceptions and limitations. There will also need to be an exception to the prohibition against circumventing technological protection measures.[18] This is because the prohibition against circumventing technological protection measures does not contain any exception whatsoever, and the law will have to add an exception for potentially tinkering with technical protections in order to allow use by persons with a visual impairment (PVI).

In short, Costa Rica will have to add to its legislation measures that will create an exception to the exclusive rights of the author for those who are considered beneficiaries under the Treaty. At the moment, it is clear that the exception is badly needed: a recent report by the University of Costa Rica has found that there is an absence of available literary works for PVI in Costa Rica.[19] While the report is not official and has not been used to shape policy, the findings are troubling and highlight the need to change the law and add exceptions for users with disabilities.

With regard to moral rights, there is nothing in the text of the Treaty that would affect the existing level of protection given to moral rights. We will need to see if the forthcoming changes to the law make any concessions in this regard.

3D printed works

Brief introduction to 3D printing and to the relevant legal issues

While it is not the place of this chapter to introduce the subject of 3D printing, it is important to introduce some of the basics for later comparative analysis

18 Ley N° 8039 de procedimientos de observancia de la propiedad intelectual, Art 5.

19 Peña Bonilla ME, 'País tiene escasez de recursos bibliográficos accesibles para personas con ceguera o baja visión' (2017), *UCR Research*, https://www.ucr.ac.cr/noticias/2017/06/02/pais-tiene-escasez-de-recursos-bibliograficos-accesibles-para-personas-con-ceguera-o-baja-vision.html.

of the existing law. The 3D printing refers to both the process of generating a computer-aided design (CAD)[20] file that contains the contour information about an object, and the process of processing that file and generating a printed copy of that information.[21] These two stages represent two different aspects of the technology: the creation of the file is the virtual element, while the process of manufacturing is the physical phase.[22] Others view this as a trichotomy; for example, there is the code in the file itself, then the design that is contained in the file, and finally the printed work.[23]

From the perspective of the file, many jurisdictions treat the CAD file as a literary work, with general agreement amongst scholars that the work falls under the definition of a computer programme, which also includes the preparatory works for the creation of the computer programme.[24]

As to the design element, the work portrayed itself could have several types of protection. If the original is protected in its own right under copyright law, say, by being a sculpture, then a reproduction of that design and its implementation into a 3D printed work would potentially be an infringement of copyright.[25] If the work has no protection, then the digital design itself is likely not to have protection either.[26]

With regard to the physical object produced after printing the file, there is no consensus as to whether it is protected at all as such. There is considerable debate and national disagreement in various jurisdictions as to whether a 3D printed work could have some sort of copyright protection, particularly because copyright does not protect functional items and many such works could be functional in nature.[27] The question may also rest on the possible lack of originality with the resulting work.

This brings us to the question of whether or not there is copyright infringement in a situation in which a 2D work has been made into a 3D article. In some jurisdictions, the answer is clear that this is infringement, both as a reproduction and as an adaptation. For example, in the UK, it is an infringement to make "a

20 Tran J, 'The Law and 3D Printing', (2015) 31 *The John Marshall Journal of Information Technology & Privacy Law* 505.

21 Negi S et al., 'Basics, Applications and Future of Additive Manufacturing Technologies: A Review' (2013) 5:1 *Journal of Manufacturing Technology Research* 75–96.

22 Ibid.

23 Daly A, *Socio-Legal Aspects of the 3D Printing Revolution* (Palgrave Macmillan 2016).

24 See: Bradshaw S et al., 'The Intellectual Property Implications of Low-Cost 3D Printing' (2010) 7:1 *SCRIPTed*; and Mendis D, 'Clone Wars: Episode II – The Next Generation: The Copyright Implications Related to 3D Printing and Computer-Aided Design (CAD) Files' (2014) 6:2 *Law, Innovation and Technology* 265–281.

25 See Bradshaw, ibid.

26 Mennell P and Vacca R, '3D Printing and US Copyright Law' (2016) UC Berkeley Public Law Research Paper No. 2859737, https://papers.ssrn.com/sol3/papers.cfm?abstract_id=2859737.

27 See for example: Simon M, 'When Copyright Can Kill: How 3D Printers are Breaking the Barriers between "Intellectual" Property and the Physical World' (2013) 3:1 *Pace Intellectual Property, Sports and Entertainment Law Forum* 59–71; see Weinberg, M, What's the Deal with Copyright and 3D Printing? (2013) Public Knowledge White Paper.

copy in three dimensions of a two-dimensional work and the making of a copy in two dimensions of a three-dimensional work".[28] In the United States, the landmark case of Rogers v Koons[29] involved an adaptation of a photograph into a sculpture, which was ruled to be copyright infringement.

Infringement, exceptions, and Costa Rican law

Assuming there is infringement in the work following what was described in "Costa Rican copyright protection and artistic works", then it could be possible to try to find an exception to copyright. Exceptions and limitations do not exist specifically for 3D printed works, so any exception would be entirely dependent on the type of use given to the work.[30] Birtchnell et al. comment:

> Although this debate also pre-dates the emergence of 3D printing, the existence of the 'fair use' defence to copyright infringement in the US (and various other jurisdictions, such as South Korea and Israel) does set a different standard of permissibility compared to the more limited 'fair dealing' defences in jurisdictions such as the UK and Australia. Given 3D printing's potential for remixes and mash-ups of objects, it may be that these would be more permissible under fair use conditions than in fair dealing conditions, but this remains to be seen in practice.[31]

As with many other issues surrounding 3D printing, there is no harmonised practice across the world, so these exceptions have to be looked at on a country-by-country basis.

Regarding Costa Rican copyright law, it contains various exceptions and limitations that could be applied to 3D printed works. Article 73 contains exceptions for private use, for research, and for educational and research purposes. Article 74 contains a relevant exception regarding printing of works for educational purposes:

> The reproduction of a didactic or scientific work, carried out personally and exclusively by the interested party for their own use and without direct or indirect profit, is also free. This reproduction must be done in a single copy, typed or manuscript. This provision will not apply to computer programs.

This may appear like a strange exception to have, but it is the direct result of widespread copying of texts around university establishments.[32] Around 2012,

28 Copyright Designs and Patents Act 1988, s17.

29 Art Rogers v. Jeff Koons, 960 F.2d 301 (1992).

30 Birtchnell T et al., '3D Printing and Intellectual Property Futures' (2018) Intellectual Property Office Research Paper.

31 Ibid.

32 'Universitarios defienden derecho a fotocopiar' (2012), UCR Vida, https://www.ucr.ac.cr/noticias/2012/10/08/universitarios-defienden-derecho-a-fotocopiar.html.

by the time of the implementation of the DR-CAFTA treaty, one of the reforms to the law imposed restrictions on the defence to copying for educational purposes, as it was felt that it was being overused and abused by businesses, particularly those around universities.[33] There was a considerable industry that would profit from selling textbooks to students, and this prompted a change in the law. The resulting change limits copying for educational purposes to one copy. While this is clearly a norm addressed to the printing and copying of literary works, it is interesting that it specifies that it does not cover computer works, which begs the question of whether it would apply to 3D printed works, especially if the definition of a computer programme includes a CAD file. Regardless of whether a CAD file falls under this definition, the limits to the educational uses tend to be very narrow, and they may not cover all uses of a 3D printer to adapt a work in order to make it available to people with disabilities.

Looking forward

It has been stated repeatedly that Costa Rican law has no exceptions for users with a disability with regard to gaining access to copyright works. It is difficult to analyse whether this has had a negative effect on the everyday experience of Costa Rican persons with a disability, and while there is limited evidence that the number of available works is low,[34] more empirical research is needed.

The recent law that incorporates the text of the Marrakesh Treaty into the corpus of Costa Rican legislation is a welcome step in the right direction, but it is too early to ascertain the effect that this will have, and we will have to wait until the existing copyright law is changed in order to begin to see real effects. The truth is that while welcome, the Marrakesh Treaty only applies to a limited range of works, so even this reform may fall short of what is needed.

It is also too early to ascertain how exactly this could affect 3D printing of 2D copyright works for the benefit of PVI. Could PVI, or another beneficiary, print a work of art under the terms of the agreement? It is difficult to say given the fact that the final wording of the law is not finalised at the time of writing. The wording of the Treaty includes a definition of "work" that includes some artistic works, so one could argue that if the Costa Rican legislation ends up with a similar formulation, then the exception would cover those artistic works. However, as we have mentioned, this would be a very generous interpretation. One way to get past this limitation is if legislators create a wider definition of "work" when implementing the terms of the Treaty, one that includes all copyright works and not just literary works and some illustrations.

Moreover, there is one case that was brought before the Costa Rican constitutional court that has created a general obligation of state entities to promote the

33 Perez Damasco D, 'El fotocopiado con fines académicos ya está garantizado en Costa Rica, afirman Gobierno y especialistas' (2012), *CAMTIC Blog*, https://www.camtic.org/actualidad-tic/el-fotocopiado-con-fines-academicos-ya-esta-garantizado-en-costa-rica-afirman-gobierno-y-especialistas/.

34 See supra note 28.

wider dissemination of cultural works to the benefit of society.[35] The case dealt with a constitutionality challenge to a piece of legislation that sought to promote the dissemination of cultural works by government institutions. The court answered the challenge negatively, and in doing so it stated a general obligation of the state to ensure a wide dissemination of cultural works. Unfortunately, the decision is worded in such a way that it is more of an ethical mandate than an actual obligation to pursue an agenda of cultural dissemination. Still, the decision sets an important precedent when it comes to the state's role in the disseminator of culture, and this could be used to put forward a more progressive copyright policy dealing with artistic works and disabilities.

For the time being, the government has welcomed the incorporation of the Treaty in Costa Rican law,[36] but it is still too early to tell the full effect until it is written into the existing law. One thing is certain, given the relative disinterest and lack of enforcement, the passing of the exceptions and limitations may not be such a vital step. Copyright infringement in Costa Rica is rampant, and new exceptions may not have much of a real impact in existing practice. However, the lack of an exception could have a chilling effect in stifling the adaptation of copyright materials for the purpose of giving access to people with disabilities, particularly from governmental entities and NGOs.

Nevertheless, in 1996, Costa Rica passed ground-breaking legislation recognising the rights of persons with a disability.[37] The law does not deal with accessibility to copyright works, and its main objective is mostly to provide physical access to infrastructure in the shape of ramps, lifts, and similar accessibility tools. However, Article 1 contains a general provision concerning disabilities:

> The integral development of the population with disabilities is declared of public interest, under the same conditions of quality, opportunity, rights and duties as the rest of the population.

This could be used in the future to argue that inclusion does not only mean physical accessibility but also requires access to copyright works. In other words, "integral development" above could be interpreted in the broadest possible sense, including access to cultural works. This could be incorporated into the Constitution, but as such a reform requires two-thirds of legislative majority, it may be easier for the Constitutional Court to interpret existing norms so as to include access to cultural works for persons with a disability based on the aforementioned principle. Needless to say, more needs to be done in this area.

35 Sala Constitucional, Resolución N° 16810–2015, 28 de Octubre del 2015.

36 Presidencia de la Republica, 'Costa Rica promueve tratado que facilita acceso a obras literarias para personas con discapacidad visual' (2017), https://presidencia.go.cr/comunicados/2017/06/costa-rica-promueve-tratado-que-facilita-acceso-a-obras-literarias-para-personas-con-discapacidad-visual/.

37 Ley No 7600 de igualdad de oportunidades para las personas con discapacidad (1996).

17 How Japanese copyright law can facilitate access to art for persons with a visual impairment

Simone Schroff[1]

The main contribution of 3D printing to persons with a visual impairment (PVI) is that it allows them to perceive art in a way not previously possible. Art works rely on visual perception and therefore can be beyond the reach of PVI. In the case of 2D art works such as paintings, the scene and setting of the painting is crucial, but touching the art work does not convey the content. Moreover, even if the work is three-dimensional, allowing museum visitors to touch it is usually out of question. As a result, art is often inaccessible to PVI. The 3D printing can bridge both of these gaps. It can turn a two-dimensional piece of art into a three-dimensional work, making the scene and setting accessible. In addition, 3D printing has advanced enough to allow for cost-effective replicas which visitors can touch. Finally, the original remains unaffected: all that is required is a detailed laser scan. However, the scanning and (3D) printing are copyright-relevant activities in Japan.

The role of copyright law in facilitating the full participation of people with disabilities in society and especially its cultural life has long been recognised.[2] On 1 October 2018, Japan ratified the Marrakesh Treaty which entered into force on 1 January 2019.[3] While the Marrakesh ratification came in the wake of a major reform package,[4] the role of 3D printing and modern technology as

1 Lecturer in Law, University of Plymouth.

2 For example, Japan signed the Convention for United Nations Convention on the Rights of Persons with Disabilities on 20 January 2014.

3 In doing so, it is in line with the European Union (see Directive (EU) 2017/1564 of the European Parliament and of the Council of 13 September 2017 on certain permitted uses of certain works and other subject matter protected by copyright and related rights for the benefit of persons who are blind, visually impaired or otherwise print-disabled and amending Directive 2001/29/EC on the harmonisation of certain aspects of copyright and related rights in the information society).

4 Copyright Amendment Act of 18 May 2018, effective from 1 January 2019. For a good summary, Current Awareness Portal, *Reforms for the Progress of Digital and Networks and the Broadening the Information Access Opportunities for Disabled Persons* (デジタル化・ネットワーク化の進展や障害者の情報アクセス機会の拡充等に対応した改正著作権法が成立) (23 May 2018) (http://current.ndl.go.jp/node/36038, accessed 19 September 2019). The copyright term was extended from 50 years after the death of the author to 70 years, catching up with both the EU and the US. Amendments also focused on making new industries viable and reduce the hindering effect

such in making art works more accessible has not stirred major debates in Japan. In fact, Japan took a narrow implementation route by drawing on the Treaty's article 4(4), which allows countries to apply the rules of the Marrakesh Treaty only to the extent that works are not available commercially. This seems to imply that Japan's approach to the issue is narrow and limited.

This chapter examines the extent to which Japanese copyright law supports or hinders sensory art, mainly in reference to the 3D printing of art works for PVI by cultural heritage institutions. It focuses on cultural heritage institutions in particular, as these are, in the first instance at least, the most likely institutions carrying out this kind of project as pilots. In the first part, the basic requirements for copyright to be relevant will be outlined. The discussion will then examine 3D printing as a process from the copyright angle to identify when and how copyright law is relevant. In the third section, the 1970 Japanese Copyright Act's mandatory exceptions are analysed, focusing on the key requirements and the extent to which they cover 3D printing for PVI. The conclusion then will make suggestions for reform to facilitate the use of 3D printing in the sensory art context.

The requirements for copyright protection

Copyright protection is dependent on meeting certain statutory requirements. This means that copyright is relevant if, and only if, the original art work to be scanned for 3D printing meets these conditions. First, the original art work must fall within the scope of copyright law. Japanese copyright law defines copyright works as the creative expression reflecting the author's emotions, especially in the fields of literature, science and scholarship, art and music.[5] The notion of originality is best understood in context, in particular in relation to the specific type of work.

The notion of work is further clarified in the list of copyright works provided by article 10. For art works, the key provision is article 10(iv) which covers the traditional forms of artistic expression such as paintings, sculptures and engravings '*and other artistic works*'. It is an open-ended definition which gives only illustrating examples, covering both 2D and 3D works. The key criterion for art works to be considered copyrightable is that they need to be perceived as primarily artistic,[6] whereby originality is expressed as a combination of the shape and colours used.[7] Photographs are also protected but are listed separately[8] because they are the result of a technical process. They only benefit from protection if the author, defined as the natural person who has created the work,[9] has shown

copyright may have on these. They address issues around the reproduction, use of databases and the storage of works for AI purposes.

5 Japanese Copyright Act 1970, art. 2(1)(i).

6 M. Kato, *Copyright Law: Article by Article Analysis* (著作権法逐条講義), p. 122.

7 M. Kato, *Copyright Law: Article by Article Analysis* (著作権法逐条講義), p. 122.

8 Japanese Copyright Act 1970, art. 10(viii).

9 Japanese Copyright Act 1970, art. 2(1)(ii). This is subject to employment provisions under art. 15.

some active decision-making when the photograph was set up. In practice, photographs will be presumed to be original if they have significant economic value.[10] For photographs that are part of art exhibitions, this threshold might be presumed to be met since their consideration for exhibition by itself marks them as outstanding and original within the definition of the law. However, not covered are photographs made automatically by machines without significant human intervention; as part of cinematographic works; and those purely made to reflect reality.[11] Taking the term 'art' more broadly, Japanese copyright law also includes protection for 'artistic' architectural works,[12] while their blueprints and figurative works of a scientific nature such as plans, charts and models are protected under article 10(vi). Therefore, it can be presumed from article 10 that all types of art works, their plans and models in exhibitions fall under Japanese copyright law.

The second requirement is that the art work in question must still be protected by copyright. The standard term of protection is 70 years after the death of the author. In cases where the author is not known (anonymous/ pseudonymous works), the relevant time point is the making public of the work or its translation. This generally refers to the publication, transmission or issuing copies to the public either by the author or with his permission.[13] For art and photographic works, this explicitly also includes their first exhibition.[14] Given the recent copyright term extension from 50 to 70 years, care needs to be taken with this requirement.[15] The law does not 'revive' expired rights (like the EU extension did in the 1990s), but instead it only applies to works still under protection on 30 December 2018 and thereafter. In practice, this means that the death of the author or the first act of making the work public needs to have occurred after 30 December 1968 for copyright protection to subsist.

In summary, copyright law is only a relevant consideration if two criteria are met. First, the work must be copyrightable and therefore fall within the scope of copyright works and meet the minimum originality threshold. Secondly, the term of protection cannot have expired. If these conditions are not met, then anyone is free to reproduce the original art work using 3D printing technology. If they are, then it is essential to proceed in a copyright-compliant manner.

3D scanning of art works

In general, the 3D printing process has three distinct stages. First, the original art work needs to be loaded into the computer-assisted design (CAD) software

10 M. Kato, *Copyright Law: Article by Article Analysis* (著作権法逐条講義), p. 125.

11 M. Kato, *Copyright Law: Article by Article Analysis* (著作権法逐条講義), pp. 125–126.

12 Japanese Copyright Act 1970, art. 10(v). Actually establishing the artistic character and artistic components can be difficult in practice as Sakka has pointed out. F. Sakka, *Detailed Explanation of Copyright Law* (詳解著作権法) (Tokyo: Gyousei, 5th ed., 2018), pp. 88–89.

13 Japanese Copyright Act 1970, art. 4(1).

14 Japanese Copyright Act 1970, art. 4(4).

15 For an explanation of the 2018 reform package, see footnote 3.

by scanning every detail of it. Under copyright law, authors[16] have the exclusive right to control the reproduction of their work which is defined as the reproduction '*in a physical form through printing, photography, or replication, by recording its sound or visuals, or in any other way…*'.[17] The definition is technologically neutral and does include the scanning of the whole work or a significant part of it. The physical form here is the image that is created in the CAD software. It should be noted that under sub-paragraph (c), the reproduction right also includes building an architectural work based on its blueprints. There has been no case law yet on the extent to which 'building' activity can be digital, but given the technological neutrality of the main provision, an argument can be made that it is covered. It can therefore be concluded that the scanning process requires permission under the right to reproduction (article 21).

Once the image has been scanned and loaded into the CAD software, the latter is used to develop the model needed by the actual printing software to make the 3D model. Making changes can potentially be an issue as authors have the right to protect the integrity of their work: the author '*shall have the right to preserve the integrity of his work and its title against any distortion, mutilation or other modification against his will.*'[18] However, this provision does not apply where the modifications made are required by the nature of the work and its intended use.[19] Given that the purpose of the 3D printing here is to enable PVI to experience the original art work as much as possible, it is most likely that the changes to be made to the scanned reproduction are limited to what is technologically necessary to enable the printing. Therefore, there are no major copyright concerns in this regard.

It can be questioned whether the image in the CAD software is sufficiently creative to give rise to a copyrightable work in its own right. In the absence of case law, this remains an open question, but a few pointers can be given. First, the list of work types is illustrative and not a closed list, leaving room for new additions. In this sense, there is nothing that prevents CAD images from falling under copyright protection. Instead, the issue is if the originality threshold is met. As previously mentioned, Japanese copyright law requires a natural person to create a work. Based on this, meeting the originality threshold crucially depends on the extent to which the technician intervenes in or after the scanning process. One possible analogy here could be the protection of photographs. Photography is essentially a reproduction technology, but photographs are copyrightable as long as the author's choices are sufficient to meet the originality requirement.[20]

16 The term is used broadly here and includes copyright owners who have been assigned the rights at some stage.

17 Japanese Copyright Act 1970, art. 2(15)- Translation by Ministry of Justice (http://www.japaneselawtranslation.go.jp/law/detail/?id=2506&vm=04&re=02, accessed 19 September 2019).

18 Japanese Copyright Act 1970, art. 29- Translation by Ministry of Justice (http://www.japaneselawtranslation.go.jp/law/detail/?id=2506&vm=04&re=02, accessed 19 September 2019).

19 Japanese Copyright Act 1970, art. 20(iv).

20 This goes back to the originality standard required for photographs which is reflected in the choices the photographer makes. For a detailed discussion, see F. Sakka, *Detailed Explanation of Copyright Law* (詳解著作権法), pp. 91–95.

The same reasoning could justify giving protection to CAD images, depending on how much human intervention is required to turn the CAD image into a usable 3D print. While the issue remains debated in the literature, there seems to be a growing consensus in favour of copyright protection.[21] Given Japan's general preference for stronger protection and support to new industries,[22] it seems reasonable to conclude that the CAD images are copyright works in their own right, at least until the issue is clarified by the courts or the legislature.

The discussion is important as it affects the status of the CAD scan under copyright law, especially if the CAD scan and the resulting replica have to be considered derivative works. Making adaptations and therefore derivative works is regulated by article 27: the author has the exclusive right to '***translate, arrange musically or transform, or dramatize, cinematize, or otherwise adapt his work.***'[23] Derivative works under Japanese law are considered copyright-protected works in themselves (二次的著作物), and therefore have to meet the originality threshold in order to get copyright protection. As a result, this provision covers turning a 2D art work into a 3D one (and vice versa), but it does not include translating a work using Braille – only foreign language translations fall within this provision.[24] If the CAD image meets the originality threshold, then it has to be considered a derivative of the original art work which, in turn, makes it copyright relevant in its own right. Since scholarly opinion currently seems to favour that CAD images are copyright works, permission is required not only to reproduce the original art work but also to make a derivative work.

21 N. Kotaro, "We Made a Penrose Triangle with 3D Printing, But…(3Dプリンターでペンローズ三角形は 作れたが…)", *Journal of Information Processing and Management*, Vol. 56(7), 2013, pp. 477–479. K. Nagai, *3D Printing and Creating an Open Creative Breeding Ground within Current Copyright Law* (*3D*プリンタと著作権の現在 —オープンな創作の土壌をつくるために)" (26 June 2014) (https://www.kottolaw.com/column/000798.html, accessed 19 September 2019); EC法務, *The Problems of 3D Printing Technology under Copyright Law Are?!* (*3D*プリント技術の著作権法上の問題点とは！？) (19 March 2019) (https://ec-houmu.com/right/3Dprint-copyright#3D-2, accessed 19 September 2019); T. Ikkanda, "Can AI Be the Author?- Technological Possibilities and Their Limits (?)- ?! (AI は著作者になれるのか —テクノロジーの可能性と限界（？）—！？)", *Kyojo Journal of Law and Politics*, Vol. 11, 2017, pp. 40–41; For an opinion to the contrary, concerning the pure scanning of an item. M. Sudo, "Copyright Issues Surrounding Online Publication of Archaeological Site Reports and 3D Scanning of Cultural Properties (発掘調査報告書のウエブ公開と文化財の3D データに関する著作権の諸問題)", *Nara National Research Institute for Cultural Properties*, Vol. 21, 2019, pp. 94–95.

22 See footnote 3. Japan considers strong copyright protection essential for the creative industries. Indeed, the TRIPs negotiations were strongly shaped by the triumvirate made up of the US, EU and Japan – all arguing for stronger levels of protection.This ethos was also evident when Japan ratified the ill-fated ACTA agreement which raised not only serious concerns within the EU but led to street protests and the first successful public opposition to a copyright agreement in the West. For a historical perspective, see J. Braithwaite and Drahos, P., *Global Business Regulation* (Cambridge: Cambridge University Press), p. 66.

23 Japanese Copyright Act 1970, art. 27, Translation by Ministry of Justice (http://www.japaneselawtranslation.go.jp/law/detail/?id=2506&vm=04&re=02, accessed 19 September 2019).

24 M. Kato, *Copyright Law: Article by Article Analysis* (著作権法逐条講義), p. 213. It should be noted though that the use of Braille would fall under article 21 and therefore the reproduction right.

Considering the CAD images as derivative works adds another layer of authorship. This is also reflected in article 28, which clarifies the rights status of the derivative work by providing the author of the original work with the same rights as the author of the derivative work.[25] This covers all of the rights which are available, and the rights are cumulative: both the original artwork and the derivative work are protected under copyright law, and each one has a distinct author and rights attached to it. However, the derivative work's author cannot give permission alone for any further use of the work: she or whoever is seeking permission also needs agreement from the author of the original artistic work.[26] Kato points out that the purpose of article 28 is to give the author control over secondary (derivative) works which are directly derived from his own.[27] As a result, the artist and the author of the derivative work both have equal rights and need to agree on how the derivative work is to be further used. This is important in terms of long-term copyright management in the context of sensory art projects. In particular, it requires that the copyright ownership of the 3D CAD images and the replica is clarified (ideally beforehand and contractually), to ensure both can be used as intended by the cultural heritage institution.

Examining the 3D printing process from a copyright angle shows that cultural heritage institutions need up to three sets of permissions. First, they need permission to reproduce the original art by scanning it. Secondly, they also need approval to make a derivate work depending on the rights status of the adapted CAD image, which will be presumed here to be a copyright work in its own right. Finally, the cultural heritage institution will have to either acquire the copyright or get permission to use the CAD image and the 3D printed replica from the author of the CAD image. While the last part will most easily be resolved by contracts as part of the 3D printing project, the permissions from the original artist are more difficult to acquire. It is here that the copyright exceptions for PVI are most important.

Limitations in the 1970 Japanese Copyright Act

Limitations in the 1970 Japanese Copyright Act can be conceptualised as four distinct situations where the public benefit outweighs the interests of the author: (1) the type of use makes the application of copyright inappropriate, (2) the public benefit involved by the use in question requires a limitation to copyright,

25 Article 28:

> The author of the original work underlying a derivative work holds exclusive rights in the same categories as the rights prescribed in this Subsection that the author of the derivative work holds in connection with the exploitation of that derivative work.

Translation by Ministry of Justice (http://www.japaneselawtranslation.go.jp/law/detail/?id=2506&vm=04&re=02, accessed 19 September 2019).

26 M. Kato, *Copyright Law: Article by Article Analysis* (著作権法逐条講義), p. 217.

27 M. Kato, *Copyright Law: Article by Article Analysis* (著作権法逐条講義), p. 213.

(3) a need to coordinate copyright with other rights that may exist and (4) customary practices which do not cause undue economic harm to the author.[28] The exceptions for PVI (article 37) and persons with a hearing impairment (article 37*bis*) fall under the first category, because for these individuals, accessing the work as such already breaches copyright in a way not faced by persons without a disability. They would be unduly affected by the law in the absence of specific exceptions.

While the general justifiability is accepted by scholars and legislators alike,[29] new technologies which provide novel ways of making copyright works accessible to persons with a disability (such as 3D printing 2D art works, as examined here) are slow to be included. First, as a member of the Berne Convention, all of the Japanese exceptions are subject to the Three-Step Test and therefore should prevent undue market harm to the rights holder. This favours narrow exceptions, covering established uses at the time of drafting. Secondly, achieving technological neutrality is difficult because of the inherent uncertainty of how future uses may relate to the law. Nonetheless, this technological neutrality is exactly what the Japanese provision for PVI seeks to create.

Permission to reproduce a work for the benefit of PVI (Article 37)

The main provision for PVI can be found in article 37.[30] Paragraphs (1) and (2) focus on the traditional view of the difficulties PVI face when accessing works: they cannot see the letters. Under paragraph (1), the user is allowed to make a reproduction of the original work in Braille. Paragraph (2) then extends the provision by adding the use of computers when accessing, storing and transmitting Braille works. Both provisions are specifically limited to Braille, and while they are open to all types of works, they are largely applicable to literary works due to the nature of the activities envisaged by the legislator. More interesting for 3D printing is the third and final paragraph of article 37. Article 37(3) aims to give PVI access to all types of copyright works in whatever manner is the most suitable for them. However, the provision is complex, and therefore this analysis will proceed examining its core requirements one by one.

Like paragraphs (1) and (2), paragraph (3) applies to all types of copyright works, as long as the work has been made public.[31] The meaning of making

28 M. Kato, *Copyright Law: Article by Article Analysis* (著作権法逐条講義), p. 277.

29 This is clearly visible in practice as article 37 was first introduced in 1970 and has since been continuously expanded to meet technological changes and the opportunities these offer to the visually blind.

30 A full translation of article 37 can be found in the Annex.

31 It should be noted here that another widely used translation by the Copyright Research and Information Center (CRIC) contains a minor but significant error in its translations. It refers to "word, made public" rather than "work". However, the original provision reads 公表された著作物 and therefore work.

public depends on the specific type of work in question, as discussed earlier in the context of the term of protection.[32] The provision then narrows the scope to works '*offered or presented to the public in a rendered form that is perceived visually*'. As a result, the visual component has to be central to accessing the work, for example, the information, emotions and impressions a painting gives to the audience is visual. Music, on the other hand, relies on hearing and therefore has the audio and not a visual component at its centre. However, this requirement only applies to the main work that is being reproduced: any other copyright works which are attached to the original work are still included within the scope of the provision.[33] This is necessary to ensure that combined works, such as having an image next to text, are not unduly preventing the application of the exception, rendering it ineffective in practice. Similarly, neighbouring rights (phonograms, broadcasts and performances) are covered via article 102(1) and 102(4), which extends the rules of article 37(3) to all neighbouring rights.

Differently to paragraphs (1) and (2), paragraph (3) is broader in practice because it is not limited to Braille as a method of reproduction. Paragraph (3) allows for the reproduction, transmission and automatic transmission (which, in EU countries, is the equivalent to making available) of the copyright work in whatever form is required to make it accessible. The key point for sensory art is its openness to the techniques used: '*or in any other form that is necessary to allow the visual work to be used by persons with visual impairments.*' It is consciously technologically neutral by not prescribing any particular method. Sakka, for example, emphasises that the provision aims to be as broad as possible and does not seek to exclude anything as long as it is suitable for the overall aim.[34] In addition, it does not limit the senses used by the accessible copy. A standard book in this context can be made accessible by using textiles or re-designing it into a 3D book (pop-up book). While 3D printing is not mentioned in the examples listed within article 37(3), it is not excluded either. Instead, it represents a similar sensory shift from vision to touch, and therefore it is in line with other, more established methods given as illustrating examples within the provision itself. However, the scope is limited to '*within the limits that are found to be necessary in order to provide the visual work for their exclusive use.*' In other words, it depends on the specific visual impairment that the individual has, assessed on a case-by-case basis. The specific visual impairment will then determine if 3D printing is suitable or necessary.

Article 37 relies on a two component definition of what 'visually impaired' means. The provision first refers to natural persons that have '*difficulties in the perception of visual renderings*' in combination with '*other impairments*' that affect vision. Kato highlights this need to be interpreted broadly and includes, for example, blindness, developmental conditions and colour blindness,[35] as long

32 See section "The Requirements for Copyright Protection".

33 "*Including a work other than the work in question which is reproduced therein or which is offered or presented to the public in a body united with the former work*".

34 F. Sakka, *Detailed Explanation of Copyright Law* (詳解著作権法), p. 348.

35 M. Kato, *Copyright Law: Article by Article Analysis* (著作権法逐条講義), p. 292.

as they affect the individual's ability to visually perceive the work in question.[36] However, it needs to be noted that this reference to the visually impaired also forms a strict condition on the use of this exception. Under article 49(1) in combination with article 49(2)(i), it is clear that if the copies made under this provision are used for any other purpose such as loaning, selling or broadcasting the copied work to persons without a visual impairment or the general public, normal copyright provisions apply. In other words, these activities constitute copyright infringement if the author has not given his/her permission. As a result, the cultural heritage institutions should clearly define which type and/or degree of visual impairment is covered by the sensory art project (and equally important, which ones are not).

Given its broad scope in terms of aims, permitted techniques and definition of visually impaired, it is not surprising that there are limitations in terms of who can actually rely on the provision. Article 37(3) only covers the action of certain organisations, namely, '*person set forth by Cabinet Order that engages in an undertaking related to the welfare of persons who have difficulties in the perception of visual renderings due to visual impairments or other impairments*'. Under the Cabinet Order, specialist institutions for PVI, all schools, public libraries and similar institutions are explicitly included.[37] In addition, the Cabinet Order also offers any institution the option to register as a designated person as long as it meets three requirements: (1) having the technical and financial skills to support the relevant activity, (2) having employees with the necessary expertise and (3) keeping a register of PVI they share information with.[38] The range of institutions that can apply for designated status is therefore very broad, but unless they are explicitly included in the list, they need to apply for permission. The secure route would be for the cultural heritage institution to apply for recognition under the Cabinet Order. While museums and archives are not explicitly mentioned, it is likely that they would also be covered given their shared public benefit missions of providing access to culture. However, the requirement to keep a register could prove difficult in practice, especially in the context of exhibitions open to the general public. Alternatively, a cooperation between a designated institution and a cultural heritage institution may be suitable.

The other major limitation within article 37(3) refers to the market for works for PVI. The legislator sees a market solution as preferable, in line with the Berne Convention's Three-Step Test, which requires all exceptions to not unduly affect the author's economic interests. As a result, article 37(3) explicitly states that if a work has been made available in a suitable, accessible format by the author, then the provision does not apply at all. In this way, authors are given an incentive for using market mechanisms, while PVI receive the access this provision intends to provide. 'Suitable' here does not refer to convenient or generally affordable,

36 Article 37(3) clarifies this explicitly by stating: "having difficulty in using that visual work in its visual form".

37 F. Sakka, *Detailed Explanation of Copyright Law* (詳解著作権法), p. 437.

38 Copyright Law Implementation Order 1970, art. 2(2).

though.[39] Instead, it has to be read from the viewpoint of offering substitutes: since the reason for this limitation is incentivising authors to license their works in suitable formats, any competing offer that undermines this (namely, offering free or lower-priced substitutes) is excluded from article 37(3).

Finally, both the author and the source have to be named.[40] The author is presumed to be the person named on the work.[41] This refers to the usual method by which authors are named according to the type of work in question, including, for example, title pages, publication data, labels or booklets, and this actually supersedes the name next to a copyright notice (if it exists).[42] However, it does not cover implied authorship references (暗示的な表現), such as only mentioning a name in the foreword of a book.

In summary, permission to reproduce an original art work through 3D printing for the benefit of PVI has to meet the following conditions:

- The art work must have been made public and offered in a way that can be perceived visually.
- The 3D printing has to be an effective way of giving access to the work in the context of the specific visual impairment: clear delineation is preferable here about which type/ degree of visual impairment should be covered by the 3D printing project.
- The managing institution needs to have recognised status or cooperate with one which does. If the institution does not fall under a default category, then the requirement to keep a register of PVI benefitting from its actions will most likely prove the most difficult condition to comply with in practice.
- If an official, commercially licensed suitable alternative is available, the sensory art project cannot rely on article 37(3).
- The authors and sources of all copyright- or neighbouring rights-relevant parts have to be named.

Permission to make adaptations

As discussed previously, permission to make a derivative work may be required in addition to the permission to make a reproduction. Article 47*Sexies*[43] covers the exploitation of copies made under previous exceptions, including making derivative works. As long as the conditions of the primary exception (here article 37(3)) are met, it allows for the making of translations, reformulations and adaptations.

39 F. Sakka, *Detailed Explanation of Copyright Law* (詳解著作権法), p. 350; M. Kato, Copyright Law: Article by Article Analysis (著作権法逐条講義), pp. 295–296.

40 For copyright works, see art. 48(1)(ii) and art 48(2). This is extended to neighbouring rights under art. 102(2).

41 Japanese Copyright Act 1970, art. 14.

42 M. Kato, *Copyright Law: Article by Article Analysis* (著作権法逐条講義) (Tokyo: Copyright Information Center, 6th ed., 2013), p. 144.

43 This article used to be article 43, but since then it has shifted. Please note that older Copyright Commentaries and the CRIC translation do not reflect this shift yet.

Translations refers to offering the work in other languages. Reformulations is not as clear from the English translation, but the original Japanese wording shows that it refers to changing the form (変形), while the concept of adaptations is broader altogether. As Kato points out, an adaptation uses the story, structure and main components (= interior form) to make a derivative work.[44] Under article 47 *Sexies*(1)(v), it explicitly refers to the copies under article 37(3). For the 3D printing project, this provision means that both the CAD image and the resulting end product (the printed art) are covered by the exception. While article 47*Sexies* does not impose any additional conditions, it should be noted that the need to name the source and author also applies to the derivative work via article 48(3).[45]

Once copies have been made, the producing institution can share them with PVI. Sakka points out that this includes (and even presumes) a transfer of copies and therefore goes beyond the lending envisaged by article 37(1) and (2).[46] This reasoning derives from article 47 *Septies*, which states that a transfer of copies is permitted as long as the transfer is for the same purpose as stated in article 37(3) – in other words, making works accessible for PVI. In practice, therefore, cultural heritage institutions can provide the replicas to PVI on a temporary or on a permanent basis.

Conclusion

In conclusion, making 3D copies of copyright protected art works is permitted under Japanese copyright law as long as it is for the benefit of and limited to PVI. However, compliance with the rules is difficult in practice, given the large number of provisions that have to be taken into account, the diverse conditions these impose and the unclear status of 3D printing under copyright law. To facilitate the access to copyright-protected art by PVI, a series of recommendations can be made. They centre on the complexity of the rules, which can potentially chill sensory art projects or lead to accidental mistakes in their implementation. First, all cultural heritage museums with a public benefit mission should be explicitly included in the Cabinet Order that defines which institutions can rely on article 37(3). This would facilitate the process not only by clarifying the institutions' legal position but also by reducing the registration-related transaction costs involved in getting sensory art projects off the ground. Secondly, the status of 3D printing (including the status of the CAD images) needs to be resolved because it is crucial to determining which rules actually apply when. Thirdly, in the absence of a specialised provision in the Copyright Act, it is necessary to provide detailed guidance to cultural heritage institutions, laying out how they can comply with the exceptions' requirements in practice.

44 M. Kato, *Copyright Law: Article by Article Analysis* (著作権法逐条講義), p. 213.

45 Depending on the situation, it may be necessary for the cultural heritage institution in charge to secure the rights in the CAD reproduction of the original art work, especially if this task is not carried out in-house.

46 F. Sakka, *Detailed Explanation of Copyright Law* (詳解著作権法), p. 348.

Annex

1 It is permissible to reproduce in Braille a work that has been made public.

2 It is permissible to use a computerized Braille processing system to record a work that has been made public onto a recording medium or transmit to the public such a work (except in a broadcast or cablecast; however, it is permissible to make the work available for transmission, if it is to be transmitted to the public via automatic public transmission; the same applies in the next paragraph).

3 A person set forth by Cabinet Order that engages in an undertaking related to the welfare of persons who have difficulties in the perception of visual renderings due to visual impairments or other impairments (hereinafter in this paragraph and in Article 102, paragraph (4) referred to as "persons with visual impairments, etc.") may reproduce a work that has been made public and that is offered or presented to the public in a rendered form that is perceived visually (including a work that has been made public and that is offered or presented to the public in a form that is perceived both visually and through other senses) (including a work other than the work in question which is reproduced therein or which is offered or presented to the public in a body united with the former work; hereinafter in this paragraph and in Article 102, paragraph (4) referred to as a "visual work"), and may transmit such a visual work to the public, with the writing in the visual work changed into sound, or in any other form that is necessary to allow the visual work to be used by persons with visual impairments, etc. who have difficulty in using that visual work in its visual form, within the limits that are found to be necessary in order to provide the visual work for their exclusive use; provided, however, that this does not apply if the visual work has already been offered or presented to the public in such a form by the copyright owner, a person authorized thereby, a person in favor of whom the print rights set forth in Article 79 have been established, a person authorized thereby to reproduce the visual work, or a person authorized thereby to transmit the visual work to the public.[47]

47 Translation by Ministry of Justice (http://www.japaneselawtranslation.go.jp/law/detail/?id=3259&vm=04&re=02, accessed 19 September 2019).

18 New Zealand

Lida Ayoubi

Introduction

It is estimated that around 168,000 New Zealanders are blind or have a visual impairment.[1] The Blind and Low Vision NZ (formerly Blind Foundation) is the biggest provider of accessible works to persons who are blind or visually impaired (PVI) in New Zealand (NZ).[2] The formats that the Foundation produces include Braille, large print, electronic text and audio books. Other entities including educational institutions may also provide PVI with accessible formats of copyright works.[3] The focus of the Blind and Low Vision NZ and similar entities, however, appears to be mainly the provision of access to literary works. Some other parties, primarily in the GLAM sector (galleries, libraries, archives and museums), work on facilitating access to artistic works for those with visual and other disabilities.[4]

The research for this chapter revealed that initiatives for provision of access to art for PVI in NZ involve both a direct reproduction of copyright works and the use of other means of facilitating access. For instance, the Museum of New Zealand Te Papa Tongarewa (Te Papa), Audio Described Aotearoa and Arts Access Aotearoa regularly provide audio descriptions of various forms of art including artistic works such as paintings, sculptures and even ballet performances.[5] Examples of access to art through touch are also available. The Govett-Brewster Art Gallery, for instance, occasionally provides tactile 'samples, models and or

1 Disability Survey: 2013 (*StatsNZ*, 2013) <http://archive.stats.govt.nz/browse_for_stats/health/disabilities/DisabilitySurvey_HOTP2013/Commentary.as> accessed 15 October 2019.
2 Accessible Information and Technology (*Blind and Low Vision NZ*) <https://blindlowvision.org.nz/how-we-can-help/technology/accessible-information/> accessed 15 October 2019.
3 See for example the New Zealand National Library <https://natlib.govt.nz/about-this-site/accessibility-standards> accessed 15 October 2019.
4 Examples of those organisations are Art Access Aotearoa <https://artsaccess.org.nz/>; Govett-Brewster Art Gallery <https://govettbrewster.com> accessed 15 October 2019.
5 For examples of such services, see 'Audio Description and Touch Tours' (*Arts Access Aotearoa*) <https://artsaccess.org.nz/audio%20description%20and%20touch%20tours>; 'Royal New Zealand Ballet's First Audio Description' (*Creative NZ*, 21 August 2017) <https://www.creativenz.govt.nz/news/royal-new-zealand-ballet-s-first-audio-description> accessed 15 October 2019.

props' of artworks. These may be 'either samples or offcuts provided by the artist' or replicas of copyright works reproduced after obtaining 'permission from the artist as the copy right holder to make samples' at the Gallery.[6] Te Papa also runs touch tours where access for the public in general and those with disabilities is provided to:[7]

> not replicas but rather original works or materials we [have] sourced from communities or the artist specifically with the intention of making them available for handling. Sometimes those we commission[ed] to create artworks have [a] product that has not made the final cut into the installation and thus does not form part of the artwork. However, these left-overs still have value as examples of textures that can be handled. As they are not copies and they are also not the final artwork there is no restriction to them being handled as part of the accessibility tour. In other cases, we [have] purchased or gathered resources for handling.

Disability rights, including the rights to equality and non-discrimination for persons with a disability (PWD), gained momentum in NZ in the 1990s.[8] The NZ Human Rights Act 1993 included disability as a prohibited ground for discrimination.[9] The trend that started in the late 1990s continued with New Zealand's close involvement and leadership in the adoption of the Convention on the Rights of Persons with Disabilities 2006, which NZ ratified in 2008.[10]

Before the government started to consider joining the WIPO Marrakesh Treaty,[11] lack of access to copyright works for New Zealanders with disabilities was not arguably part of the official discussions around disability rights.[12] The first New Zealand Disability Strategy, adopted in 2001, recognised the provision of

6 Email from Govett-Brewster Art Gallery staff to author (15 October 2019).

7 Email from Victoria Leachman, Rights Manager, Te Papa to author (8 October 2019).

8 Margaret Bedggood and Claire Breen, 'The Rights to Equality and Non-Discrimination' in Margaret Bedggood and others (eds), *International Human Rights Law in Aotearoa New Zealand* (Thomson Reuters New Zealand Ltd 2017).

9 Human Rights Act 1993, s 21(1)(h).

10 See for a discussion of these developments Judy McGregor and others, *Human Rights in New Zealand: Emerging Faultlines* (Bridget Williams Books 2016) 118–122.

11 World Intellectual Property Organization, Marrakesh Treaty to Facilitate Access to Published Works for Persons who are Blind, Visually Impaired, or Otherwise Print Disabled, WIPO Doc VIP/DC/8 (opened for signature 27 June 2013, entered into force 30 September 2016) (Marrakesh Treaty).

12 See, for example, the First New Zealand Report on Implementing the United Nations Convention on the Rights of Persons with Disabilities, March 2011, that briefly mentions that Ministry of Social Development funds Royal NZ Foundation of Blind 'to provide a talking books service to people who are blind or vision-impaired'; the Human Rights Commission, 'Disabled Children's Right to Education', 2009, that discusses inclusive education but does not mention accessible print material; the New Zealand Human Rights Commission, 'Discussion Paper The Wider Journey: The Rights of Disabled People', March 2012, that discusses access to information, but does not mention accessible print material.

the best possible education for PWD as one of its objectives. It required that 'disabled students ... have equitable access to the resources available to meet their needs'.[13] In 2012, the NZ Human Rights Commission referred to the Disability Strategy in one of its Discussion Papers when addressing access for PWD to information.[14] However, the Disability Strategy was seen by some as out of date and requiring amendment.[15] Over the years, there were references to access for PWD to information.[16] In addition, the rights of students with a disability to primary and tertiary education were highlighted, but the need for accessible textbooks or other educational material, which may include artistic copyright works, was not explicitly discussed.[17] The recent Disability Strategy 2016 also counts 'inclusive education' and 'accessibility' (including accessible information and communication) among its outcomes, but there is no direct reference to the need for accessible material or copyright works.[18]

This might in part be attributed to the fact that copyright law in NZ has for some time contained fair dealing exceptions for different purposes, including for the benefit of PVI.[19] Furthermore, in 2017, the NZ government indicated its intention to join the WIPO Marrakesh Treaty.[20] Subsequently, in 2019, the Parliament approved the Copyright (Marrakesh Treaty Implementation) Amendment Bill 2018 ('the Marrakesh Amendment'), amending the Copyright Act 1994 (the CA or the CA 1994). Soon after the adoption of the amendment, NZ deposited its instrument of accession to the Treaty, bringing into force both the Amendment and the Treaty on 4 January 2020.[21]

This chapter evaluates the existing general flexibilities in the CA 1994, as well as the implications of the new Marrakesh Amendment, for access to artistic works for PVI and PWD in NZ. Following this Introduction, section 'Copyright

13 Office for Disability Issues, Ministry of Social Development, 'New Zealand Disability Strategy' (April 2001)16.

14 New Zealand Human Rights Commission, 'The Wider Journey: The Rights of Disabled People' (March 2012).

15 See Association of Blind Citizens of New Zealand (ABCNZ), 'Submission to Human Rights Commission in response to Discussion Paper the Wider Journey: The Rights of Disabled People' (March 2012) 4.

16 See for example ABCNZ, 'The Great Barrier Brief: Register of Issues' (22 July 2008) 3.

17 Ibid. 7 calling upon the government to 'fund and resource the education of blind children to a level that enables them to access and receive a quality education equivalent to that received by their non-disabled peers'. See also ABCNZ, 'As We See It: Accessing New Zealand via Non-visual Means' (July 2003) 35 recommending the adoption of legislation for promotion of 'a mechanism by which uniform standards for electronic data storage can be managed and circulated thus facilitating rapid production of Braille for students enrolled in both compulsory and tertiary study'.

18 Office for Disability Issues, Ministry of Social Development, 'New Zealand Disability Strategy 2016–2026' 24 and 32.

19 Copyright Act 1994, Part 3 (CA 1994).

20 'New Zealand to Join Marrakesh Treaty' (*Beehive*, 22 June 2017) <www.beehive.govt.nz/release/new-zealand-join-marrakesh-treaty> accessed 15 October 2019.

21 'New Zealand Joins Marrakesh Treaty' (*WIPO*, 4 October 2019) <www.wipo.int/marrakesh_treaty/en/news/2019/news_0008.html> accessed 15 October 2019.

flexibilities and access to art in New Zealand' discusses a number of general fair dealing exceptions in the CA that might be relevant to access to art for PVI. Section 'Copyright flexibilities for the PWD' then provides an analysis of the newly introduced disability exception. Finally, section 'Access for PWD and rights of Māori' briefly highlights the interface of copyright exceptions and the rights of Māori, the indigenous people of New Zealand. For the purposes of brevity, the terms PVI or PWD are used throughout the chapter when discussing persons who require accessible format copies to enjoy copyright works.

Copyright flexibilities and access to art in New Zealand

Copyright protection of art

The CA 1994 (and its amendments) is the main legislation governing copyright protection in New Zealand. The CA protects original 'artistic works'[22] that are defined as belonging to any of these three categories:[23]

- i a graphic work, photograph, sculpture, collage or model, irrespective of artistic quality; or
- ii a work of architecture, being a building or a model for a building; or
- iii a work of artistic craftsmanship, not falling within subparagraph (i) or subparagraph ii).

A 'graphic work' is further defined as including 'any painting, drawing, diagram, map, chart, or plan' as well as 'any engraving, etching, lithograph, woodcut, print, or similar work'.[24] The CA does not define a work of artistic craftsmanship.

Reflecting NZ's international treaty obligations, the CA grants the owner of the copyright in an artistic work the right to enjoy a bundle of economic rights for a limited term of protection.[25] Authors of works also have several moral rights in relation to their works.[26] Of most relevance to this chapter is the right to copy a work, which relates to producing an accessible 3D copy of an artistic work for the benefit of PVI.[27]

The CA adopts a broad definition of copying, meaning 'reproducing, recording, or storing the work in any material form (including any digital format), in any medium and by any means' and specifically 'in relation to an artistic work, the making of a copy in 3 dimensions of a two-dimensional work'.[28] The interface of access to artistic works for PVI and the rights of copyright holders are discussed in the following sections.

22 CA 1994, s 14(1).
23 S 2.
24 Ibid.
25 CA 1994, ss 16 and 22.
26 Part 4.
27 S 16(1)(a).
28 S 2.

General limitations and exceptions

The fair dealing provisions of Part 3 of the CA permit certain uses of a copyright work for diverse purposes. This section analyses only those exceptions that are most likely to serve the interests of PVI in relation to access to art.

Fair dealing for research or private study

Section 43 of the CA allows fair dealing with a copyright work for the purposes of research or private study and adopts factors[29] similar to those highlighted by Lord Denning as applied in *Hubbard*[30] and followed in *CCH Canadian*.[31] Those factors require the courts to consider the purpose of copying, the nature of the work, whether the work could have been obtained within a reasonable time at an ordinary commercial price, the effect of the copying on the potential market for, or value of, the work and the amount and substantiality of the part copied taken in relation to the whole work.

While potentially of use to PWD, several issues would need to be addressed regarding the application of s 43 to artistic works. First, s 43 uses the term 'work', indicating a broad application of the research and private study exception to all types of copyright works. This is also confirmed by the reference to reproduction of any artistic works which may be included in a published edition.[32] Furthermore, copying under s 43 could be 'by means of a reprographic process or by any other means'.[33] A reprographic process under the CA relates to the processes for making facsimile or other forms of copies including electronic ones.[34]

This section could, therefore, arguably be applied to copying of artistic works either from 2D to 3D or from 3D to 3D in the form of replicas or copies if done for the purpose of research or private study. Relying on this section, PWD could produce an accessible copy of an artistic work as part of their private academic, professional or personal interest studies and research efforts.

The copying for research and private study must be done by, or at the direct instruction of, the researcher and not without his or her request. In the *Longman v Carrington* case, decided under those provisions of the 1962 copyright legislation similar to the current s 43,[35] the Court agreed with the plaintiffs that 'use for research or private study must be that of the compiler'.[36]

Therefore, a PWD who is a student or researcher can arguably copy an artistic work or can ask for it to be copied into an accessible format so long as such copying is done in the course of research or private study.

29 S 43(3).
30 *Hubbard v Vosper* [1972] 2 WLR 389 (CA).
31 *CCH Canadian Ltd v Law Society of Upper Canada* [2004] 1 SCR 339 (SCC).
32 CA 1994, s 43(2).
33 S 43(3).
34 S 2.
35 Copyright Act 1962, ss 19(1), 20(1) and 21(1).
36 *Longman Group Ltd v Carrington Technical Institute Board of Governors* [1991] 2 NZLR 574 (HC) [6.9].

It is trite law that fair dealing is an issue of 'fact and impression having regard to all the circumstances'.[37] It does not appear that the criteria for consideration of the fairness of the dealings under s 43 would pose a problem for PWD. The determination of the purpose of the copying and the nature of the work copied would be possibly approached in a similar manner for users with and without a disability, and this relates to courts' definitions of research and private study. PWD should be also able to satisfy the commercial availability test under s 43. Replicas or 3D representations of artistic works are not normally easily available in the same way that non-accessible copies of copyright works may be.

New Zealand courts have underlined the importance of whether the infringing work competes with or rivals the copyright work.[38] Reproductions of an accessible format arguably would not affect the market or the value of the copyright work in the same way that photocopying books into coursepacks would. Accessible format works do not compete with the original works as the work, be it literary or artistic, in its original state, is normally of no use or interest to PWD. The substantiality of the part copied would be justified in view of the fact that the purpose of the copying is to provide access to the work for PWD. PWD are unlikely to benefit from a work unless it is copied in its entirety.

Finally, in determining fair dealing for research or private study, NZ courts have considered the availability or lack thereof of reliable licensing schemes.[39] Thus, fairness in dealings with artistic works for PWD may depend on whether easy-to-use and reliable licencing opportunities are available for accessible format reproductions of such works.[40]

Copying of 'any literary, dramatic, or musical work'[41] for the purpose of research or private study can also be done by the librarian[42] of a prescribed library.[43] Arguably, this allows the 3D copying of an artistic work included in a literary work that was made accessible to PVI.

Copying for educational purposes

Like the research or private study exception, s 44 of the CA can also provide arrangements for PWD, but specifically in the context of education. This section

37 Ibid. [6.1].

38 Ibid.

39 In the late 1970s and early 1980s, attempts to reach an agreement between the Book Publishers Association of New Zealand Incorporated (BPA) and educational institutions did not yield an outcome, leaving the scope of permissible 'dealing' for educational institutions unclear. *Longman* (n 36) [5.16]–[5.19].

40 At the time of writing this chapter, Copyright Licensing New Zealand, as the main rights management entity in NZ that has long had a focus on the publishing industry, introduced its new 'Visual Arts Licence' covering works such as paintings, photographs, drawings and sculptures. The success of this new licensing scheme, and in particular its application to accessible format copies for PVI, remains to be seen. <www.copyright.co.nz/licences-and-permission/visual-arts-licence> accessed 1 November 2019.

41 CA 1994, s 51(1).

42 S 51.

43 S 50(1).

does not use the terms 'fair dealing', as copying the whole of a work is permitted in certain cases upon meeting the prescribed conditions.[44] These conditions mainly relate to the act of copying relating to instruction, preparation for it and receiving it as well as the number of copies made on any one occasion.[45]

Limits on how much of a work can be copied are imposed when the copying is 'done by or on behalf of an educational establishment' and for 'an educational purpose' which appears broader than relating to instruction.[46] In *Longman*, Doogue J opined that copying for instruction purposes can be done by an agent so long as it is 'for the teacher or student in the course of instruction'.[47] In *University of Auckland*, the Court confirmed that, as previously found in *Longman*, [48] a master copy of a copyright work cannot be made with the intention of making further copies in the future on a recurring basis.[49]

This section may assist students and researchers with a disability and those engaged in their instruction and general education to make accessible 3D copies of artistic works when doing so serves an educational purpose. Frankel, however, argues that the conditions the section imposes on educational institutions make the exception 'virtually useless in the context of materials prepared for distribution to a class'.[50] While this may be true in relation to mass copying and distribution of material commonly known as coursepacks for sighted students, the section can arguably be used for one-off 3D printing of artistic works that are to be used in the course of instructing students with an impairment.

The following section discusses flexibilities in the CA that specifically address the needs of PWD.

Copyright flexibilities for the PWD

As Frankel points out, the inclusion of an exception for the benefit of PVI in the CA 'appears to be the result of lobbying during the passage of the Act'.[51] The subsequent amendments to the CA[52] did not affect the originally adopted Braille exception.[53] This was until recently, when the government introduced and passed the Marrakesh Amendment with the intention to join the WIPO Marrakesh Treaty. The old and the newly enforced exceptions are both discussed below in relation to access to artistic works by PWD.

44 In *Longman* (n 36) [8.10], commenting on s 21(4) of the 1962 statue which is the equivalent of current s 44, Doogue J stated that no restriction was imposed on the length of what can be copied from a work in the provision, and as such he saw no basis for imposing one.

45 CA 1994, s 44(1)–(2).

46 S 44(3).

47 *Longman* (n 36) [8.8].

48 Ibid. [8.4]–[8.7] and [8.11].

49 *Copyright Licensing Ltd v University of Auckland* [2002] 3 NZLR 76 (HC).

50 Susy Frankel, *Intellectual Property in New Zealand* (2nd edn, LexisNexis 2011) 365.

51 Ibid. 378.

52 See for a list of these amendments, Duncan Laing and Ian Finch, *James & Wells Intellectual Property Law in New Zealand* (3rd edn, Thomson Reuters 2017) 371–372.

53 CA 1994, s 69 replaced (Provision of Braille copies of literary or dramatic works) (s 69 replaced).

Type of copyright works

Under the old s 69, 'prescribed bodies' could make or communicate Braille or otherwise modified copies or adaptations of 'published literary or dramatic works' for use by persons with a print disability. At first glance, the section's notable lack of any reference to artistic works seems to have excluded the possibility of reproduction of artistic works in accessible formats. However, since this section was not limited to the production of Braille copies, it could be interpreted to have permitted the 3D reproduction of an artistic work as part of the process of making accessible a literary work containing the art.

That question is now moot. The Marrakesh Amendment introduced the new s 69A, which states that 'an authorised entity does not infringe copyright in the relevant work' when producing an accessible format copy. An accessible format copy, under the amended s 2, is defined as meaning 'a copy of a published literary, dramatic, musical, or artistic work'. As such, the new exception explicitly permits the reproduction of artistic works into accessible formats, including a 3D copy. This wording goes beyond the more limited definition of 'works' in the Marrakesh Treaty as

> literary and artistic works within the meaning of Article 2(1) of the Berne Convention for the Protection of Literary and Artistic Works, in the form of text, notation and/or related illustrations, whether published or otherwise made publicly available in any media

and is a welcome approach by the drafters of the Marrakesh Amendment.[54]

Accessible formats

As discussed earlier, a broad range of accessible formats could have been provided to PVI under the old s 69, which allowed the production of Braille as well as 'otherwise modified' accessible copies.[55] This approach, in line with the language of the Marrakesh Treaty,[56] was carried over into the new exception. Section 2 of the CA now defines an accessible format as a copy of a copyright work 'in an alternative manner or form that gives persons who have a print disability access to the work'.

This language is a departure from the traditional approach to accessibility for PWD which may have been focused on access to print material in Braille or audio form and acknowledges the need for an all-encompassing approach to access equality. This is consistent with the recognition of 'the principles of non-discrimination, equal opportunity, accessibility and full and effective

54 Marrakesh Treaty (n 11) art 2(a).
55 CA 1994, s 69(1) replaced.
56 Marrakesh Treaty (n 11) art 2(b).

participation and inclusion in society' in the Marrakesh Treaty[57] as well as the objectives of NZ's new Disability Strategy 2016 discussed earlier.

The beneficiaries

The old s 69 provided a relatively broad definition of end beneficiaries by stating that accessible copies were for the use of 'persons who have a print disability'.[58] A print disability was defined as relating to blindness, severe visual impairment, the inability to 'hold or manipulate books' or 'a handicap with respect to visual perception'.[59] The same approach appears to have been adopted in the new exception. The amended s 2 defines print disability as meaning 'an impairment that prevents the person from enjoying a printed copyright work to the same degree as a person who does not have that impairment'.

A literal reading of this definition may imply that the new disability exception is limited to provision of access to printed copyright works for the blind. This, however, would not be in line with the explicit reference to artistic works (which includes 2D and 3D works) as well as the meaning of an accessible format copy including a copy in 'an alternative manner or form'.[60]

The scope of the beneficiaries, therefore, appears to be those with visual or other disabilities that mainly impact access to print. This would include persons who are deaf-blind but does not seem to include other forms of disability, for instance, a hearing impairment. Despite the calls for explicit inclusion of other types of disability in the new provision,[61] the definition of beneficiaries was not expanded.[62]

The authorised persons or entities

The Marrakesh Amendment extends the reach of the permissible acts under the disability exception in NZ to cover the activities of both PVI (including those acting on their behalf) and an 'authorised entity'.[63] Under the old s 69, an accessible copy could only be produced by a 'prescribed body', which under the

57 Preamble.

58 CA 1994, s 69 (1) replaced.

59 S 69(4) replaced.

60 S 2.

61 See, for example, submissions on the Copyright (Marrakesh Treaty Implementation) Amendment Bill by Nicola Owen on behalf of Audio Described Aotearoa Ltd (February 2019) 1; The Braille Authority of New Zealand Aotearoa Trust (February 2019) 2.

62 The Select Committee in its report on the Marrakesh Amendment bill stated that since the purpose of the bill is for NZ to accede to the Marrakesh Treaty only, the new exception need only cover print disabilities, and provisions for other types of disabilities could be considered as part of the wider review of the CA 1994 that was ongoing at the time of writing this chapter. 'Copyright (Marrakesh Treaty Implementation) Amendment Bill', as reported from the Economic Development, Science and Innovation Committee (8 May 2019) 4–5 (SC Report).

63 CA 1994, s 69A and B.

now revoked Copyright Regulation 5 was one of only six listed entities.[64] The Marrakesh Amendment, in contrast, allows PVI themselves or persons acting on their behalf within the GLAM sector or in the arts space, in addition to the traditional blind institutions, to engage in production of accessible format copies of artistic works. However, the scope of what can be done with such accessible copies is a matter for further consideration, depending on who creates the copy.

An 'authorised entity' under the Marrakesh Amendment is defined as an educational establishment or educational resource supplier, a prescribed library or a charitable entity serving persons with a print disability.[65] While this definition is more inclusive than the previously exhaustive list of prescribed bodies, it remains limited. This limit on the definition, as well as the conditions imposed on the conduct of authorised entities, is perhaps due to the broader freedom they enjoy as compared to PVI.[66] An authorised entity can make or reproduce an accessible copy;[67] import into NZ a copy from another authorised entity;[68] share the made, reproduced or imported copy with PVI or other authorised entities;[69] and, finally, export an accessible copy to an authorised entity or PVI in another Marrakesh country.[70]

By contrast, individuals with a print disability, whose rights were not explicitly recognised under the previous provision, can only produce accessible copies or import such copies from an authorised entity abroad, in addition to receiving copies that NZ's authorised entities produce.[71] Unlike an authorised entity, they cannot share the copy they have made or imported with other PVI in New Zealand or elsewhere. This can arguably only be done if the PVI share the work with an authorised entity in NZ first, for it to then be shared with another PVI in NZ or elsewhere. A question remains regarding the possibility of a NZ PVI exporting a work to a foreign authorised entity. The Marrakesh Amendment allows NZ PVI to 'provide the accessible format copy that he or she made or imported [...] to an authorised entity',[72] but it is unclear whether this includes foreign-authorised entities or is limited to NZ entities only.

The inclusion of PVIs and the expansion of the definition of an authorised entity under the Marrakesh Amendment is potentially beneficial to provision of

64 S 69(3) replaced.

65 S 69(1).

66 An authorised entity must take all reasonable steps to notify the copyright owner of its intention to create the accessible copy (s 69A(2)(b)), ensure to respect the integrity of the original work when creating an accessible copy (s 69A(2)(d)) and keep a record of all the accessible works it has made, provided, reproduced, imported, exported or received (s 69C(1)(a)). Out of these three requirements, PVI are only bound by the second, regarding respecting the integrity of the original work as per s 69B(2)(a).

67 S 69A(2) and (4)(b).

68 69A(3).

69 S 69A(4)(c).

70 S 69A(4)(a).

71 S 69B.

72 S 68B(2)(c).

better access to artistic works for those with a print disability. This is particularly important because much of the practical and cost burden of providing accessible format copies has historically fallen to Blind and Low Vision NZ.

However, the disparity in the scope of permissible acts for authorised entities and the PVI is arguably not fully in line with the goal of facilitating equal access to copyright works for PVI. The requirement that PVI need to use an intermediary, meaning an authorised entity, to share an accessible copy is an unnecessarily narrow and potentially paternalistic approach to the disability exception that imposes an undue burden on an already disadvantaged group. While the Marrakesh Treaty only explicitly refers to distribution of an accessible copy 'by an authorised entity',[73] art 5(3) arguably allows countries to adopt measures beyond the explicit wording of the Treaty regarding cross-border exchange of accessible copies. The opportunity to do so was evidently not fully exploited in the adoption of the Marrakesh Amendment.

Moral rights issues

Of particular relevance to the reproduction of artistic works by authorised entities or PVI and persons acting on their behalf is the requirement under the Marrakesh Amendment that the accessible copy 'respects the integrity of the original work, as far as is reasonably possible and taking into account changes needed to make the work accessible in the alternative format'.[74]

This new requirement, as dictated by the Marrakesh Treaty,[75] was not part of the old s 69 exception. As such, currently, there are no guidelines or precedent as to what respecting the integrity of the original work means in the context of producing accessible formats.[76] The use of the word 'integrity' may imply moral rights considerations such as the right of the author to object to derogatory treatment of his or her work.[77] If so interpreted, the author of an artistic work can object to reproduction of the work in 3D or other accessible formats if they regard such reproduction as a derogatory treatment.

73 Marrakesh Treaty (n 11) art 5(1).

74 Ss 69A(2)(d) and 69B(2)(a).

75 Marrakesh Treaty (n 11) art 2(b).

76 The authors of the World Blind Union Guide on the Marrakesh Treaty suggest that the provision in the Treaty

> clarifies that Marrakesh Treaty beneficiaries and authorized entities are entitled to modify copyrighted works if necessary to make such works accessible to print-disabled individuals. The E&L adopted in national implementing legislation must therefore permit changes that may constitute derivative works under domestic copyright laws, as well as changes that may interfere with the integrity of a work under Article 6*bis* of the Berne Convention.

Laurence Helfer et al., *The World Blind Union Guide to the Marrakesh Treaty* (OUP 2017) 109–110.

77 CA 1994, s 98.

However, currently, the threshold of derogatory treatment under NZ law seems rather high. First, treatment does not explicitly include copying or reproduction but is defined as 'any addition to, deletion from, alteration to, or adaptation of the work'.[78] However, while neither 'alteration' nor 'adaptation' is defined with regard to artistic works under the moral right of integrity, these terms may arguably apply to an accessible format copy of an artistic work. Furthermore, the treatment, 'whether by distortion or mutilation of the work or otherwise', must be 'prejudicial to the author's honour or reputation'.[79] The indicative words 'distortion or mutilation' imply that the treatment would have to involve change that degrades the work and does more than merely make the work accessible to PVI without altering its essence. This is arguably confirmed by the requirement in the Marrakesh Treaty that when creating an accessible copy, an authorised entity 'does not introduce changes *other than those needed* [emphasis added] to make the work accessible to the beneficiary person'.[80] This suggests that changes necessary for making the work accessible alone, even if seen as alteration, would not normally harm the integrity of the work.

Finally, case law involving derogatory treatment of copyright works that may be prejudicial to an author's honour or reputation is mainly around commercial[81] or political contexts,[82] and it is difficult to categorise the non-commercial production of accessible copies of art for PVI as a derogatory treatment.

However, it may be possible that an author or his or her estate would view a certain reproduction of a prominent work of art as against the reputation or artistic values of the artist. As such, the new integrity requirement may increase the risk of criticism or even legal action that PVI or those acting on their behalf would have faced previously.

One solution to this would be an attempt to engage with authors or owners of moral rights when such works are the subject of reproduction. It is, however, important not to treat this engagement as an expectation, as it would be imposing an obligation on PVI where no such obligation exists legally.

Authorised entities, on the other hand, are required to notify the copyright owner of the production of the accessible format.[83] Consultations with the author, who may or may not also be the copyright owner, could perhaps form part of this process. This is also particularly important when access to the original artwork for the purposes of reproduction is crucial but not readily available, and such access would be dependent on the agreement of the artist or the copyright owner.

78 S 98(1)(a).

79 S 98(1)(b).

80 Marrakesh Treaty (n 11) art 4(2)(a)(ii).

81 See, for example, *Snow v Eaton Centre Ltd* 70 CPR (2d) 105 (OJ); *John Radford v Hallensteins Bros Ltd* [2009] DCR 907 (HC); *Prise de Parole Inc v Guerin* (1995) 66 CPR (3d) 257; *Schott Musik International GmbH v Colossal Records of Australia Pty Ltd* (1997) 36 IPR 267.

82 See for example *Shostakovich v Twentieth Century-Fox Film Corporation* (1948) 80 NYS 2d 575.

83 CA 1994, s 69A(2)(b).

However, identifying or contacting the relevant individual by PVI or authorised entities, for either notification or consultation purposes, may not always be possible or straightforward for a multitude of reasons, including when dealing with an orphan work or one published under a pseudonym.

Commercial availability

The proposal to include a commercial availability test in the Marrakesh Amendment, which requires a search of the market for any already available commercial accessible copies before one is created, proved to be the most controversial aspect of the reform of the disability exception.[84] On the advice of the Select Committee, the test was removed from the Marrakesh Amendment.[85] This removal is justified considering the difficulties with the vague wording of the test in the old s 69[86] that could create bureaucratic burdens and delays in the reproduction of accessible formats. This is particularly significant considering that commercial copies of accessible artistic works are even less likely to be available compared to accessible literary works, which were the focus of the movement to end the global book famine, leading to the adoption of the Marrakesh Treaty.

Cross-border exchange of accessible formats

The lack of clear and consistent rules around international exchange of available accessible formats has complicated access to copyright works for PVI for decades.[87]

84 For arguments in support of the test, see for example, the submissions by Copyright Licensing New Zealand suggesting that not only authorised entities but also visually impaired individuals should be required to meet the commercial availability requirement; the Publishers Association of New Zealand, 2; The Royal New Zealand Foundation of the Blind, 19.4. For arguments against the test see the submissions by the Blind Citizens NZ, [2.1]; the International Federation of Library Associations and Institutions, 2; the Library and Information Association of New Zealand Aotearoa, 2; and the Universities New Zealand Copyright Expert Committee, 5.1. <www.parliament.nz/en/pb/bills-and-laws/bills-proposed-laws/document/BILL_80988/tab/submissionsandadvice> accessed 15 October 2019.

85 Copyright (Marrakesh Treaty Implementation) Amendment Bill, As reported from the Economic Development, Science and Innovation, 2–3 stating that 'we consider that a formal requirement for a commercial availability test would disadvantage print-disabled people disproportionately to the benefit gained by copyright holders'.

86 The section used phrases such as 'reasonable efforts', 'reasonable time' and 'ordinary commercial price' without defining them.

87 See Wanda Noel, 'Copyright Problems Raised by the Access by Handicapped Persons to Protected Works', report to the Intergovernmental Committee of the Universal Copyright Convention and the Executive Committee of the Berne Union, Paris, 1985, IGC(1971)/VI/11 – B/EC/XXIV/10 ANNEXII; World Intellectual Property Organization, Standing Committee on Copyright and Related Rights, Study on Copyright Limitations and Exceptions for the visually impaired, prepared by Judith Sullivan, SCCR/15/7, 20 February 2007, 47–61, for a full analysis of export and import possibilities in international and some national copyright laws; and ten stating that 'in countries with fairly comprehensive provisions regarding the making of

The old s 69 was silent on the issue, and such import and export appear to be have been done mainly through private contracts.[88] The Marrakesh Amendment, consistent with the Marrakesh Treaty,[89] allows a NZ's authorised entity to import an accessible copy from an authorised entity in another Marrakesh country[90] or export such copy to an authorised entity or PVI in another Marrakesh country.[91]

As discussed earlier, PVI in NZ can import accessible copies from an authorised entity in a Marrakesh country but not from another PVI.[92] It remains unclear whether they can export a copy to a foreign authorised entity. These limitations on actions of PVI arguably can have an overall negative impact on facilitating cross-border exchange of accessible works.

Access for PWD and rights of Māori

In NZ, reproducing accessible artistic works raises issues around the use of *taonga* and *taonga*-derived copyright works. *Taonga* (often translated as sacred or treasure) are defined as cultural or artistic works 'founded in and reflecting the body of knowledge and understanding known as mātauranga Māori … Some of them are ancient, others not'.[93] Some *taonga* works may fall under copyright protection if they fit the statutory requirements of NZ copyright law.[94]

Because of the *kaitiaki* (kinship or guardianship) relationship between *taonga* works and their creators,[95] application of copyright exceptions to such works should be considered from an indigenous rights perspective. Te Papa Museum has in the past produced 3D replicas of copyright *taonga* works. Reportedly, 'any creation of such replicas is only actioned after discussions with and support of the *iwi* (source community) to which the *taonga* has *whakapapa* (lineage) connections'.[96]

---

accessible copies under exceptions to copyright, there may still be problems where it is desired to move accessible copies between countries'.

88 Emails from Jennifer Ashton (Pre-Production Co-ordinator, Accessible Format Production, the Blind Foundation) to author (9 July to 12 August 2013).The Blind Foundation, for example, reportedly receives accessible works from Blackstone (audio books), Ulverscroft (audio books and some large print), Royal National Institute of the Blind in the UK (audio books and Braille), Vision Australia (audio books and braille). Accessible copies are purchased from Blackstone, Ulverscroft and RNIB; although RNIB provides the Foundation with a reduced rate. The Blind Foundation also has an exchange agreement with Vision Australia that allows the two countries to exchange accessible works.

89 Marrakesh Treaty (n 11) arts 5, 6 and 9.

90 CA 1994, s 69A(3).

91 S 69A(4).

92 S 69B(2)(b).

93 Waitangi Tribunal Report, Wai262 'Ko Aotearoa Tēnei: A Report into Claims Concerning New Zealand Law and Policy Affecting Māori Culture and Identity' (2011) 31.

94 CA 1994, Part 1.

95 Ibid.

96 Email (n 7).

As Lai explains, the problem with copyright permitted acts in general 'is that they were created with the interests of Western society in mind' and as such 'can undermine indigenous customary laws, which do not share the same norms and values, and in which permitted acts are either non-existent or very different'.[97] The application of the disability exception to *taonga* works is part of the bigger mismatch between copyright law and the rights of indigenous peoples in their cultural expressions. As such, the conflicting interests should be addressed in a holistic way that goes beyond reforming the Marrakesh Amendment.[98]

Reconciling the interests of Māori and PWD could involve the introduction of a registrar for *taonga* works, a decision-making body that would oversee the use of such works and any necessary consultations with *kaitiaki*, under the disability exception.[99] Alternatively, the moral rights provisions in the CA can be amended to create new norms that are compatible with *kaitiaki* interests and protect *taonga* works against 'derogatory and offensive public use'.[100] Meanwhile, rights of Māori could, and arguably should, be included in the consideration of respecting the 'integrity' of a copyright work under the Marrakesh Amendment.[101] It is, however, worth noting that the 'integrity' requirement currently appears to relate to changes beyond what is necessary for making the work accessible, while in certain cases any treatment of a *taonga* may be against Māori *tikanga* (customs or practices) or *kaitiaki* interests.[102]

Conclusion

This chapter discussed the exceptions under NZ copyright law that can facilitate access to works of visual arts for PVI and PWD. The focus was on the Marrakesh Amendment that implements the Marrakesh Treaty in NZ. This new exception permits the reproduction of artistic works into accessible, including 3D, formats and as such would be of benefit to PVI and individuals or organisations serving their interests.

97 Jessica Lai, *Indigenous Cultural Heritage and Intellectual Property Rights: Learning from the New Zealand Experience?* (Springer 2014) 82–83.

98 Considerations for the rights of Māori are part of the review of the CA 1994 that is ongoing at the time of writing this chapter, and the outcome of the review could inform the interface of Māori rights and access to artistic works for PVI. Ministry of Business, Innovation and Employment, Issue Paper: Review of the Copyright Act 1994, November 2018, Parts 1 and 8.

99 Waitangi Tribunal Report (n 93) 99–100.

100 Ibid. 91.

101 CA 1994, s 69A(2)(d).

102 See, for example, *Yumbulul v Reserve Bank of Australia* [1991] FCA 332; (1991) 21 IPR 481 where the image of an indigenous artwork was reproduced on a bank note. The indigenous community to which the artist belonged deemed the use inappropriate, while the reproduction of the copyright protected artwork would have been unlikely to meet the threshold of derogatory treatment under Australian copyright law. See also, for a discussion of indigenous rights and copyright moral rights, Lida Ayoubi, 'Copyright Harmonisation in the Asian Pacific Region: Weaving the Peoples Together?' in Susan Corbett and Jessica Lai (eds), *Making Copyright Work for the Asian Pacific: Juxtaposing Harmonisation with Flexibility* (ANU Press 2018) 66–67.

A few questions remain regarding the limiting approach of the new exception to what an authorised entity is and the scope of the activities of PVIs or persons acting on their behalf regarding sharing of accessible formats. Additionally, the interface of the rights of Māori in *taonga* works and the application of the disability exception requires further consideration in the future. If PWD do not meet the definition of those with a print-disability under the Marrakesh Amendment, the general fair dealing provisions may be of benefit if the purpose qualifies. Such gaps, however, should be addressed in further amendment of the CA. A useful step forward would also be further development of best practices through cooperation between the stakeholders involved. As discussed, there are some initiatives in place for provision of access to artistic works for PWD in NZ. These can be built upon and expanded for 'developing voluntary guidelines, or a self-regulation regime for authorised entities' and rightholders that would further improve access to arts for PWD.[103]

103 SC Report (n 62) 5.

19 Conclusion

Ana Ramalho and Jani McCutcheon

A fragmented legal framework

The 3D printing of a 2D copyright-protected artistic work involves performing certain acts that are the exclusive rights of the copyright owner. First, it is necessary to scan the 2D work, which amounts to the exclusive economic right of reproduction. Upon scanning, a file (called STL, an abbreviation of stereolithography) is created. To proceed with the process of 3D printing, the next step may involve modifying the STL file with a modelling programme.[1] The modelling stage is necessary where the agent wants to, for example, change the picture (e.g., turn the picture of a vase with sunflowers into a vase with roses); or because some fine-tuning is needed to make the 3D model as close to the 2D work as possible. This may be necessary if blind spots remain after the scanning process and must be readjusted. The modelling stage involves exclusive economic rights of the author as well. Depending on the jurisdiction, modifying the STL file might infringe the exclusive right of adaptation or again the right of reproduction.

Moreover, modifying the STL file might – depending on the jurisdiction and the concrete alterations made to the work– amount to an infringement of the moral right of integrity. Moral rights pose an additional challenge in this regard, because their recognition and strength vary greatly from one country to another. Indeed, while most jurisdictions would recognize the act of 3D printing of 2D art works as a reproduction, when it comes to moral rights, the legal landscape is more fragmented. Even though most jurisdictions have some version of moral rights (chiefly, the moral rights of attribution and integrity), their scope is less harmonized internationally than the scope of the economic right of reproduction. For example, in France, Article L121-1 of the Intellectual Property Code defines the moral right of integrity quite broadly as a right to "respect for [the] work". This means that any modification of the work risks violating the right of integrity.[2] By contrast, the United States, for instance, displays weak moral rights at the federal level, and only a significant alteration of the 2D work in the

1 One example of such modelling programmes is ZBrush (which works in similar terms to photoshop) – see https://www.zbrushcentral.com/ (last accessed 15 January 2020).

2 Sundara Rajan, M (2011). *Moral Rights*, Oxford University Press, Oxford, p. 66.

3D printed reproduction would constitute an infringement of the moral right of integrity.

Most jurisdictions (but not all; note, for example, Costa Rica) provide a technologically neutral disability exception, where the technology used to reproduce works for the benefit of PVI is not relevant. The 3D printing could thus be seen as a legitimate means to reproduce works. However, as suspected, very few jurisdictions are able to accommodate 3D printed versions of 2D works of visual art. Most jurisdictions examined have a disability exception, either as a result of the Marrakesh Treaty or pre-dating it. However, the exception is often – sometimes expressly, sometimes impliedly – limited to literary works and/or related illustrations. The failure to acknowledge a broader disability exception can, of course, be explained by technological developments that simply did not exist when the law was enacted. Until very recently, making 3D copies of artworks was not a realistic possibility. However, failure to address that legislative gap can also be a symptom of a disconnection between human rights and copyright, or, in other words, of a poor accommodation of the human rights framework within copyright law. For example, in Europe, the Court of Justice of the EU has unhelpfully ruled that Member States are not allowed to derogate from the exclusive rights of the author beyond existing exceptions, as it considered that the latter enshrine fundamental rights considerations within copyright.[3] According to the Court, the mechanisms that balance the different rights and interests at stake (i.e., copyright and fundamental rights) are already contained in copyright legislation.[4] These rulings make it more difficult to find leeway to expand existing copyright (disability) exceptions.

Another issue that ought to be considered is the interaction between technological protection measures (TPM) and exceptions. The regime of TPM and how they might hinder beneficiaries of a disability exception are also not harmonized and vary from one country to another. Should a 2D artwork be protected by a TPM, it is not always straightforward whether and how a beneficiary of a disability exception might circumvent the TPM to carry out a legitimate reproduction of the work. In fact, even if such circumvention is allowed, different laws mandate different procedures for beneficiaries to be able to legitimately make use of an exception.

Further challenges

From the point of view of museums and galleries, sensory art projects may represent challenges that go beyond legal obstacles, such as low budgets and lack of skilled staff. Nevertheless, absent a legal exception to copyright, sensory art projects are encumbered with the need to secure licences from a variety

3 Case C-469/17 *Funke Medien*, ECLI:EU:C:2019:623, paras. 60–62; Case C-516/17 *Spiegel Online*, ECLI:EU:C:2019:625, paras. 45–47.

4 Case C-467/17 *Pelham*, ECLI:EU:C:2019:624, para. 60.

of stakeholders, which, as described in the introduction, is impractical and, at times, impossible. The fact that such an exception does not exist at the international level (and in many instances, it does not clearly or workably exist at national level) might have undesirable effects on the existence of sensory art projects. There is a real need for follow-up empirical research that will ascertain to which extent the lack or the uncertainty of exceptions has chilled sensory art projects for the benefit of PVI, and which type of concerns or measures stakeholders have adopted to face such deficient legal frameworks. From the small sample of stakeholders that contributed to this book, it seems that 3D printing companies fear intellectual property infringement and yearn for legal certainty, (some) museums have an interest in pursuing sensory art projects (either for the benefit of PVI or for reaching a wider, more diversified, audience) and PVI see as their inalienable right the ability to access cultural works.

In relation specifically to PVI, and as Torrente's chapter has made clear, an important issue to consider is the question of translation. Since the sense of touch has a lower ability of perception than the sense of sight, transforming a 2D artwork into a 3D model might not always amount to an exact copy of the former, but rather one that fully enables the "aesthetic enjoyment" by the PVI. The problem becomes then who should be in charge of this translation, which should ideally require a good knowledge of the artwork and of the artist's style.

Moreover, a transformation of this kind must respect the vision of the author. The role of the artist and her relation to the work must be borne in mind, but this is all the more challenging if one considers that the relation between original and copies is a complex, dynamic one. As explained by Saaze, copies of original works are increasingly accepted, not as weak versions of the original work but rather as part of its biography, helping the user to explore the original. If one considers this evolution of the relation between a work and its copies, then the vision of the artist should be considered both in the context of the original work and of its copies.

Another challenge is difficulty in accessing the works. Acts of 3D printing imply, first and foremost, access to the original 2D artworks. However, access to artistic works is often conditioned by the *physical* access to them. For example, unlike other works (e.g., literary works), online access to artistic works is rare, at least in the high resolution necessary for effective 3D printing. Access is also made difficult by the practices of many institutions, where exclusion is the default mode and access the exception.

What would a broad and operative disability exception look like?

The 3D printing of 2D artworks allows for a more effective and subjective interpretation of the visual art. Subjective interpretation of artworks was usually very difficult for PVI, who often could only access visual artworks through someone else's words describing the works. This rendered a "second-hand" interpretation of the artworks, filtered through the (necessarily personal) interpretation of another person. The 3D printing can then change the way PVI are able to experience art. Therefore, a broad disability exception allowing for the 3D printing of 2D artworks found its normative basis on international human rights instruments and/or on national constitutional rights granted to people with disabilities. Such an exception would comply with and foster the goals of inclusion and non-discrimination of people with disabilities in general and PVI specifically: enabling PVI to independently experience and interpret visual works fulfils their human rights to participate in culture and society.

The fact that many jurisdictions already have a disability exception – albeit in some cases limited – shows that disability considerations have their place within copyright law. As mentioned earlier, the limited character of the disability exception is, one might think, often due to an outdated copyright law, that did not consider it possible to have disability exceptions for visual works because the necessary technology simply did not exist until very recently.

As a preliminary point, a broad disability exception should be operationalized. If exclusion is more common, as mentioned earlier, some steps must be taken towards a paradigm where access is the rule and exclusion is the exception. For example, digital rights management tools and TPM might provide some guarantee for institutions that are reluctant to grant open access to digital copies of copyright works – although especially TPMs are an obstacle to access to begin with.[5] As stated in the introduction of this book, institutions might struggle with the practical impossibility of limiting user reproductions to those with a permissible exempted purpose; however, combining the use of the full range of possibilities of new technologies with sound contractual practices might provide some relief in that regard.

A prospective disability exception should expressly include artistic works within its scope, so as to accommodate 3D printing practices of works of visual art for the benefit of PVI. Since, depending on the jurisdiction, the rights of reproduction and/or adaptation might be affected by 3D printing practices, the exception should cover at least these rights and – where possible, again depending on the particular jurisdiction – the moral right of integrity.

Another issue to be considered is the beneficiaries of the exception. Different jurisdictions display different approaches to this matter. It is of utmost importance that not only PVI themselves but also their representatives and cultural institutions (such as museums or galleries) can benefit from the disability exception. It is also important to ensure that stakeholders in charge of the technical means of copying – such as 3D printing companies – can be accommodated within the exception as well.

5 It should be noted moreover that in some jurisdictions, TPMs are both a *technical* obstacle – as they prevent the actual access to and/or copy of the work – and a *legal* obstacle. In the EU, for instance, Article 6 of the Information Society Directive protects effective TPMs against their circumvention, and also sanctions preparatory acts of circumvention such as the manufacture, import, distribution, sale, rental, advertisement for sale or rental or possession for commercial purposes of circumventing devices and components.

Any disability exception thus crafted should also be made mandatory to ensure its wide applicability and effectiveness.

Despite these suggestions, which provide a modest contribution to the definition of the broad contours of a possible disability exception, it is important to consult widely with the stakeholders concerned – PVI, museums/galleries, 3D printing companies, artists – in the framework of any legislative process. A sound disability exception must consider all the interests at stake and be able to express a balance between them. The "nothing about us without us" principle, widely used in the context of disability rights, should in that sense be widened to consider all of the interests involved.

Index

Note: Page numbers followed by "n" refer to notes.

For Product Safety Concerns and Information please contact our EU
representative GPSR@taylorandfrancis.com
Taylor & Francis Verlag GmbH, Kaufingerstraße 24, 80331 München, Germany

www.ingramcontent.com/pod-product-compliance
Ingram Content Group UK Ltd.
Pitfield, Milton Keynes, MK11 3LW, UK
UKHW010958180926
475701UK00004B/441

* 9 7 8 0 3 6 7 5 5 3 4 6 3 *